The Hypocrisy
of Justice in
the Belle Epoque

The Hypocrisy of Justice in the Belle Epoque

Benjamin F. Martin

Louisiana State University Press
Baton Rouge and London

Library of Congress Cataloging in Publication Data

Martin, Benjamin F., 1947–
    The hypocrisy of justice in the belle epoque.

    Bibliography: p.
    Includes index.
    1. Trials—France. 2. Criminal justice, Administration of—France. 3. France—History—Third Republic, 1870–1940. I. Title.
LAW   345.44'02   83-16263
ISBN 0-8071-1116-3   344.4052

for
Janis
maintenant et toujours

CONTENTS

ILLUSTRATIONS

PREFACE AND ACKNOWLEDGMENTS

From June to August, 1977, I participated in a summer seminar of the National Endowment for the Humanities directed by Eugen Weber at the University of California, Los Angeles. The seminar considered the interrelationships of high culture and popular cultures in nineteenth- and twentieth-century Europe. I pursued in particular the interaction of national and local political cultures in rural France. The experience led me to question to what extent the practice of politics and the attitudes that derive from the combination of politics and social prejudice influence justice. This book grew out of that questioning.

The project was made less difficult and more pleasant through the encouragement and suggestions of Lamar Cecil, Roy Watson Curry, David H. Pinkney, Vincent Milligan, and John Raymond Walser. Gérard Poisson and Jean-Louis Ginhac, of the Archives de la Préfecture de Police, Paris, and Ségolène de Dainville-Barbiche and Geneviève Le Moël, of the Archives Nationales, were excellent guides to the treasures they administer. Generous grants from the Andrew W. Mellon Foundation allowed me to spend precious months in France and underwrote the cost of preparing the final manuscript. I am grateful to the French Institute/Alliance Française of New York for permission to adapt and reprint material I first published in the magazine of the American Society of the French Legion of Honor: "The Steinheil Affair, 1908–1909," Laurels, L (Winter, 1979), 137–52, and "The Caillaux Affair: Justice as a Political Statement," Laurels, LII (Winter, 1981), 143–62; and for the right to reproduce the illustrations from its archives that accompany the text. Leslie E. Phillabaum, Beverly Jarrett, John Easterly, and the capable staff of the Louisiana State University Press made the process of shepherding the manuscript through publication more enjoyable than tedious. My research assistants, Jane Catherine Overton, Carol Louise Bird, and Linda Elaine Patterson, did much to maintain order in the project and compiled the index. My greatest debt is owed to my wife, Janis Kilduff Martin. This book is dedicated to her.

The Hypocrisy
of Justice in
the Belle Epoque

INTRODUCTION

France's Third Republic was born in 1870 during the lost Franco-Prussian War and was the eighth change in the governmental structure since 1789. The constitution was the shortest and most ambiguous in French history and consequently the most lasting. It was a conservative republic: a republic because the monarchists were unable to decide among three pretenders; conservative because the Jacobin traditions had been discredited—aggressive nationalism by the defeat in war, economic egalitarianism by the crushing of the Paris Commune in 1871. The society of the Republic was a stalemate. Political freedom would be the opium of the masses, for whom there was little opportunity to rise in the rigid social structure of family, correct schools, and old-boy networks. "Bourgeois" was a compliment, "arriviste" an insult. The very slow expansion of the economy and the long period of deflation in the 1880s and 1890s prevented the growth of a working-class consciousness and increased the importance of rentier wealth and of the mentality that went with it. Peasants and artisans believed that the modern world would not overtake them and maintained their patterns of life and deference unchanged. Faced with no necessity ever to work, the scions of the bourgeoisie and the aristocracy could become leisured dilettantes, pursuing politics as a pastime or adopting a literary or artistic culture. It was not difficult to do both: Maurice Barrès, Charles Maurras, and Charles Péguy, among others, provided Roger Martin du Gard with the example for his *Jean Barois*, in which political action becomes founding a critical journal.[1]

France, so goes the epigram, is a nation of calm people governed by overwrought politicians. For most of the country, politics were local politics, the struggle for dominance by powerful families whose rivalries went back many years and who adopted the colors of national issues only for effect. Affairs of state were mysterious to the average Frenchman in the late nineteenth century, and politicians in Paris were to be mistrusted. From Paris, the view was equally extreme: only in France is everything outside the capital considered the provinces. Government was carried on by career bureaucrats because the politics of the Third Republic were more drama than action. The theater was the Chamber of Deputies and the Senate, a legislature that so often turned out the premier and his cabinet that between 1870 and 1914 no ministry lasted longer than three years, and most toppled in less than twelve months. Looking on benignly was an impotent chief of state, the president of the Republic. During the first forty years of the Republic, the office was occupied by eight men, each one the inferior of his predecessor: Adolphe Thiers (1871–1873), a former royalist turned founder of the Republic, who was deposed by the monarchists he had betrayed; Marshal Patrice de MacMahon (1873–1879), the military leader with the fewest defeats, who resigned under pressure after unsuccessfully trying to influence the composition of the legislature; Jules Grévy (1879–1887), last truly a leader in 1848, who resigned in disgrace after ordering the police to destroy the evidence for influence-peddling against his son-in-law; François Sadi-Carnot (1887–1894), elected because his grandfather had organized revolutionary victories ninety years before, and assassinated by a crazed Italian anarchist; Jean Casimir-Périer (1894–1895), a millionaire businessman who promised law and order but became bored and impatient enough to resign after six months; Félix Faure (1895–1899), whose virile appearance was his greatest asset and who died in the arms of his mistress of heart failure;

1. The best political narrative is Denis W. Brogan, *The Development of Modern France, 1870–1939* (London, 1940). For the nature of society, bourgeois and peasant, see Stanley Hoffman *et al.*, *In Search of France* (Cambridge, Mass., 1963); and Eugen Weber, *Peasants into Frenchmen: The Modernization of Rural France, 1870–1914* (Stanford, 1976), and "Inheritance and Dilettantism: The Politics of Maurice Barrès," *Historical Reflections*, II (Summer, 1975), 109–31.

Emile Loubet (1899–1906), elected largely because he had been able to hush up the Panama Canal scandal in 1894; Armand Fallières (1906–1913), who was little more than a peasant made good.[2]

With this leadership, the single unchanging feature of Third Republic politics was the pork barrel. Grévy's son-in-law Daniel Wilson and the Panama Canal scandal were the most obvious examples, but there were recurrent raids on the public treasury and the national welfare by all of those with influence. Large landowners and peasants alike put off the day of rationalization and reckoning with world competition through hefty tariffs. Industrialists hid their inefficiencies in similar fashion, although their demands were less reactionary. The Freycinet railway program, which, more than any other legislative act, modernized and opened up France, directly benefited the businessmen who sat in the Chamber and Senate and voted the law. Corruption among the deputies and senators was rampant, and even the most upright of them campaigned for reelection on the claim of having diverted large amounts of government funds to their districts. It was in this manner that national politics most frequently impinged on the provinces— and to the good, as the schoolhouses and schoolmasters, the new roads and the railways brought manifold changes. This was France's civilizing mission at home: peasants were being turned into Frenchmen—that is, bourgeois Frenchmen.[3]

The world that was placed before the peasant masses to emulate was elitist, hierarchical, and in retrospect after the horrors of World War I, the Belle Epoque, the "good old days." It was a man's world, but a man in suit, overcoat, top hat (later bowler), all in black, with beard, moustache, and pince-nez, ready to make his contribution to a France where the right sentiments of order, justice, law, and fortune were—he thanked God or science, depending upon his belief—solidly in power. His wife and daughters were armored against nature and the natural with ankle boots, garters, complicated and oppressive underwear, long dresses, veils, and multiple accessories: purses, gloves, handker-

2. See Jacques Chastenet, *La France de M. Fallières, une époque pathétique* (Paris, 1950); Jean-Marie Mayeur, *Les Débuts de la IIIe République, 1871–1898* (Paris, 1973); and René Eschaich, *Les Monstres sacrés de la IIIe République* (Paris, 1974).

3. Weber, *Peasants into Frenchmen*; Sanford Elwitt, *The Making of the Third Republic: Class and Politics in France, 1868–1884* (Baton Rouge, 1975).

chiefs, brooches, hatpins, and muffs. The image was dignity and respectability, but the truth behind the facade was in many cases different. Bourgeois wives contrived to escape their constricting clothing often enough to make adultery a cult in some circles. Their husbands made themselves foolish with a fascination for underwear and pornographic postcards. Fathers and sons supported the enormous number of cabarets, brothels, and apartment buildings that specialized in bachelor rooms. The demimondaines, especially the "grande trois" of Liane de Pougy, Caroline Otéro, and Emilienne d'Alençon, were celebrated to such an extent that notoriety became fame.[4]

The facade of suffocating dress and manners with the undercurrent of decadence appeared in the endless courses of heavy foods. This was the age of banquets, of Auguste Escoffier and sauces. Furnishings were heavy, solid, graceless, durable enough to pass on to heirs, but designed for a crushing comfort. Rooms were dark, tapestries somber, wainscotting black or chocolate brown, unrelieved by the taste for false gothic in candelabra, stained-glass windows, knickknacks, heroic bronzes, and sepia-tint photographs. Official art was sober and dignified: the correct landscapes, interior studies, and nudes. The excitement of Impressionism and Postimpressionism was looked at askance. So too were the experiments in music by Claude Debussy or Erik Satie and in poetry by Guillaume Apollinaire or Arthur Rimbaud. There was, instead, an approved literature of the bourgeoisie: Hector Malot for children, Zénaïde Fleuriot for young girls and sensible women, Paul Bourget for serious men, François Coppée for those who insisted on poetry. But these prescriptions did not limit the readership for Aristide Bruant's novel of two prostitutes, *Les Deux gosses*, Edouard Drumont's hysterical diatribe against the Jews, *La France juive*, or the growth of occultism, which was sponsored by the circle of the eminently respectable Juliette Adam.[5]

4. Among the many sources that could be mentioned, see in particular Paul Morand, *1900*, trans. by Mrs. Romilly Fedden as *1900 A.D.* (New York, 1931); Count Marie Paul Ernest Boniface de Castellane, *Confessions of the Marquis de Castellane* (London, 1924); and Michael R. Marrus, "Social Drinking in the Belle Epoque," *Journal of Social History*, VII (Winter, 1974), 115–41.

5. See Winifred Stephens, *Madame Adam (Juliette Lamber), la grande française: From Louis Philippe Until 1917* (New York, 1918); Saad Morcos, *Juliette Adam* (Cairo, 1961); James Webb, *The Occult Establishment* (La Salle, Ill., 1976); and Roger Shattuck, *The Banquet Years: The Origins of the Avant-Garde in France, 1885 to World War I* (Rev. ed.; New York, 1968).

This attitude of ambiguity and hypocrisy in life spilled over from personal to public codes, particularly in the exercise of law, order, and justice. Based ostensibly on the Napoleonic Code, French law regards as valid any statute from centuries past that has not been specifically repealed. With laws covering every aspect of life, the question becomes not one of enforcement—because that would be impossible without a dictatorial police state—but one of discretion. The police decide which of the laws they will enforce, and because everyone will eventually transgress some statute or another, they can arrest anyone, almost at their pleasure.

Particularly during the Third Republic, the process was simplified by the procedure of compiling dossiers on any person who came to the notice of the police. Although the information was often of dubious veracity, gathered as it was from police spies and informers who were usually petty criminals allowed at liberty only so long as they provided useful reports, the police preferred to be able to find in their files at least the excuse for an arrest should one appear desirable. Once arrested, an individual was at their mercy. For good reason, the French have always had great faith in their police, knowing them to be brutal, rough, and corrupt. Men who were "awkward" or potentially embarrassing to those in power had a way of being shot "trying to escape." Anyone who caused the death of a police officer could expect to be killed in retaliation even if he surrendered himself. To avoid injuries when suspects took refuge in a building, the police commonly dynamited it, saving themselves the effort and risk of extricating their prey. For a suspect taken into custody, there was no right of habeas corpus and no limit to the time during which he could be held pending an investigation into his alleged crime. If he had no connections, he could expect to be beaten until he confessed to everything charged—the so-called *passage à tabac*. Then, the tasks of the police having been finished, he would come under the protection of the courts.[6]

Few Frenchmen, and certainly not the bourgeoisie, seem to have questioned seriously the justice either of the police or of the courts, at least not until the Dreyfus affair. In the simplest terms, the Dreyfus af-

6. Probably the best introduction to this question is Hubert Leuthy, *Frankreichs Uhren gehen anders*, trans. by Eric Mosbacher as *France Against Herself* (New York, 1955), 60–65, although it is treated briefly in many sources.

fair resulted from the failure of *military justice* to function, but these deficiencies were essentially the same ones that afflicted *civilian criminal justice*. The most remarkable question surrounding the affair is not why military justice should have come under first public scrutiny and then public attack but why criminal justice should have escaped unscathed without examination.[7]

The Dreyfus case began in 1894 when the French army's Second Bureau (the intelligence service) began an investigation to determine the source of secret information transmitted to the Germans. The chief clue was the so-called *bordereau*, a thin piece of blue paper fished out of a wastebasket from the German embassy in Paris by a cleaning woman in the army's employ. It listed a number of technical specifications and handbooks that its author, an anonymous French officer who had clearly done business with the Germans before, promised to procure for sale. In the opinion of the Second Bureau, the *bordereau* provided four important indications in the search for the traitor. First and most obvious, it was in his handwriting. Second and third, because of the specific information offered, it seemed extremely likely that the man was an artillery officer and a probationer rotating through the divisions of the General Staff for training in strategic planning. Fourth, he seemed to have participated recently in maneuvers. It was relatively easy to draw up a list of the officers who met the last three requirements, but without examining the dossiers of all of the potential suspects, the Second Bureau settled upon Captain Alfred Dreyfus as the traitor.

One of the relatively small number of Jewish officers in the French army, Dreyfus had few enemies but almost no friends. Quiet, wealthy, and respectable, he seemed a poor candidate for a traitor, but he fell victim to the latent anti-Semitism of an officer corps made up principally of men from old aristocratic Catholic families. The intelligence service remembered that its greatest success in recruiting spies within foreign armies had come with Jews—but failed to comprehend how this result derived from concentrating all of their efforts among Jews

7. For the Dreyfus affair, there can be no better guide than Douglas W. Johnson, *France and the Dreyfus Affair* (London, 1966); Guy Chapman, *The Dreyfus Case: A Reassessment* (London, 1955) and David L. Lewis, *Prisoners of Honor: The Dreyfus Affair* (New York, 1973) are also excellent.

in foreign armies. Dreyfus had prejudice against him, and he satisfied three of the four criteria for the authorship of the *bordereau*. His handwriting superficially resembled that on the blue paper, and although graphologists differed, the army accepted the conclusions of those experts, the famous criminologist Alphonse Bertillon among them, who declared Dreyfus to be the author of the note.

All of the evidence thus far was circumstantial, and the intelligence service might have reconsidered its conclusion if the initial arrest of Dreyfus had not been made public by the minister of the army, Auguste Mercier, who saw in the detection of a traitor a boost to his sagging political fortunes. At this point, although anti-Semitism continued to play a role in the case, it was overshadowed by the combination of Germanophobia and desire for revanche that characterized French nationalism between 1870 and 1914. If a traitor had been located, he had to be punished; if the army admitted doubts now, it would appear indecisive and weak, no match for Germany. Mercier could expect to lose his ministry in that case. All of these feelings were compounded by Dreyfus' origins in Alsace, one of the lost provinces. Under public pressure, the army quickly convened a court-martial board, but midway through the deliberations, it was clear that the evidence against Dreyfus was too ambiguous for a conviction. The panel of judges was then secretly shown other documents collected by the Second Bureau and implied to refer to Dreyfus, documents alleged to be too sensitive to be shown to the defense. This additional evidence convinced the judges, and they voted unanimously for conviction. Dreyfus was condemned to suffer military degradation in public ceremony and then life imprisonment on Devil's Island.

The proceedings against Dreyfus had been manifestly unjust. At their conclusion, Charles Demange, the eminent attorney who had accepted the defense only after satisfying his Catholic conscience that Dreyfus was innocent, declared, "Your condemnation is the greatest crime of the century." The trial was held in camera, and the judges did not include a single artilleryman. Most serious, the secret evidence submitted to the judges by the prosecution could not be challenged by the defense because Demange and Dreyfus were not even told of its existence. Mercier justified this tactic because the most damaging document, which spoke of "this scoundrel D"—who was assumed without any proof to be Dreyfus—was a letter between the German and Italian military attachés, both France's enemies in the Triple Alliance with Austria-Hungary. The public embarrassment of these men might mean war when France was ill-prepared, or so argued Mercier. The maneuver and the conviction were a triumph for *raison d'état* but a travesty of justice.

With the trial over in December, 1894, and Dreyfus transported to Devil's Island, public opinion forgot him. But at the Second Bureau, there were continued problems: the flow of secret information to the Germans had not ceased with the arrest of Dreyfus, and every interpretation of this fact meant difficulties for the army. Dreyfus might have had an accomplice; there might be a second spy with no relationship to Dreyfus, who had been a spy himself; Dreyfus might have been innocent. By the middle of 1895, Lieutenant Colonel Georges Picquart, the newly assigned head of the Second Bureau, had come to believe the last of these three options and began to amass evidence that the real author of the *bordereau* was Major Ferdinand Walsin-Esterhazy, an infantry officer exceptionally curious about artillery matters, debt-ridden, and known about Paris as a rake. The most damning item was the *petit bleu*, a letter intercepted by the Second Bureau, from the German military attaché to Esterhazy, which made it clear that Esterhazy was a traitor.

Picquart consulted his superior, General Raoul Boisdeffre, the chief of the General Staff, and disclosed to him the obvious case against Esterhazy and his opinion from reading the dossier compiled against Dreyfus that an innocent man was rotting on Devil's Island. Picquart also informed Boisdeffre that the Dreyfus family knew of the suspicions about Esterhazy and that the judges from the court-martial had indiscreetly revealed the role of the secret documents. Demange and Mathieu Dreyfus, Alfred's brother, were preparing to demand a new trial on procedural grounds and on the basis of new evidence. The army, Picquart argued, could avoid intense embarrassment only by admitting its errors before being forced to do so.

Boisdeffre carried Picquart's comments higher, and the response of the army command was to reassign the head of the Second Bureau to Tunis, out of the way. Once he was gone, another intelligence officer, Major Hubert Henry, destroyed the usefulness of the *petit bleu* by erasing Esterhazy's name and then writing it back in, as if it had been forged. Henry also set about to forge absolute proof of Dreyfus' guilt, concocting a letter between the German and Italian military attachés in which Dreyfus was named directly. What the army did not know was that Picquart had suspected this reaction and had confided his suspicions to an attorney, Louis Leblois, who in turn communicated them to Auguste Scheurer-Kestner, the vice-president of the Senate.

The army's treatment of Picquart and the forgeries by Major Henry need not be seen as entirely Machiavellian. Undoubtedly, the army had come to feel that its honor was at stake in Dreyfus' conviction. If it were overturned, if it could be proved that the army had erred in so important a question as treason, public confidence in the military and the high command might decline drastically, a situation that would invite an attack by Germany. It was easy to portray Picquart as overexcited and perhaps untrustworthy, a careerist trying to advance by discrediting his predecessors. Dreyfus might have been convicted irregularly, but he was nonetheless guilty; Henry's forgeries would prevent the naïve from questioning the army's judgment. As for Esterhazy, he could be watched.

Unfortunately for this brand of thinking, too much about the case was already known outside the high command and the Second Bureau. In November, 1897, Mathieu Dreyfus publicly accused Esterhazy of being the real traitor and demanded a new trial for his brother. Scheurer-Kestner also called for "revision" of the first verdict. They had behind them a growing number of intellectuals and politicians, mostly of the ideological left. The "case" was now an "affair," converted into a political question because the Chamber of Deputies and Senate were then under the control of a Right-Center coalition personified by the premier, Jules Méline. Convinced by the high command of the army's version of the case, Méline refused to consider a new trial for Dreyfus until there was absolute proof of his innocence. This attitude allowed the Left to claim "revision" as its own whether they truly cared about the fate of Dreyfus and justice—as did Scheurer-Kestner, Georges Clemenceau, who led his newspaper *L'Aurore* into the fight, and many intellectuals—or saw the agitation as a stick with which to beat the Méline ministry and seek its fall—as was the case for some members of the Radical party.

Accused, Esterhazy demanded an inquiry to clear himself. The court-martial convened to try him disposed of the allegations rapidly on January 12, 1898, deliberating only three minutes before finding him innocent. The following day's *L'Aurore* bannered Emile Zola's "J'Accuse," an open letter to Félix Faure, the president of the Republic, charging the army and the government with having knowingly convicted an innocent man. Brought to trial for libel, Zola was himself convicted and sentenced to a year's imprisonment—avoided by a flight to England. Nevertheless, his attorneys managed to establish publicly the irregularities at Dreyfus' court-martial. The army did not dare to deny them, but its defenders countered with the claim that there existed a copy of the *bordereau* annotated by Kaiser Wilhelm II himself. Obviously, it could not be produced for fear of precipitating war, but it was proof positive. Later, this absurd story would be used as the excuse for the forgeries: since the true evidence had to be concealed, an equivalent had to be manufactured.

The legislative elections of May, 1898, distracted notice from the affair and led to the replacement of Méline's ministry by one more clearly of the Center. In July, the minister of war, Godefroy Cavaignac, made the mistake of insisting before the Chamber of Deputies that there was a letter explicitly naming Dreyfus, referring to Henry's forgery, which he thought to be authentic. His words forced the government to subject the letter to close examination, closer than it could stand. By the last week in August, Cavaignac had resigned in chagrin, Esterhazy had fled to England, and Henry had been arrested. On August 31, Henry was found dead in his cell, leaving behind a note to his wife asserting that the forgery had actually been a true copy of a genuine letter and writing as his final words the cryptic phrase: "You know in whose interest I have acted." Whether suicide or murder, no one knew, but the defenders of the army claimed him as their martyr.

Even the revelation of the forgery did not make a new trial for Dreyfus inevitable, because the fate of the man had become secondary to a much grander question: Which is more important, *raison d'état* or justice? For the proponents of Dreyfus, many of them organized in the Ligue des Droits de l'Homme (League of the Rights of Man), the issue of justice to each individual was paramount. Their opponents, in the Ligue de la Patrie Française (League of the Fatherland), vowed that a *hypothetical* injustice must not damage the prestige and self-confidence of the army and endanger France: defeated, France could defend justice for no one. It required the obscene death in February, 1899, of President Faure, a determined foe of Dreyfus; a ludicrously unsuccessful attempt at a coup de'état by ultranationalist Paul Déroulède at Faure's funeral; the election of Emile Loubet, a "revisionist," as president; and a physical assault on Loubet four months later, in June, by more nationalists before the "Dreyfusards" finally swung sufficient sentiment in public opinion and the government to win a retrial.

The highest French court, the Cour de Cassation, which could not overturn the conviction but could require a rehearing of the evidence, was convened to consider the case. On June 3, its forty-six justices did order a new trial, and Clemenceau splashed the single word JUSTICE across the front page of *L'Aurore*. During the weeks that followed, Dreyfus began the journey back from Devil's Island to face a second court-martial; Esterhazy, safe in London, admitted writing the *bordereau*; Zola returned from London to Paris; and Picquart, who had been imprisoned in August, 1898, for having made his revelation of sensitive information to Leblois, was released. Confident that right would conquer, the Dreyfusards even talked of arresting Mercier and such generals as Boisdeffre, who had resigned after Henry's suicide. This spirit of optimism ended soon after the opening of the trial on August 7.

This time, there were distinguished artillery experts among the seven judges, and far from taking place in camera, the court-martial was covered by the press from every European nation and the United States. Unfortunately, the truth about the case remained elusive. Two of the stars in the affair were absent, Henry dead and Esterhazy unwilling to leave London. Dreyfus himself, his health broken by five years on Devil's Island, produced a poor impression. Demange again led the defense, assisted by a brilliant younger attorney, Fernand Labori. Their best efforts were handicapped by the army's now deeply ingrained prejudice against Dreyfus and by testimony from Mercier. The former minister of the army hinted at the existence of an original *bordereau* annotated by Wilhelm II, which could not be produced, and made Esterhazy appear to have been a French agent who had traced the *bordereau* onto thin paper—thus his admission. On September 9, after hearing a month of confusing evidence, the judges deliberated for less than an hour. By a vote of five to two, they again found Dreyfus guilty, but with extenuating circumstances. As a result, the sentence of life imprisonment was to be reduced to imprisonment for ten years, half of which had already been served.

The verdict was ludicrous: treason has no extenuating circumstances. With the military unwilling to certify Dreyfus innocent, René Waldeck-Rousseau, who had been named premier in June, 1899, with the mandate to resolve the affair, convinced President Loubet to issue, and the twice-convicted Dreyfus to accept, a pardon on September 19. The decision was a necessity for Dreyfus, who very clearly could not have survived many more months on Devil's Island, but it infuriated many of his partisans, among them Clemenceau and Picquart. They had come to the ironic conclusion that Dreyfus should be a martyr if necessary for "justice"—as the army had made him a martyr for its "honor." They argued passionately that by accepting the pardon, Dreyfus was acknowledging guilt and forgoing any chance for full vindication; by issuing it, the government was affirming the innocence of Mercier and the high command, preventing forever legal retribution for their persecution of an innocent man. Nearly seven years later in July, 1906, when he finally became premier for the first time, Clemenceau arranged for the Cour de Cassation to quash the second court-martial conviction and declare Dreyfus innocent, although it did not legally have the authority to do so and the act was a clear infringement of civilian justice onto the realm of military justice. Dreyfus was restored to the army at the rank of colonel; Picquart was made a general and entered Clemenceau's cabinet as minister of the army. Eventually, the end justified the means for both sides.

The Dreyfus affair was a combination of many factors. The investigation by the Second Bureau was so sloppy that even now the full extent of Esterhazy's treason and whether or not he worked alone cannot be determined. Public opinion made it impossible for the army to back away from its initial conclusion that Dreyfus was the traitor and later to admit its mistake. Prejudice afflicted almost everyone concerned: against Jews, "civilians," and "faint-hearted idealists" by the army and its defenders; against military justice, nationalists, and the aristocratic, Catholic officer corps by the Dreyfusards. The fate of an individual was submerged by the relationship of the case to passionate issues: anti-Semitism, nationalism, and Justice. Most important, politics intervened in the process of justice from the beginning to the end, making injustice all but inevitable.

But what exactly was this "justice"? Reflecting upon the war cry of the 1789 Revolution, Henri Frédéric Amiel wrote in his *Journal Intime* on December 4, 1863: "Liberty, equality,—bad principles! The true principle of humanity is justice."[8] At least, it is the popular principle. For the last two centuries, Western democratic societies have exalted the ideal of rendering justice to those accused of crime. As is the case for most ideals, it is sullied in the practice. Justice is never entirely blind and is rarely evenhanded. The manner in which it departs from the ideal—what may be called the "hypocrisy of justice"—describes the tensions in a society, in its laws, mores, conditions, politics. For the historian, the knowledge of who was punished for what, and the converse, makes possible the analysis of an enormously varied array of social statistics and the ordering of priorities of time and place. But this analysis begs the question what is "justice."

Here, the inquiry refuses to proceed straightforward. If the "justice" of a society is to be judged, whose justice is to be applied? Should it be the standards contemporary to the period? Or should it be the retrospective hindsight of the historian passing judgment from another era? Justice, flung about so blithely in headlines and slogans, is one of the perennially popular topics for philosophers and theologians. But their complex, many-faceted definitions are too cumbrous for use in the hugger-mugger of history and too much the expression of an ideal.[9] What historians need is a working definition that takes account of the compromises necessitated by practical considerations.

Such a definition might be that justice is the entire process by which a crime is investigated and tried. "Fair justice" would then be compliance with the written law. Common-sense understanding confuses "justice" with "equity," and this interpretation leads to the corollary

---

8. Henri Frédéric Amiel, *Journal Intime*, trans. by Van Wyck Brooks and Charles Van Wyck Brooks as *The Private Journal of Henri Frédéric Amiel* (Rev. ed.; New York, 1935), 181.

9. See Chaïm Perelman, *The Idea of Justice and the Problem of Argument* (New York, 1963); John Rawls, *A Theory of Justice* (Cambridge, Mass., 1971); and Hans Kelsen, *What Is Justice? Justice, Law, and Politics in the Mirror of Science* (Berkeley, 1957).

that justice is the discovery of the truth and the due apportionment of guilt and innocence to each individual. The extent to which justice departs from these formulations is the measure of its hypocrisy during any period. This measure is known for the Dreyfus affair but not for the civilian criminal justice of the Belle Epoque. It is provided by an analysis of the remarkable, sensational cases of Marguerite Steinheil, Thérèse Humbert, and Henriette Caillaux. In these three "affairs," justice departed so far from its ideals that it was seen not as an opportunity for the strict application of the law but for a system of rewards and punishments meted out in accordance with an idiosyncratic view of social utility.

The explanation for what happened to these three women, and the reason that their experiences have broad implications for an interpretation of Third Republic France, must be sought in fundamental ironies of the Belle Epoque. Implicit in this stalemate society was an inner tension created by the combination of ostensible rigidity and the rich possibilities of upward mobility through illicit means. The republican politics of the period had an often overlooked savage aspect that found significant expression through interference in the judicial process. Finally, the Belle Epoque was less than *belle* even among the affluent and privileged: the outwardly sober and respectable upper-bourgeois society had a distinctly sordid side that was revealed in pervasive personal and public corruption. Justice reflects the society in which it is rendered, and the justice of the Steinheil, Humbert, and Caillaux affairs was hypocritical in the extreme.

Chapter 1

THE STEINHEIL AFFAIR
Sex, Sin, and Murder

Qui culpae ignoscit uni, suadet pluribus.
Syrus, *Sententiae*, No. 578

I

The Steinheil affair began on a stormy night in May, 1908, with all the trappings of a lurid detective novel: a beautiful woman gagged and bound to her bed, disguises and wigs, a watchdog mysteriously absent, the pendulum of the clock stopped, and two corpses, those of the noted painter Adolphe Steinheil and his mother-in-law, Mme Emilie Japy. Steinheil's wife, Marguerite, was the woman found tied and gagged, alone able to tell the tale of a night of terror. Tell a tale she did, until she trapped herself in a web of lies and transfixed a fascinated public. The truth seemed impossible to find, and everyone connected with the case stepped onto a slope of conjecture and hypothesis. A bizarre double murder came to be transformed into a celebrated "affair" that passed judgment not merely on Mme Steinheil but on the French judicial process as well.[1]

---

1. Accounts of the Steinheil affair have been invariably controversial, semihistorical, or both. Meg Steinheil's contribution is *My Memoirs* (London, 1912), ghosted by freelance journalist Roger de Chateleux. It is a tissue of many lies but also some truth and must be used with extreme care. The press of the period, notably *Le Figaro*, *L'Echo de Paris*, and *Le Matin*, took great interest in the case and gave it much space. Where *Le Figaro* is cited alone in the notes, it should be understood that similar information was published in most of the Parisian daily newspapers on the same day. Even the semiofficial *Gazette des Tribunaux, Journal de jurisprudence et des débats judiciaires* emphasized the Steinheil affair. It is fair to conclude that the journalists were as confused as anyone else about the facts and contributed to the confusion by becoming participants in the investigation and publishing the most outrageous rumors. The sensational aspects of Meg Steinheil's life have attracted a number of popular writers, all of whom neglect to one

Jeanne Marguerite Japy, always known as Meg, was born on April 16, 1869, at Beaumont in the department of Belfort to a wealthy and conservative Protestant family. With her two sisters, Julie and Mimi, and her brother, Julien, she spent the comfortable childhood of a bourgeoise learning to play the piano and gracefully to ride horses. But there were tensions in the family. The Japys had traditionally been hardware manufacturers, and Meg's father, Edouard Japy, had for a time managed one of the family factories in nearby Montbéliard. After retiring to the country, he became an alcoholic, watching his wealth slip slowly away. His marriage had been a disappointment. As a young man, against the wishes of his family, he had wed a pretty teenaged girl, Emilie Rau, whose parents owned the modest Lion Rouge Inn outside Montbéliard. After a few years had passed, the love in the relationship had gone, but the stigma of mésalliance remained.

Meg was her father's favorite child, but in 1888 when she was nineteen, she also failed him. She had grown tall and beautiful, her oval face and plump lips alluring, her dark deeply set eyes mysterious and accentuated by the copper chestnut color of her hair, her figure stunning. At the same time, she retained a pouty innocence, a look she would lose only in middle age. There were many suitors, and she fell in love with a handsome lieutenant, Robert Scheffer. He was a friend of her brother, and both were stationed with the Thirty-fifth Infantry at Belfort. Scheffer had every romantic virtue but no money. Meg's father became apoplectic when he learned that the initial interest had by the late fall of 1888 turned into a love affair. Remembering the reaction of his parents to his own marriage and the increasingly precarious state of the Japy finances, he forbade his daughter to enter into this mésalliance and for her sins sent her into quasi exile to the home

---

degree or another the elements of scholarship: Armand Lanoux, "La Mystérieuse affaire Steinheil," in Gilbert Guilleminault (ed.), *Le Roman vrai de la Troisième République: La Belle Epoque* (Paris, 1957), 267–305, a convenient summation of his "L'Affaire de Mme Steinheil" in *Paris-Presse-L'Intransigeant*, December 20–28, 1955; René Floriot, *Deux femmes en cour d'assises: Madame Steinheil et Madame Caillaux* (Paris, 1966); Rayner Heppenstall, *A Little Pattern of French Crime* (London, 1969); Roland E. Schacht, *Madame Steinheil: Drama in Elf Bildern* (Berlin, 1933); Ernest Dudley, *The Scarlett Widow* (London, 1960); Michel Chrestien, *L'Affaire Steinheil* (Paris, 1958); and René Tavernier, *Madame Steinheil, ange ou démon: Favorite de la République* (Paris, 1976). There is a cryptic reconstruction of the night of the crime by France's most famous criminologist, Edmond Locard, in his *Le Crime et les criminelles* (Paris, 1925).

Adolphe Steinheil and his beautiful young wife, Meg

The house in the Impasse Ronsin in which Meg Steinheil was found bound and gagged (window 3), with her husband and her mother dead in adjoining rooms (windows 1 and 2)

The headlines announcing Meg Steinheil's acquittal, with photographs of Meg and her attorney, Antony Aubin

In her youth, Meg Steinheil posed for this statue by Jean Hugues, which is now in the Palais du Luxembourg, where the French Senate meets.

of her married sister Julie in Bayonne. A few days later on November 14, he raged himself into the heart attack that caused his death.

Meg was now out of sight, but her romantic indiscretions with Lieutenant Scheffer had been noticed. They fueled the additional rumors that hang like an albatross in conservative society about the neck of a girl who seems errant and wild. There was talk of an earlier affair with the son of a grocer and even of a bastard son. It made little difference that these stories were inventions without substance: Meg's value in the marriage market had plummeted.

Suddenly widowed and her daughter a scandal, Emilie Japy was delighted to find what seemed to be a relatively painless means of alleviating a portion of her embarrassment. At Bayonne, Meg had been introduced to Adolphe Steinheil, a Parisian artist working on frescoes and stained-glass windows in the cathedral. Odd-looking with his large moustache overpowering a weak face and small eyes, forty years old, self-effacing, he was hardly the stereotype of the nineteenth-century profligate artist. For one of the few times in his life, this gentle and timid man succumbed to emotion. He fell helplessly in love with the beautiful young Meg and pressed his suit by offering her lessons in painting. At first, neither mother nor daughter found this attention attractive, but Mme Japy grew much less hostile when she learned that Steinheil had an excellent artistic reputation—derived largely from an association with his father, Louis Steinheil, who had restored the windows of the cathedral at Chartres and of the Sainte Chapelle, and from his uncle, Jean Louis Meissonier. In the 1950s the sculptor Constantin Brancusi would recall, "In Steinheil's time, he was something like what Bernard Buffet is today." Meg was brought around to appreciate the painter by the thought of living in Paris. Steinheil lacked a fortune and he was a Catholic, but here was an opportunity to marry Meg off before she found another romantic but unacceptable suitor. The marriage was arranged, and after a proper period of mourning for Edouard Japy, it took place on July 6, 1890.

After an Italian honeymoon, the Steinheil ménage moved into the artist's large house at 6 *bis* Impasse Ronsin, in the Vaugirard district (15e *arrondissement*) of left-bank Paris. There was an enormous amount of room in the four storeys, and the house easily served as both a residence and a studio for Steinheil. Meg became pregnant almost immediately, and in June, 1891, she gave birth to her only child, Marthe. Nevertheless, the marriage failed from the beginning. The allure of being the wife of an artist disappeared before the reality of being the wife of this artist, the very opposite of a man of the world, unexciting, unambitious, too much like his canvases, which were praised more for their careful and precise technique than for their originality. He was twenty years her senior and content that each year since 1870 the official state exhibition had selected one his paintings for hanging, content to lead a mediocre existence on a minimum income: no new clothes, no new furniture, no new anything. Most serious, he also had homosexual tendencies, leading Jules Roche, the Progressive politician, to remark cruelly, "This shifty Steinheil prefers to look at men from the rear than face to face."[2]

Bored by her life and frustrated at her inability to play the role she had envisioned for herself, Meg soon sought the satisfaction of her dreams outside her marriage. In 1893, she took a state prosecutor, Manuel Baudouin, as her first lover. Like others later, he would be fascinated by the combination of her availability and her schoolgirl appearance; like them he would be alternately attracted and repelled by the lack of passion in her embrace and the calculation and innocence that coexisted in her eyes. She could be both virgin child and serpent. Baudouin was amazed at how easily she accounted to Steinheil for her long absences and for the gifts he showered on her during their four-year liaison. She invented the story of an "Aunt Lily," the natural sister of one of her cousins, claiming to have reunited them and to pay visits to Aunt Lily, who gave her jewels and knickknacks in gratitude. This excuse was pathetically transparent, and Steinheil was aware of her infidelity very early. He allowed it to continue and even agreed to live with Meg at the Impasse Ronsin as brother and sister because he remained profoundly in love with her and feared losing his daughter if he insisted on a divorce. There was also a less elevated reason to feign

2. For Meg's early life and marriage, see the background piece in *Le Figaro* written as a prelude to the trial, November 2–3, 1909. See Meg's version, *Memoirs*, 1–32; as well as Chrestien, *Steinheil*, 27–47, the judgment by Brancusi from p. 44, n. 1; Dudley, *Widow*, 14–21; and Tavernier, *Steinheil*, 24–57. For the remark by Roche, see the report of November 28, 1908, in the Archives de la Préfecture de Police, Paris (hereinafter cited as APP), B A/1584, Affaire Steinheil.

indifference. To bring additional money into the household, Meg badgered the prosecutor, and later his successors to her favors, into posing for portraits by her husband, thereby providing a steady source of income.

Upon the departure of this first lover in 1897, Meg was ready for a liaison of higher status and set out to win the ardor of Félix Faure, the newly elected president of the Republic who had always cut a wide swath through the ladies. Faure had met both Steinheils at receptions in 1894, when he was as yet only minister of the navy. As president after 1895, he was immensely more attractive and also had within his gift the commission of great tableaux for the state. He found Meg's allure irresistible; Meg delighted in pretending to be a republican Pompadour. Steinheil's reward was the appointment to produce the mammoth *Remise des décorations par le Président de la République aux survivants de la Redoute Ruinée (8 août 1897)* of 1898, for which he was paid thirty thousand francs and created a knight of the Legion of Honor.

Meg began almost daily visits to the Elysée palace, entering by a small door in the gardens at the corner of the Rue du Colisée and the Avenue des Champs Elysées. In her memoirs, she would claim that these visits were to help Faure with the composition of *his* memoirs and to carry out secret errands for him. The secret errands were essentially a single one, to wait for him in the Blue Salon of the palace as his chief mistress, a fact known by many in fashionable Paris. It was in this capacity that she provoked his death of stroke and heart failure on February 16, 1899, at the height of the Dreyfus affair. Louis Le Gall, the secretary of the Elysée, discovered her beneath Faure, naked in his arms, helpless as he clutched her hair in his struggle for a last breath. Hastily summoned palace domestics desperately prized her loose and rushed her out half-dressed—without her corset—as a priest was led in from the street in a vain effort to hear Faure's confession. During the next two weeks, several of the more sensationalist newspapers accused a certain Mme S—— of knowing a great deal about the death of the president and of carrying off undisclosed papers from his office. The government had hushed up her role in the business, and Meg found no grounds for suit since she was not named explicitly by the press. The insinuation about purloined papers had no basis in fact and no consequences except to inspire Meg's later comment in her memoirs.[3]

From the early 1890s to 1908, Meg conducted a weekly salon at the Impasse Ronsin, entertaining three to four hundred people during the course of an afternoon in her spacious drawing room. Her goal was to heighten the appreciation of Parisian society for Steinheil's paintings and thus to bring him more sales, although it is doubtful that the increased income much more than covered her expenses. Steinheil refused to hawk his wares so blatantly and found the salon embarrassing. He was also aware that whatever the avowed purpose of these afternoons, Meg was the main attraction. Pretty, seductive, an excellent musician, receiving with exquisite grace, she attracted all of artistic, literary, and eventually political Paris. François Coppée (poet), Pierre Loti (novelist), Auguste Bartholdi (sculptor), Charles François Gounod (composer), Ferdinand de Lesseps (of the Suez canal), Emile Zola (novelist), Léon Bonnat (portraitist), Jules Emile Massenet (composer), Camille Groult (art collector), François Sadi-Carnot (deputy, minister, president of the Republic), Jules Méline (deputy and premier), Admiral Alfred Gervais (of the Kronstadt mission), Hippolyte-François Alfred Chauchard (founder of the Louvre stores), nobility and diplomats from several countries, cabinet ministers, and even the Prince of Wales crowded into her salon. Some repaid her hospitality by purchasing the period studies that were Steinheil's speciality. Some became the lovers of this woman whose code of morality was so singular for one of her position and later commissioned portraits and other subjects from her husband. In such fashion, the household sought to meet expenses: Meg offering her delectable charms for sale, with the coin of purchase a canvas from Steinheil's studio.

The artist occasionally bemoaned his existence as perpetual cuckold to his brothers-in-law and to a few other friends, particularly several of his longtime male models. For the most part, he had come to terms

3. For the relationship with Faure, see APP, B A/1017, B A/1072, B A/6022–27, Mort de M. Félix Faure. See also Charles Braibant, *Félix Faure à l'Elysée: Souvenirs de Louis Le Gall* (Paris, 1963); Steinheil, *Memoirs*, 68–126; Dudley, *Widow*, 22–31; Chrestien, *Steinheil*, 9–25, 47–53; Tavernier, *Steinheil*, 65–103. In the February 17, 1899, *L'Aurore*, Clemenceau wrote: "Le président Félix Faure est mort. Cela ne fait pas un homme de moins en France." The February 28, 1899, *La Libre Parole* accused a Mlle S—— of the crime, referring to actress Cécile Sorel; the *Journal du Peuple* more accurately identified Meg but called her Mme S—— on February 22, 1899.

with this life in which Meg was his wife in legal fashion only. He tolerated all of her lovers, whether those who bought her favors once with a single purchase or those whose attentions lasted longer and thus were more lucrative to his brush. By 1905, however, it was doubtful that this arrangement could last much longer. Steinheil himself was fifty-five and no longer able to work consistently because a habit of taking opium at night to aid sleep had caused him to age prematurely. He produced fewer canvases each year, and income from sales declined proportionately. Meg was now in her mid-thirties. She remained a stunningly beautiful woman—described by Gustave Téry as a madonna by Andrea del Sarto—who could be mistaken easily for her daughter's elder sister, but she could not hope to attract wealthy lovers for very many more years. There was also the question of Marthe, who was now in adolescence. Although she knew nothing of her parents' lives apart, this secret could not be kept from her forever.[4]

Meg's lovers had always been replacements for Steinheil, but up to this point, they had served principally to satisfy her mythomania, her delusions of prestige, wealth, and, not incidentally, dominance over men. In choosing to compromise herself, she placed them in her thrall while she remained untouched emotionally. Now, there was an increasingly pressing need of a permanent substitute for Steinheil. In early 1905, she met Emile Chouanard, director of the Forges de Vulcain, very wealthy, about forty years old, a man who never allowed guilt to interfere with his pleasures. In the beginning, he was willing to play the game of purchasing paintings from Steinheil and meeting Meg in hotel rooms to carry on an affair. After a few months, he tired of this and proposed that Meg rent a hideaway where they might meet at leisure and offered to pay whatever bills for it that Meg presented to him. From this suggestion came the acquisition of a villa, the Vert-Logis, outside Paris overlooking the Seine in the small town of Bellevue. The location was convenient—only forty-five minutes away by train from both the Montparnasse and Invalides stations—and Meg arranged to rent the villa in the name of one of her friends, Mme Mathilde Prévost, who lived near the Impasse Ronsin at 10 Boulevard

4. For the salon, Meg's role, and her husband's reaction to it, see Steinheil, *Memoirs*, 38–67, 127–34; Chrestien, *Steinheil*, 54–73; Locard, *Crime*, 239; Lanoux, "Mystérieuse affaire," 279–80, the description by Téry quoted on p. 272; Tavernier, *Steinheil*, 58–64.

Edgar-Quinet. To take charge of the housekeeping, she had her trusted chambermaid, Mariette Wolff. Steinheil made no objection to this arrangement except to insist that he be welcome at Bellevue when Meg did not have other male visitors. To the curious, both husband and wife explained that Meg's trips to the villa were to meet her Aunt Lily.

Chouanard was very generous with his money, paying the entire cost of the villa at Bellevue and many of Meg's other bills as well. Meg may have entertained some hopes of marrying him eventually, but in November, 1907, the affair came to an end. The specific incident was a dispute over Chouanard's choice for his daughter's fiancé, but the larger issue was Meg's presumption in claiming to interfere in Chouanard's family concerns. She was, after all, only a mistress, and the affair had run its course after more than two years.

Perhaps Meg was disconsolate; surely she was disappointed. These emotions may have contributed to a fainting episode that occurred while she was riding the Métro a few weeks later in December. Or perhaps it was Meg the actress. An elegant young nobleman with a gold-headed cane, Count Emmanuel de Balincourt, walked her home, and by the time they reached the Impasse Ronsin, Meg had decided to make him her next conquest. Balincourt was handsome and appeared wealthier than he was. Meg invited him to dine at the Impasse Ronsin and to see her husband's paintings. He paid the visit, spoke at length with Steinheil about art, and found the artist sympathetic. He commissioned a portrait in riding habit. A week later, he traveled to Bellevue for a tryst with Meg and then was overwhelmed with guilt. He finished the poses for his portrait and bought two other canvases as if in private amends. He did not see Meg again.

These experiences left Meg desperate. She was now thirty-eight years old and could not expect to find many more Chouanards or Balincourts. This sense of despair made her all the more delighted when she met Maurice Borderel on February 15, 1908. He was nearly fifty years old and a recent widower with three adolescent children, a son and two daughters. Tall, pot-bellied, and bald, with a blond beard and russet moustache, a rustic from the Ardennes, gentle, but for all that a wealthy landowner, his emotions were not a match for the supreme Parisienne. He succumbed to Meg almost immediately and paid his first visit to the villa on March 6. Like Chouanard, he paid her debts. Unlike him, he fell in love. From the start, he insisted that he could not marry her. He would not disgrace the memory of his first wife by taking a divorced woman as his second. Neither did he intend to impose a stepmother on his children. In perhaps ten years' time, when his children would be grown and married, if Meg had been freed by Steinheil's death, they could then discuss the matter of marriage. Even under these conditions, there were to be no promises, no certainties.[5]

It is easy to imagine how Meg felt. Borderel seemed her last chance to win a new husband while she was still young. He had made his intentions clear, but he was in love with her and kept returning to the villa ever more entranced. His mind could be changed. Everything was still possible if only Steinheil were not an obstacle. Divorce could not be considered, because neither would surrender Marthe and because Borderel would be very reluctant to marry a divorcée. Steinheil would have to die. And die he did, along with Meg's mother, on the night of May 30–31, 1908.

Sunday, May 31, was Pentecost, the day of the derby, extremely hot and uncomfortable. At 6 A.M., the Steinheil valet, Rémy Couillard, came sleepily down the stairs from his room in the fourth-floor attic to hear moans from the bedroom on the second floor where Marthe usually slept. But Marthe was at the villa in Bellevue, where Steinheil, Meg, and Mme Japy, who had arrived two days earlier for a visit, were to join her that afternoon. Racing into the room, Couillard found Meg tied hand and foot to Marthe's bed, her nightgown—he was to say—pulled up about her face, leaving her body naked. Beside her head lay what appeared to be a wad of cotton wool that she had finally managed to force from her mouth. She cried out something about robbers in the house and that Rémy should call for help. These words were all that an already jumpy twenty-year-old boy needed to make him throw open a window and scream.

The Steinheil house was located quite near a printing shop on the Impasse Ronsin, and a night watchman heard the cries. He ran to investigate. So did a neighbor, Maurice Lecoq, and a policeman just coming off duty, Agent Ponti. They found the iron gate to the yard open

5. For these three lovers, see the report of December 4, 1908, APP, B A/1584, Affaire Steinheil; *Le Figaro*, November 29–30, December 1–2, 1908, Steinheil, *Memoirs*, 135–50; Floriot, *Deux femmes*, 21–26; Tavernier, *Steinheil*, 104–13.

and the outside door to the house unlocked. Alerted by Couillard's screams, they warily looked for intruders on the ground floor of the house and then rushed up to the second floor. There, they found a frantic Couillard trying to untie the knots binding Meg, who seemed in shock. Stepping into the next rooms, they discovered the bodies of Adolphe Steinheil and Emilie Japy. Steinheil was on the floor of one adjoining bedroom, his legs curled beneath him; Mme Japy was in the bed of the other. Ordinary household cord was wrapped about their necks, and both appeared to have been strangled. Within minutes, a police commissioner, M. Buchotte, and his men had been summoned, and the search for the murderers began.

It was a strange tale that Meg told, the words coming in a rush as though she had been severely traumatized by her experience. She had been awakened about midnight from a deep sleep by the touch of a cloth on her face. She sat up in bed and saw dim figures and shrouded lanterns. Immediately, three men and a woman threw themselves upon her, the woman wielding a revolver. They seemed to take her for her daughter, because the woman hissed: "Your father has sold some paintings, no? Where is the money? No tricks! Or we'll have your skin, slut!" One of the men said quickly, "We don't kill brats!" Meg told them that the money was kept in a small study off from the bedrooms, felt herself struck on the head, and then fainted, waking only much later to find herself tied and gagged. After what seemed like hours of effort, she had finally dislodged the gag from her mouth and had begun calling for Couillard, who heard her only when he came down from the attic. Before she fainted, however, she managed to see glimpses of the intruders: the men wore long, black shirts or coats, the woman had brilliant red hair.

Around 9 A.M., Octave Hamard, the dapper and meticulous chief of the Sûreté (the criminal investigation division of the Paris police), appeared in person at the Impasse Ronsin with no fewer than seven assistants—a principal inspector, a brigade commander, a deputy brigade commander, and four inspectors. This singular deployment of forces was increased by the presence of Examining Magistrate Joseph Leydet, who had requested assignment to the case and who had been a close friend—some said a lover—of Meg Steinheil. Hamard took the unusual step of personally directing the investigation, and Meg recounted to him and Leydet the story she had already told, adding only that a number of jewels and perhaps Fr 7,500 appeared to have been taken during the crime. She was then confined to her bed by her doctors, who had added to the crush in the house. The men from the Sûreté overran the rooms looking for clues, while the famous Dr. Alphonse Bertillon directed the taking of fingerprints from various objects. A few hours later, the bodies were taken to the morgue.

In a statement to the horde of reporters who had gathered near the house, Hamard offered his preliminary opinion that this was a case of thieves surprised at their work who had managed to kill Steinheil before he could act against them. The artist's iron-cored walking stick—an alpenstock—had been found near his body and had perhaps been meant by him as a weapon. The death of Mme Japy was less easy to explain. Also curious was the apparent intimate information possessed by the intruders. They had picked a night to rob the house when only Couillard was supposed to be in residence. The Steinheils had planned to join their daughter at Bellevue for the night and had decided not to make the trip only at the last moment, when Mme Japy's rheumatism flared up and the weather turned stormy. There were, Hamard concluded, many clues and indications to follow, but the most promising was the possibility that one of Steinheil's former models had led the band, as Mme Steinheil seemed to remember having seen one of the men before. This statement was the epitome of moderation and restraint, but public opinion, sensationalist, and "tous les Sherlock Holmes de café" insisted from the beginning that this was a crime of passion.

On the following day, Meg, still in her bed, received Hamard and the goateed Leydet to provide a more complete account of the night of terror and murder now that she had had some rest. She thanked them for their concern for her health and volunteered that her sleep had been interrupted continually by nightmares. Nevertheless, she was anxious to do all she could now to find the murderers of her husband and mother. Mme Japy, Meg began, had arrived from Besançon on May 29, and the entire family had planned to spend the night of May 30 at the villa in Bellevue. With a thunderstorm in the air and Mme Japy's legs aching, they had decided after dinner to postpone the trip a day. Marthe would be perfectly safe at Bellevue under the care of Mariette

Wolff, and Louis Buisson, the father of Marthe's fiancé, could look in at the Vert-Logis because he had a villa quite close by.

At the Impasse Ronsin, everyone had gone to bed around 10 P.M. after drinking rum toddies Meg made. Her mother had severe pain in her legs and slept in Meg's bed for the night because it was larger and more comfortable than Marthe's. Meg took her daughter's bed, and Steinheil kept his own bedroom. At around midnight—she knew because she heard the chimes of the clock—Meg felt the cloth on her face and awoke to the scene she had described before. Now she was able to add that the hair of the woman was frizzy as well as red and that she seemed a slattern. The men wore ankle-length black garments that "resembled the vestments of the pope." One had a long black beard laced with silver streaks, an angular face, and thin bony hands. The other two men had red and brown beards, respectively, and wore hats. Meg added that she would probably recognize them if she saw them again but that she was less certain that one of the men might have been a model for her husband.[6]

This additional description gave Hamard and Leydet important new evidence as they began the process in French judicial procedure known as the *instruction*, essentially an inquiry combining investigation and interrogation. The examining magistrate (*juge d'instruction*) assigned to the case presides over an investigation by the Sûreté, weighs the evidence, and determines which suspects should be arrested. Once an arrest has been made, the magistrate presents this evidence—whether witnesses or exhibits—in the presence of the suspect (*inculpé*), who has the right to counsel. There are always confrontations between the suspect and his accusers; in murder cases, there is often a confrontation of the suspect with the corpse. In either instance, the suspect's reactions are carefully noted. At the conclusion of this presentation, the magistrate decides either that the case against the accused should be dismissed or that there should be an indictment. If the later, the *inculpé*, then termed a *prévenu*, is brought before the Chambre des Mises en accusation, a five-judge panel that serves the function of a grand

6. This description of the scene of the crime and the first steps of the investigation is taken from the report of May 31, 1908, APP, B A/1584, Affaire Steinheil; *Le Figaro*, June 1–2, 1908; Steinheil, *Memoirs*, 151–80; Floriot, *Deux femmes*, 27–35; Lanoux, "Mystérieuse affaire," 269–73; Dudley, *Widow*, 32–42; Tavernier, *Steinheil*, 114–19.

jury. If this indictment court finds the work of the magistrate proper, it binds the accused over to the criminal court (Cour d'Assises), where guilt must be proved before a jury. This action by the indictment court causes a final change in nomenclature, the accused now being designated formally as the defendant (*accusé*).

The process of a French *instruction* is normally a long one, and in the case of the murders at the Impasse Ronsin, there were particularly vexing questions. Although there had been a heavy rain the night of the murders, there was no trace of water on the carpets inside. There was also no evidence of forced entry. One of Steinheil's favorite models, a part-time grocer named Blaise Antemzio, volunteered to the police that the painter chose those who posed for him carefully and used them time after time, never recruiting ones he did not know. But if the criminals had never been inside the house before, how did they know its disposition so well? Only a few of Meg's jewels had been stolen, and the silver in the dining room had not been touched. How could professional thieves—since amateurs could hardly have been expected to leave so little evidence—have been so careless? Why had Steinheil and Mme Japy been *strangled*? This perplexing problem loomed especially large because it quickly became apparent that the cord used in the murders and to tie up Meg had come from the Steinheil kitchen. In the face of these unanswered questions, the Sûreté did not publicly abandon its initial conclusion that Meg's version of the crime was generally correct, but there were immediate rumors in the sensationalist press that Meg herself was the murderess. There were also veiled references to her lovers and wounding nicknames: Du Barry de Montparnasse, Circé de Vaugirard, and most commonly, Veuve Rouge—the Red Widow.

These rumors were fed by a sudden dearth of news from the Sûreté. All that Hamard and Leydet would reveal was that they were pursuing "several leads." A curious public made what it could of the revelation that the villa in Bellevue had been rented in the name of Mme Prévost and that Louis Buisson, the head of a chain of tobacconists, issued a strong statement supporting the mother of his son's fiancée. The attitude of the press led Meg to seek asylum from the "agony" and "persecution" of the case at the palatial townhouse of her friends the Count and Countess d'Arlon off the Champs de Mars (12 Rue Edmond

Valentin) until she felt stronger. She continued, her doctors declared, to suffer from nightmares, and the many servants of the d'Arlon entourage could shield her from an unfriendly world. The only item of significance that the press could exploit was the list drawn up by Meg on June 11 of the twelve pieces of jewelry she claimed had been stolen. The Sûreté counted on apprehending the murderers when they attempted to sell their plunder. Newspapers and the Agence Azur, of 24 Boulevard Sébastopol, which cataloged lost and stolen articles, were asked to give the list maximum publicity. This was done, but the response most often heard was that what had been stolen was not very valuable: the costliest item was a sapphire ring worth four hundred francs. Why would thieves murder for such minor booty?[7]

While the press and a fascinated public pursued rumors, the Sûreté was quietly following an important lead that promised to substantiate Meg's version of the crime. The Hebrew Theatre (Théâtre Hébreu) at 133 Rue Saint-Denis was a specialized institution, presenting all of its plays in Hebrew and filling the roles from a largely floating cast of actors, many of them immigrants from eastern Europe who did not speak French. On the night of May 30, the troupe was to produce *Cain and Abel*. Costumes for the play had been rented on May 27 from the Agence Guibert at 14 Boulevard Saint-Martin and included four long black vestments. At the last moment before the performance when the actors were donning their costumes, three of the vestments were found to be missing. Critically, they matched closely the description given by Meg Steinheil of the clothing worn by the three male murderers. In addition, on May 31, the day after the crime, a certain Villemant, a ticket-taker of the Métro system, picked up an astounding piece of evidence from the floor of a second-class compartment in a subway car at the Villiers station. It was an invitation to the exhibition of paintings that Steinheil arranged at the Impasse Ronsin for the week beginning April 7. On the reverse of the invitation, there was the penciled notation "Guibert, costumier pour théâtres." Within the fold was the greeting card of Mme Jane Mazeline, a noted painter in her mid-sixties.

At the Sûreté, there was a general conviction that someone con-

7. Reports of the June and July, 1908, APP, B A/1584, Affaire Steinheil; *Le Figaro*, June 3–7, 12–13, 17–18, 26, 28, July 21, 29, 1908; Steinheil, *Memoirs*, 173–94, 208–20; Dudley, *Widow*, 43–49; Tavernier, *Steinheil*, 120–24.

nected with the Hebrew Theater had led the intruders. That individual had stolen the invitation directed to Mme Mazeline—who was above suspicion because of her age and because her handwriting did not match that on the reverse of the invitation—and gained entrance to the Steinheil residence during the exhibition, thereby learning the plan of the house. Told of this story, Meg conveniently remembered that one of her husband's models had volunteered to deliver some of the invitations. He might be the culprit. There were inquiries at the Hebrew Theatre, but they led no further because no one there but the manager, a M. Goldstein, spoke French and except for four permanent actors, all of the members of the troupe had left Paris. Undaunted, Sûreté agent Pouce showed Meg pictures of several frequent visitors to the Hebrew Theater. When she came to that of a shaggy, blond-bearded American poet and painter Frederick Harrisson Burlingham, who was said to have a red-haired mistress named Mlle Moretti, she cried out, "That's the one!" There was brief elation because Burlingham seemed a prime suspect—disciple of Ruskin, milk drinker, and vegetarian—but it was quickly clear that she was mistaken. Burlingham was in the habit of wandering about France in leather sandals on long walking tours. There was undeniable proof that he had been at Montbard in Burgundy at the end of May. Further investigation showed that his mistress was named Mlle Crozette, who had brown hair, not red.

None of these details came to the attention of the press until November, 1908, partly because Hamard and Leydet did not want to reveal that their investigation had led to no great success and partly because from July to late October Meg vacationed on the Normandy coast at Saint-Laurent-sur-mer and was unavailable for comment. When she returned to Paris, she seemed much changed, less the helpless victim, more like herself, the director of her fate. She was also considerably friendlier to reporters.

Meg's new attitude brought the murders of the Impasse Ronsin back to the front pages of the Paris newspapers. On October 25, she had interviews with Ferdinand Monier, the public prosecutor, and Hamard, both of whom gave her the impression that the investigation was *classé*, filed as unsolved, because there were no new leads. Meg then retained an attorney, Antony Aubin, and demanded that Leydet allow Aubin to inspect the dossier of evidence thus far compiled. Rather taken aback, Leydet quite properly refused. On October 30 in a letter to *L'Echo de Paris*, she declared that she intended to find the murderers with or without the assistance of the Sûreté and revealed for the first time that they had carried off four valuable tapestries on the night of the crime. Finally, during the last ten days of November, Meg began a series of accusations that would end with her own arrest and incarceration in Saint Lazare prison.[8]

Meg began her accusations by charging that her valet, Rémy Couillard, had been in league with the murderers. As she told the story, on November 19 she had needed the address of Couillard's parents at a moment when the valet was out on an errand. The chambermaid, Mariette Wolff, suggested that they look for the address in Couillard's wallet, which he had left behind in his overcoat. When they opened the wallet, they were shocked to find in it a letter addressed to Pierre Buisson (à la Touche, par Mesland, Loire et Cher), Marthe's fiancé. Couillard had been entrusted with mailing the letter the day it was written, October 30, but he had apparently opened it and kept it for himself. After replacing the wallet, Meg thought it best to inquire more deeply into the matter of her valet's character.

On November 20, she asked the advice of her cousin, Edouard Chabrier, one of Steinheil's relatives who with his wife had moved into the large house to keep her company. She also consulted a friend, the Countess de Toulgoët, and Henri Barby, an editor at *Le Matin*, one of her several new acquaintances among the press corps. All three urged her to contact Hamard, and Chabrier undertook the mission. The Sûreté chief refused to have anything to do with this minor "act of indelicacy." Chabrier then returned to the Impasse Ronsin, and the group decided to act on their own, calling in Couillard and demanding that he show them the contents of his wallet. There was no way to hide the letter, and Couillard began to stammer excuses. Barby then suggested that the wallet be searched further to discover what else the valet might

8. Reports of June–November, 1908, particularly those of June 1, June 15, and August 10, APP, B A/1584, Affaire Steinheil; Reports of September–November, 1908, particularly those of September 28, October 31, and November 1, Archives Nationales (hereinafter cited as AN), BB 18, 2369 (1908), dossier Affaire Steinheil; *Le Figaro*, November 1–2, 4–6, 12–16, 1908; Steinheil, *Memoirs*, 195–248; Chrestien, *Steinheil*, 96–117; Lanoux, "Mystérieuse affaire," 273–74; Dudley, *Widow*, 50–77; Tavernier, *Steinheil*, 125–37.

have secreted away. Once again, the Sûreté was notified, and once again Hamard declared his disinterest. Barby proceeded to the search himself. In one of the pockets of the wallet, he found a pearl wrapped in new silk paper. Meg immediately identified it as having come from an art nouveau ring stolen during the crime, and this time, when called, Hamard sent two inspectors. A nearly hysterical Rémy Couillard admitted to having stolen the letter but denied any knowledge about the pearl. A hundred times he cried, "Je suis t'innocent!"

During the next few days, the newspapers delighted in revealing all of the details of Couillard's personal life: how he had lied about his past as a construction worker for the Métro in order to get the position with the Steinheil household, how he had a young mistress, and how this mistress had a friend with brilliant red hair. Meg seemed delighted with the course events had taken. "I have complete confidence in the Chief [Hamard]," she avowed. "I have suspected Couillard for a long time. . . . Did he commit the crime? . . . I don't know! But he will talk!"

But when Rémy Couillard talked, it was to deny any involvement in the murders, even as an accomplice who let the intruders into the house. If he had been involved, he boasted, much more would have been stolen, as he knew the secret locations in every room. He also pointed to the silk paper in which the pearl had been found. If it had been in his wallet for six months, it would not be fresh, as it was. In the meantime, Meg gave a complete statement about the discovery of the pearl to Hamard and Leydet. Very coolly, she recounted how she had suspected Couillard from the beginning but had not spoken because her doubts were based only on circumstantial evidence. She had a long list of complaints about him: he had lied about his origins, lied about breaking a vase, and lied about misplacing a key to the house. More important, on the morning after the crime, he had seemed tempted to strangle her when he found her bound to the bed and had called for help from the window instead of looking for Steinheil—as if he already knew that the artist was dead. Finally, anonymous letters had arrived that claimed Couillard had become infatuated with Marthe Steinheil and hoped to break up her engagement to Pierre Buisson. That would explain his stealing the letter.

It was not easy to fit this new development into the previous conception of the case. If Couillard had been in league with the intruders, he could have shown them where the most valuable possessions of the household were stored and surely would have warned them that instead of an empty house, there were three adults sleeping on the second floor. He would also have prevented their mistaking Meg for Marthe. Nevertheless, the Sûreté methodically pursued this new trail by searching Couillard's room on the fourth floor of the Steinheil residence and the rooms he occasionally occupied with his uncle and aunt in another part of Paris. Meg assisted in the search at Impasse Ronsin, and it was she who noticed and picked up a tiny diamond brilliant from the floor of Couillard's attic room. The evidence against the valet now seemed conclusive, and it would have been, had the case not taken a sudden and dramatic turn.[9]

On November 25, two days after the discovery of the diamond brilliant, Meg came to the interrogation room of Sûreté headquarters along the Quai des Orfèvres at the request of Hamard and Leydet. To her surprise, she found three men waiting for her in addition to the Sûreté chief and the magistrate: Lucien Gaillard, the jeweler who had created the art nouveau ring in which the pearl from Couillard's wallet had originally been mounted, Georges Boin-Taburet, a gemmologist on retainer from the Sûreté, and Léon Souloy, another Parisian jeweler. Meg listened in horror as Souloy asserted that the famous pearl supposedly stolen on May 30 and in the possession of Couillard since that time had actually been in his shop in mid-June, carried there by Meg Steinheil herself. She had brought the art nouveau ring to him with instructions to dismount the pearl and to create a new mounting for the rest of the stones in the ring. The request was a simple one and had been accomplished on the same day, June 12. Souloy himself had forgotten about it, but one of his assistants recognized the description of the pearl from the press accounts of Couillard's arrest. He had remembered it because the pearl was unusual in shape and had been drilled oddly in preparation for its mounting in the art nouveau ring.

This testimony overturned all of the assumptions previously held by the Sûreté. If true, Meg had contrived the accusation of an innocent

9. Meg justifies her role in the accusation in her *Memoirs*, 249–68. See also the reports of November 22–24, 1908, APP, B A/1584, Affaire Steinheil. There was excellent coverage of this breaking story: see *Le Figaro*, November 22–25, 1908, Meg's quotation coming in the November 22 issue.

Rémy Couillard and at the very least lied about what had been stolen on the night of the murders. Souloy's revelations could also make Meg the prime suspect in the murders themselves. Vehemently, she denied the account, but Souloy produced his records for June 12 showing her name and a description of the pearl that had been dismounted at her request. Hamard then brought in Couillard to confront Meg. The valet again protested his innocence and claimed that either Meg or Mariette Wolff had placed the pearl in his wallet without his knowledge.

At this point, a discouraged Leydet advised Meg that she should seek the counsel of her attorney, and Antony Aubin and his assistant Benjamin Landowski quickly responded to her urgent request for their presence. Aubin convinced Leydet and Hamard to suspend the interrogation, and he led Meg back to the Impasse Ronsin. Rumors about the day's events at the Quai des Orfèvres had already circulated, and by the time Meg arrived home, seven police agents had taken up positions around the house. Officially, they were to guard the property and to prevent the entrance of unauthorized individuals. Unofficially, they were to prevent any attempt at flight.[10]

The night of November 25–26 is known in the lore of the Steinheil affair as the "night of confessions." A weeping and distraught Meg Steinheil, her daughter Marthe, the Chabriers, Mariette Wolff, and two journalists, Marcel Hutin of *L'Echo de Paris* and Georges de Labruyère of *Le Matin*, who claimed to be sympathetic to Meg's plight and whom Meg had asked for advice, played out a drama at the Impasse Ronsin. Because the accusation of Couillard had clearly proved false, Hutin and Labruyère urged Meg to tell the truth to Hamard, whatever the truth was. Sobbing, Meg admitted lying. She claimed that she had done so to avoid having to name the real culprit, Alexander Wolff, the son of her chambermaid, Mariette. Wolff, she told them, had threatened either to kill her or to insist that she had been his accomplice if she were to go to Hamard with his name. His motive for the crime had been greed and resentment against the family that could hire his mother as a mere chambermaid. He had spared her, Meg finished, because he intended

10. Report of November 25, 1908, which includes an anonymous letter accusing Meg of framing Couillard, APP, B A/1584, Affaire Steinheil; *Le Figaro*, November 26, 1908.

to rape her after finishing his murders and theft, but he had been frightened away before he could do so.

By now it was midnight. Hutin and Labruyère hardly knew what to make of this new account of the murders and especially what to think of Meg. She appeared devastated and terrified, anxious above all that Mariette Wolff not be told of the accusation. Hutin learned that another journalist, Barby from *Le Matin*, had persuaded the police to allow him to join his colleagues, and he asked Barby to watch Mariette carefully while he and Labruyère went to file their stories. Sensing headlines, Barby instead sought out Meg and heard her asking for strychnine. For herself? Meg then belied her earlier wishes and met privately with Mariette for some minutes. Afterward, distraught and in despair, Meg murmured that if she were arrested, Mariette would deny everything. Barby was mystified by this cryptic confession. Everyone in the house was in a state verging on paranoia. Upstairs, Meg sat on her bed and called for poison. Downstairs, the Chabriers waited in terror for Alexander Wolff to appear and kill everyone. Mariette sat in an armchair in the salon with a revolver in her hands. Asked what she was doing with it, Mariette replied that the pistol was her "last plank of safety."

Because Meg knew that the morning papers would carry her new accusation, she had to take some action. At 4 A.M. she set off for the Quai des Orfèvres. Her motions were almost mechanical as she put on her coat and opened the front door. Then she turned suddenly, clutched her daughter, and cried out: "My child, have courage! We are all lost! You, me, all of us!"

Hamard was roused from sleep and came to his office to hear her story. Sûreté agents quickly picked up Wolff at a hotel near the Impasse Ronsin (77 Rue Brancion) where he lived with his mistress, but his demeanor hardly gave credence to Meg's accusation. He seemed genuinely surprised that his name had been connected to the crime in any fashion and vigorously protested his innocence. As soon as he could be brought to the Quai des Orfèvres, he was confronted with Meg. In her presence, he grew even firmer in his denial of guilt. Within minutes, Meg began to equivocate, eventually saying that perhaps the murderer—now singular—had merely resembled Wolff. But if that were the case, how could she have been threatened by him if she were to accuse him to the police? It was clear that she was caught in another damaging lie.

Sensing that the case was about to break open completely, Hamard brought first Rémy Couillard and then Mariette Wolff into the interrogation room to confront Meg. Mariette declared her son innocent and claimed that if he were guilty, she would have been the first to call for his arrest. By then, it was early afternoon, and Rémy Couillard was formally released. Twice more in the next few hours Meg and Wolff were brought together, each confrontation ending in a screaming match with Meg accusing him of wanting to rape her and Wolff denouncing her as "a vile lying whore." Hamard could see little point in continuing these sessions, as it was clear that Wolff was entirely innocent. After a warning that his movements would be watched, he was released. Meg was asked to remain. Leydet entered the room with some reluctance and presented her with a warrant calling for her arrest on the charge of "complicity in murder." "We think," he added, "that by your lies and your concealment of evidence, you have misled justice and placed obstacles in the way of the seizure of the murderers."[11]

Scandalmongers had barely had a chance to savor the incarceration of Meg Steinheil in Saint Lazare prison when the Ministry of Justice on the Place Vendôme issued a terse and never fully explained announcement. Public Prosecutor Monier, acting in the name of the minister of justice himself, Aristide Briand, replaced Leydet as examining magistrate of the Steinheil case with Louis André. Such a change in examining magistrates was not unknown in the French system, but in this instance it seemed remarkable. Leydet could claim to have solved the case. André, although an eight-year veteran as a magistrate, studious, capable, circumspect, and ponderous, had not seen even a single piece of evidence from the crime. With André at its head, the *instruction* would have to begin anew. The change implied criticism of Leydet and a lack of confidence in his ability to complete the *instruction* he had opened. Later, his name would be struck forever from the promotion list.[12]

11. Reports of November 26–27, 1908, APP, B A/1584, Affaire Steinheil; *Le Figaro*, November 27, 1908; Steinheil, *Memoirs*, 269–93.
12. See the extensive series of memoranda generated by the investigation of the Ministry of Justice into the role played by Leydet in this case: November 30–December 4, 1908, AN, BB 18, 2369 (1908), dossier Affaire Steinheil. There is also Leydet's personnel

Ignoring the general puzzlement at his appointment, André started to work energetically, checking to see whether any evidence might have escaped his predecessor. He interviewed and reinterviewed all of the principals in the case and commissioned experts to examine once again all of the physical evidence. The bodies of Steinheil and Mme Japy were exhumed for a second autopsy. Their viscera, maintained at the Sûreté laboratory, were tested again. All of the rooms at the Impasse Ronsin and the Vert-Logis were thoroughly searched anew and the furnishings checked for fingerprints. Very slowly out of all of this activity, André believed that he saw a pattern emerge, a pattern that could account for the murders only through the complicity of Meg Steinheil.

Mariette Wolff provided the first dramatic revelations. Her original loyalty to Meg seemed broken by the accusation of her son, and she now named Chouanard, Balincourt, and Borderel as Meg's lovers. Interest obviously centered on Borderel, as he had been Meg's latest conquest. Widower and father of three children, large landowner in the Ardennes, and mayor of the village of Balaives et Bute, he had found Meg irresistible. Nevertheless, after an affair of only three months, he told her that he could not marry her. André concluded that Meg took Borderel to mean that he would not marry a divorcée. On May 30, she telephoned him at Balaives et Bute. The connection was bad, and Borderel could catch only her comment that she was "happy to hear [his] voice" and then her laugh. Since he did not receive the Paris newspapers, he learned of the crime through a brief note from Meg's confidant, Count d'Arlon. Borderel was horrified. He hurried to Paris to offer his condolences and then returned to the Ardennes. After some months of hesitation, he sent his friend Félix Auguste Martin to Paris on October 25 with money to pay some of Meg's expenses and with the message that Borderel would see her again only if she removed all suspicion from her name. According to Martin, Meg's reaction was to blurt out: "I have lost the love of the man I loved. Everything is over

file: AN, BB 6 II, 1025. See the story in *Le Figaro*, November 28, 1908. Reports of November 27–28, 1908, APP, B A/1584, Affaire Steinheil, reveal widespread criticism by deputies and senators of Leydet and the criminal investigation he headed. See also Lanoux, "Mystérieuse affaire," 275, 280; Floriot, *Deux femmes*, 35; Chrestien, *Steinheil*, 116–17; Tavernier, *Steinheil*, 153. Meg would remain in Saint Lazare prison until her trial almost a year later; her *Memoirs*, 294–329, include an overwrought account of her life as a prisoner.

for me." Here was the motive for Meg's series of accusations in November.[13]

Less dramatic were nagging bits of information that seemed to have escaped Leydet. Early in the evening of May 30, Meg had ordered Couillard to take the watchdog Turc back to Mariette Wolff's daughter and son-in-law, who regularly loaned the dog to the Steinheil household during the summer. Meg complained that Turc failed to bark at strangers and had developed a nasty odor. The dog had also soiled a sketch executed by Steinheil, ruining a week's work. Couillard had disagreed with her on every count but ended by returning Turc to its masters and leaving the house, he claimed, less protected. Sûreté agents had noticed several gloves left about near the murder scene. Meg asserted that they had been worn by the murderers: this explained the lack of fingerprints. But Mariette Wolff told André that the gloves had been a gift to Meg from her lover Chouanard, who gave her his worn-out pairs to save her hands when she helped occasionally with light household chores. Meg could not explain this flagrant lie. She also could not explain why the cords used in the murders had come from a drawer in the kitchen. What manner of criminals would wait until they entered a house to look for their tools?[14]

There were inconsistencies in Meg's version of the crime. The first police agents on the scene noticed a small spot of ink on Meg's left knee. This was assumed to have come from an inkstand found overturned in a short corridor off the upstairs study connecting Marthe's bedroom, where Meg was found tied and gagged, to Meg's bedroom, where Mme Japy had slept and had been found dead. Drops of ink led from the pool next to the overturned inkstand to the bed where Mme Japy was discovered. Meg explained the spot on her leg by saying that there must have been ink on the hand of one of the criminals and that it had marked her as she was tied up. But the mark resembled a splash much more than a fingerprint. There was also disagreement about how securely Meg had been tied to her bed. Couillard at first called the knots very difficult to release but later reversed his judgment. The head of

13. Report of November 30, 1908, APP, B A/1584, Affaire Steinheil; *Le Figaro*, November 29–30, December 1–2, 1908; Dudley, *Widow*, 85–90; Tavernier, *Steinheil*, 138–42.

14. Reports of December, 1908, APP, B A/1584, Affaire Steinheil; *Le Figaro*, December 13, 16, 18, 1908; January 26, February 19, 1909.

the Sûreté's scientific section, Dr. Victor Balthazard, had been unable to find traces of saliva on the gag that Meg claimed to have forced from her mouth. It was possible that with so many agents rushing about in the early confusion of the investigation the wrong piece of cotton wool might have been picked up by mistake. But there was no mistaking another troubling piece of evidence. The neighbor Lecoq, who was first to the rescue, had heard Couillard scream that because the door was locked, a window would have to be smashed to gain entrance to the house. Lecoq checked the door nevertheless and found it unlocked. When he reached the second floor and saw Meg, he immediately thought that she had been tied too loosely—too loosely for security. There was also the impression of Steinheil's brother-in-law, Albert Bonnot. He arrived at the house soon after the Sûreté and before the removal of the bodies. His thought was that he was on the set of a detective play, looking at a cleverly contrived crime.[15]

All of this evidence was more suggestive than conclusive, but Leydet seemed to have ignored it completely. He had also disregarded a disturbing suggestion in the first autopsy report that was substantiated by an examination of the exhumed bodies. There was no proof that either victim had been drugged in any fashion—some had hypothesized that Meg could have carried out the murders alone had she drugged the victims. But there was absolute proof that Mme Japy died not of strangulation but of suffocation—from her own dental plate. A gag of cotton wool had been forced into her mouth with such force that it pushed her plate deep into her throat. The cord found around her neck had done its work after she was dead. Leydet had refused to grasp the implication of this discovery. Mme Japy would not have retired for the night with her dental plate in place: therefore, she had been murdered before she went to sleep. From that deduction, the only possible conclusion was that Meg's story of being awakened from sleep about midnight had to be just that, a story. The murders were done earlier.[16]

There were other pieces in the puzzle that involved Meg, but how they matched up with the murders was unclear. Rémy Couillard told

15. Reports of December, 1908, particularly December 14, 1908, APP, B A/1584, Affaire Steinheil; *Le Figaro*, December 13, 16, 20, 31, 1908; January 16, 1909.

16. The second autopsy report does not appear in APP, B A/1584, Affaire Steinheil. See *Le Figaro*, December 18, 1908, and the conclusions by Locard, *Crime*, 241.

André that he had been quite surprised at the Steinheils' decision to stay overnight in Paris because Mme Japy's legs were giving her pain. To him, she seemed to be suffering no more than usual and had even taken a short walk by herself early in the afternoon on May 30. Even more difficult to explain was the revelation that Meg made a quick trip out to the villa at Bellevue around 11 A.M. on May 30 and returned just before dinner. She claimed to have made the visit to check on Marthe and Mariette, but doing so implied that she already knew that she was not returning that evening with her husband and mother. Yet all along, Meg had insisted that the decision not to make the trip had been made very late in the day, after dinner, and had come in response to the gathering rainstorm and the pain of her mother's rheumatism. Finally, Meg's correspondence indicated clearly that both her husband and her mother were well informed about her lovers. Only Marthe was kept ignorant. Did this knowledge have any bearing on the crime? Only a few days before the murders, Auguste Steinheil had written a despairing but cryptic note to his wife. It was found by his other brother-in-law, Adolphe Geffroy, at the Impasse Ronsin:

> My Dear Child,
> I do not know how to tell you the state of my soul since Tuesday evening, but that is of little matter and this letter is not to reproach you. I found a letter from M. B[orderel], transmitted through the intermediary of M. M[artin]-F[euillée, a mutual friend]. He let it drop, and it was picked up during housework. May Marthe not have seen it. I come to talk to you in the name of your father, who must see from on high what takes place below. You are going to trap yourself on a path that will lose you infallibly. Remember what happened with M. L[emercier, a magistrate with whom she had a brief affair] and M. C[houanard]. The awakening has been more than hard. You have every good quality. I hope that it is not too late for you to come back. I adore you profoundly.
>
> "S"

Clearly, he was still in love with her in spite of everything. But what did he mean by "trap yourself" and "lose you infallibly?"[17]

17. Report of December 12, 1908, APP, B A/1584, Affaire Steinheil; *Le Figaro*, December 9, 19, 1908; the letter from Steinheil is quoted in the January 16, 1909, issue.

And what was anyone to make of a sensation in the press early in January, 1909, when a *Le Figaro* reporter discovered that on April 27, 1885, at Montbéliard—a few miles from Meg's home in Beaumont and when she was barely sixteen years old—there had been a mysterious crime. Two men, wearing long black shirts, their faces blackened, were supposed to have broken into the house of a former calvalryman turned tax collector named Peuillard. His wife had been tied up and forced to reveal the location of the strongbox. Peuillard had been overcome by the intruders and kicked so hard in the stomach that his skin bore the imprint of the hobnailed sole. When the police investigated, they found no sign of forced entry and no marks of violence on either Peuillard or his wife except the mark of the boot, and that was proved to have been self-inflicted. The tax collector had contrived the crime in order to account for the disappearance of taxes that he had received and spent. He was sentenced to five years in prison at hard labor, but the term was commuted because he had lost an arm during the Franco-Prussian War. The proceedings were amply covered by the *Quatorze Juillet* of Montbéliard and the *Petit Comtois* of Besançon, and Meg could hardly have failed to read about it. The resemblance of the crime in 1885 to that in 1908 was remarkable.[18]

But if there was great deal of evidence that pointed to Meg, there were also elements in the case that raised doubts about her guilt. Most important, there was no credible motive. Borderel claimed to have made Meg absolutely no promises of marriage. Instead, he had all but declared that he could never marry her. Meg did not love her husband, but relations between them had not noticeably worsened, and he had been aware of her lovers for fifteen years. Despite some rumors to the contrary, Meg and her mother were quite affectionate. Meg's sisters both claimed that Meg had loved her mother dearly, and they rushed to her defense. Certainly, she could not benefit monetarily from the deaths. Mme Japy left only a medium-sized estate, of which Meg's share yielded an annual income of about three thousand francs. Steinheil's income had come from his brush, and with him dead, there would be no more of his paintings to sell. His legacy to his widow was prin-

18. *Le Figaro*, January 13–14, 1909, story by Georges Bourdon. This was an exclusive for *Le Figaro*.

cipally the house at the Impasse Ronsin, which was worth seventy-five to eighty thousand francs. Meg could even explain away much of the evidence against her, including the question of her jewels. She claimed that she had moved her most valuable jewels from the Impasse Ronsin to the Vert-Logis because only Couillard would be at the house in Paris to protect them. She had exaggerated the number of jewels that had been stolen, because she had become confused about which ones were supposed to be where. When she discovered her mistake, she felt too embarrassed to go to the Sûreté with a correction. She was sensitive about answering questions about her jewels, because many of them had come not from Steinheil but from her lovers, and she was anxious that Marthe not learn of her affairs.[19]

Finally, there were questions that had no answers at all. The tall clock at the Steinheil residence had its pendulum stopped at 12:10 A.M. on May 31. The only fingerprints on the pendulum were of unknown origin. Who stopped the pendulum? Why? Did it occur at 12:10 A.M. or at some other time? What was the significance of that hour except that it corresponded with Meg's version of events? Any murder investigation attracts anonymous tips and outlandish stories, but one had the ring of truth. A respected attorney, Victor-Charles Monteils of 163 Rue de Vaugirard, looked out of his window about midnight on the night of the crime and saw a large car parked at the intersection of his street and the Impasse Ronsin. Standing next to it was a man dressed in elegant clothes, holding an umbrella, and smoking a cigar. He seemed to be watching and waiting as another man ran down the Impasse Ronsin from the direction of the Steinheil house toward him. Both climbed into the car and drove off.[20]

Despite these baffling questions, André, who had developed a singular antipathy to Meg, concluded that the *instruction* was sufficient to place before the indictment court. He manipulated the evidence to indicate her guilt:

1. She had sufficient motive in desiring her freedom from a husband who would not grant her a divorce.

19. Report of December 15, 1908, AN, BB 18, 2369 (1908), dossier Affaire Steinheil; *Le Figaro*, November 29, December 4–9, 1908; January 10, 15, 1909.
20. Report of December 1, 1908, APP, B A/1584, Affaire Steinheil; *Le Figaro*, December 3, 5, 1908.

2. She prepared the act by sending away her daughter and the watchdog.
3. She was part of the act—the ink spot resulted when she knocked over the inkstand while moving from her bed to that of her mother.
4. She prepared her defense before the crime by carrying away jewels from the house on the Impasse Ronsin to the villa at Bellevue in order to claim that they had been stolen.
5. She continued her defense through lies—she was not tightly bound, she was not gagged, she acted out her nightmares and delirium in the days following the crime, and she accused innocent principals of having committed the murders.

But Meg could just as easily manipulate the evidence to indicate her innocence:

1. She could not have been the lone assassin unless the victims had been drugged, and the autopsies revealed no drugs.
2. If she had had an accomplice, as André implied, the Sûreté could not name him. In addition, the official reports noted unknown fingerprints on the clock pendulum and showed that no ink was found on any of Meg's clothes. How could she have overturned an inkstand and escaped with only a single splash mark?
3. She had never fully abandoned the version of the four assassins, a woman and three men, except when a moment of weakness made her accuse Couillard and Wolff. How could the Sûreté explain the coincidence of the costume theft at the Hebrew Theater and the card found on the Métro?
4. What of the report of attorney Monteils?
5. Finally, what was the motive? She loved her mother; the man she wanted to marry would not marry her; she could receive little monetary gain from the deaths.[21]

On March 13, 1909, concluding an *instruction* that had run nine and a half months (three and a half under his direction) and produced 3,442

21. Reported in *Le Figaro*, March 10–12, 1909. The law of January 3, 1979, regulating the communication of documents from the Archives Nationales raises from fifty to a hundred years the length of time before a dossier of *instruction* may be communicated; the Steinheil dossier is therefore unavailable until 2009.

pieces of evidence and 13,500 pages of analysis and deposition, André formally charged Meg Steinheil with the premeditated murder of her husband and mother (*homocide volontaire avec préméditation sur la personne de votre mari et parricide*). Assistant prosecutor Guillaume Grandjean then drew up an indictment (*réquisitoire*) of nearly a hundred pages accusing Meg as the principal author of the two murders. André added a thirty-page exposition of the grounds for the indictment (*motifs*). The indictment court took up the case on April 27 with solicitor general Fernand Rome reading the reports of Grandjean and André before the court and concluding with his own recommendation that Meg be indicted for murder and bound over to appear before the Cour d'Assises de la Seine for trial. The chief justice, Antoine François Grenier, promised a quick decision and named one of his four associate justices, Paul Tournade, as reporter for the case.[22]

The decision took three weeks. On May 18, the indictment court ruled that before Meg Steinheil was brought before a jury in criminal court, the Sûreté should carry the investigation further. The obvious motive for the decision of the indictment court was the apprehension of a petty thief at Versailles, Baptiste Allaire, who claimed that one of his mates in the underworld of crime, Angelo Tardivel, had bragged of committing the murders at the Impasse Ronsin. The Sûreté had investigated and proved false literally dozens of such tales during the course of the long inquiry, and it seemed likely that the words of the court were meant as a discreet warning that the evidence against Meg was not conclusive and would prove insufficient for a jury to convict. There was even controversy about the case between André, who believed Meg the principal author of the crime, and Rome, who privately thought that she could have been no more than an accomplice.[23]

The rumors about Tardivel took until June 11 to disprove defini-

22. *Le Figaro* and *Gazette des Tribunaux*, March 14, 26, 28, 31; April 28, 1909. For a summation of the course of the *instruction* under André, see Steinheil, *Memoirs*, 342–73; Lanoux, "Mystérieuse affaire," 280–84; Chrestien, *Steinheil*, 117–35; Dudley, *Widow*, 78–120; Tavernier, *Steinheil*, 142–51, The case won André a promotion: see his personnel file, AN, BB 6 II, 620. The charge of *parricide* was shocking to the French, as the crime was rare: only 156 cases were charged between 1901 and 1913, with 14 for 1908. Premeditated murder (*assassinat*) was much more common: 1,603 during the same period, with 142 for 1908. See the annual report of the Ministry of Justice: *Compte général de l'administration de la justice criminelle*. For a view of how the police normally investigated murders, see APP, B A/81–85, B A/1612, Crimes.

23. *Le Figaro* and *Gazette des Tribunaux*, May 19, 1909.

tively and merely added more weight to an already bulging dossier. The indictment court was in recess for the summer by then, but the presiding justice of the Cour d'Assises, Charles-Bernard de Valles, exercising the discretionary power vested in him by Article 268 of the Penal Code, ruled that the intention of the indictment court had been met and that Meg would stand trial beginning November 3, 1909, with the case for the state presented by the solicitor general of the Cour d'Assises, Paul Trouard-Riolle.[24]

The trial was previewed during the first days of November by lengthy reports in the Paris newspapers. Everyone in the capital seemed fascinated by this mysterious Steinheil affair that remained an enigma in spite of now four thousand pieces of evidence, two examining magistrates, the personal participation of Hamard, and the careful attentions of an army of Sûreté agents tracking down every rumor and anonymous tip as well as more solid evidence. *Le Figaro* was not alone in predicting cynically that "the trial will likely lift few of the shadows of this bloody history."[25]

II

The trial opened on November 3 in the Cour d'Assises de la Seine of the Palais de Justice. The competition for places in the audience was intense because the publicity had made the trial not just a sensation but an occasion. A number of foreign ambassadors had successfully solicited the president of the Republic for seats. Marcel Proust even put in one of his few daylight appearances. Poet and dandy Count Robert de Montesquiou ridiculed the case, saying it proved that parvenus do not know how to kill, but he came to watch Meg. So did the Countess Elisabeth Greffulhe, née Caraman-Chimay, who called Meg "stirring and so feminine," and others from the faubourg Saint Germain. So did representatives from different levels of society, although only one hundred spectators were allowed in the court each day apart from the nearly ninety members of the press.

The courtroom itself lent an impression of ponderous dignity with its heavily decorated ceiling and the sunken panels in the walls depicting the sword and scales of justice. It was that dignity that Presid-

24. Reports of May 18, 1909, AN, BB 18, 2369 (1908), dossier Affaire Steinheil; *Le Figaro*, May 17–19, 21–23, 27–28, 30–31; June 1, 3, 5, 9, 11–12, 29; July 18, 1909.
25. *Le Figaro*, November 2–3, 1909, the quotation from the latter.

ing Justice de Valles, the president of the court, and his two associate justices wanted to maintain despite the sensational aspects of the case. Gray-bearded and dressed in the red robes of French justice, all three sat on an elevated platform with the bulging dossier of the *instruction* before them. De Valles himself was a tall man, severe and sad, of great firmness and refinement. After the first day's session, he would bar the presence of women in the audience.

Prosecutor Trouard-Riolle, an obese figure whose double chin contrasted sharply with his hawklike face and ferret eyes behind a pince-nez, also wore a red robe. Aubin and Landowski for the defense wore black robes. Aubin was among the most famous barristers of Paris and exactly the one the public would have expected Meg Steinheil to choose: strikingly handsome with his curly black hair, moustache, and beard. Between them was the exhibit table overloaded with evidence. To one side, twelve Frenchmen—four "proprietors," two mechanics, two commercial clerks, one musician, one bricklayer, one baker, and one cook—made up the jury. To the other side was the witness bar, a semi-circular rail on three uprights. When everyone else was seated, there was a hush, and Meg entered the court, very pale and dressed entirely in black crepe.

Most of the spectators knew her only from photographs in the newspapers, but even they could tell that the more than eleven months in Saint Lazare had had a baleful effect upon her beauty. Her cheeks had hollowed, and there was a new fold at the corner of her lips. She had suffered and aged. Her large dark eyes had retained their luster and brightened a waxy complexion. She appeared gentle from the front, but her profile had turned hard, accented, heavy, almost vulgar. Little shivers of rage would pass over her face when the prosecution pressed her to answer questions. She would bite her pale lips. There was every reason for her to appear too little, too thin, too frail for this contest. But she was mistress of herself; she had girded herself for this combat. Her very appearance excited an unwonted tension in the court because she was all nerves, on fire, dramatic, even melodramatic. And her voice would pass from tears to wrath, by turns caressing and violent. The court would be her stage.[26]

26. For de Valles and Trouard-Riolle, see their personnel files, AN, BB 6 II, 1267 and 1256, respectively. For the trial, see Steinheil, *Memoirs*, 416–55; Floriot, himself a member of the Paris bar, *Deux femmes*, 59–71; Chrestien, *Steinheil*, 136–63; Dudley, *Widow*,

The rules of French judicial procedure called for the trial to begin with a direct examination of the defendant before the jury by the president of the court, the *interrogatoire*. It was immediately clear that de Valles intended to exert this prerogative to the full, and to many, his partiality was blatant: in his eyes, Meg was guilty. The first questions had to do with Meg's youth and were designed to paint her as wild, impetuous, and a liar from childhood. There was the story of her affair with Lieutenant Scheffer and her exile to Bayonne, where she met Steinheil. He was from a notable family, Meg interjected; otherwise she would have been forbidden to marry him. Next there were questions about her married life with the artist. Had she been happy living in Paris and creating a salon? Meg's reply was that the salon had served to further Steinheil's career, as he thought only of painting. He was, she sighed, "a simple man, too simple." De Valles then baited her: "Yes, an effaced man, a humiliated man!" Rising to the lure, Meg cried passionately the reverse of what the justice had expected, that her husband had been an "honorable man," who knew nothing of her lovers. She denied utterly ever telling anyone, much less the Sûreté, that Steinheil took opium or that she wanted to divorce him. De Valles was startled but replied that Meg had told such things to Borderel, that she had called Steinheil "evil." With a smile, Meg won this exchange by replying, "A woman never tells her lover anything good about her husband."

Then, setting upon the name Borderel, Meg began a tirade. It had been Borderel's suspicions of her, she asserted, that had led to her arrest and imprisonment. Correcting this illogical argument, de Valles exclaimed that she had been imprisoned because of her lies and because of her guilt. Meg hardly heard him. She had already launched a denunciation of the Sûreté, the system of justice, the press, the law, the prison administration, preventive detention, and public opinion. There was no order to her thoughts, only a tumult of deeply held resentments forcing themselves to the surface. She had never, she claimed, identified Burlingham as the murderer—"I said someone who resembles him!" She stuck to the story of the three men in long black

121–79; Tavernier, *Steinheil*, 152–65; Lanoux, "Mystérieuse affaire," 284–92, the remarks by Countess Greffulhe and Montesquiou from p. 285; *Le Figaro* and *Gazette des Tribunaux*, November 4–14, 1909.

robes and the red-haired woman. It was true, she granted, that she had denied this version in accusing Alexander Wolff, but those had been desperate days for her. The press had given her no peace and printed the vilest rumors about her possible involvement in the crime. Accusatory anonymous letters had rained into the house at the Impasse Ronsin. When she had found the stolen letter in Rémy Couillard's wallet, she had wanted so badly to believe him guilty. She had believed Wolff guilty. She repented of these mistakes now. But her husband had still not been avenged! Through all of this, her voice rose and fell in sobs. She pointed wildly, grasping in her hand a white handkerchief to wipe her frequent tears. It was a compelling performance: reaching for effect, she passed her hand across her forehead and then struck her breast. De Valles was affected, admitting, "In perhaps no other case have we felt so clearly the fear of judicial error."

Meg then began a new defense of Steinheil. He had adored her as a child, she confessed, and she repented of having failed him as a wife. Her constant lovers were a search for a friend in whom she could confide. Renting the villa at Bellevue was to avoid hurting her husband by receiving lovers at home. De Valles listened to these remarks with impatience. He counterattacked by forcing Meg to admit that it had been only with Chouanard that she had rented the villa and then only because he paid for it. It was also blatant falsehood to claim that Steinheil had been unaware of her lovers. De Valles read aloud portions of the letter Steinheil had written to Meg only days before the murders, emphasizing how Steinheil asked her to break off her relationship with Borderel if only to spare Marthe from learning the truth about her parents. The artist had concluded pathetically, "I adore you profoundly."

Intense emotion seemed to flow through everyone at these words. For a moment, Meg herself was unable to control her feelings but finally recovered to say stiffly that she had tried, and failed, to defend her husband from being labeled publicly a willing cuckold. At least, she added, he had never learned that she received money from her lovers, although he may have suspected that the paintings they bought were not purchased entirely out of admiration for his art. Besides, Chouanard was the only one of her lovers to give her large sums of money, and she had not asked for even a sou. She had never, she declared proudly, "sold" herself. She "gave" herself to her lovers. It was love that was free in the best sense of the word. She had never even contemplated marriage with any of them, just as she had never contemplated leaving Steinheil.[27]

It was a bad day for the prosecution. Meg managed to portray herself very sympathetically. The only slip in her defense came near the end of the day's testimony. Meg was unable to explain why she had gone out to Bellevue on the morning of May 30 if the decision to spend the night at the Impasse Ronsin was not made until late in the evening that day. In particular, she could not explain why she had approached Buisson about stopping by the villa that night before she knew that Marthe and Mariette would be alone. But if de Valles and Trouard-Riolle thought that they could exploit this slip and create others to counter the impression she had produced the first day, they misjudged her. On the second day of the trial, she emerged unscathed, and there was even new sympathy as the result of an absurd attempt by a young man, René Colard (who called himself Jean Lefèvre), to confess to the murders. After he admitted that he had been led to this act by infatuation with Meg and order had been restored in the court, Meg continued to play her role perfectly, surprised when any of her answers were questioned. If she had committed the murders, it was reasonable to expect that she would defend herself with the energy of a murderess. If she had not committed them, it was reasonable to expect that she would defend herself with all the energy of a woman wronged and falsely accused. Henri Rochefort, the savage wit of *L'Intransigeant*, had at first dismissed Meg as a "Bovary de XVe." Now he called her "the Sarah Bernhardt of the Assises."

Asked why she had sent away the watchdog Turc, Meg replied that the dog did not bark and that the proof lay in its failure on the night of the crime to warn of the four intruders, although its owner lived only a few doors away on the Impasse Ronsin. Asked about preparing the rum toddies and the choice of beds—Mme Japy in Meg's, Meg in Marthe's—she merely recounted her previous deposition to the Sûreté. Occasionally, she was impertinent, replying that of course her mother was given the better bed. She repeated once more the version of the crime with the three men in black robes and the red-haired

27. *Le Figaro* and *Gazette des Tribunaux*, November 4, 1909.

woman. It was, she maintained stoutly, the truth. If she had varied in any details from one interrogation to another, it was because everything had happened so rapidly and horribly.

De Valles took a new tack. He noted that in *Les Cinq doigts de Birouk* by the prolific detective story writer Louis Ulback there was a crime remarkably similar to the one she described. Meg's library contained a number of Ulback's books but not that one. Had she read it, he asked coyly? Meg's reply was equally coy: no, but she was certain that she would find it as interesting as she had found Ulback's other mysteries. Of the resemblance of her version to the crime in Montbéliard when she was sixteen, Meg could say only that there was a coincidence and that she was quite certain that she had not heard of the Montbéliard case as a youth.

These questions were too easy for Meg to parry, and the presiding justice returned to problems about the night of the crime. Why had she been tied so loosely? The knots had not seemed loose to her. Why had the Sûreté not found saliva on the cotton wool Meg claimed to have had in her mouth? The agents had incompetently picked up the wrong piece of cotton wool from the room. Why had the murderers killed with cords when they carried revolvers? These were, de Valles commented ironically, very peculiar criminals who would take out a length of cord from the Steinheil kitchen cabinet, cut off what they needed, and replace the remainder. "They told you all of this?" Meg asked in seeming innocence and to barely suppressed laughter in the courtroom. Meg herself had no explanation for such curious behavior. Now angry, the presiding justice suggested that the murder of Mme Japy had been committed to produce an alibi for Meg, since the Sûreté would surely suspect her to be the author of the murder of her cuckolded husband had he been found as the single victim. The Sûreté might be less likely to believe her capable of murder and parricide both. This supposition was a dangerously clever explanation of the crime, and Meg had to respond to it carefully. She refused to be trapped into arguing the hypothesis. Instead, she launched another emotional speech in which she claimed to have loved her mother even more than she loved her daughter. She could never, she claimed, never have killed her mother, even to save herself. De Valles rebuked her for failing to reply to the question, but Meg interrupted and silenced him by crying, "I defend myself as I am able, with my heart, with my imagination, and I need not observe either order or method!"

After this outburst, Meg handled the remainder of this second day's questions routinely with one exception. Asked why the murderers had stopped the pendulum of the clock, why they dressed so strangely, and why they failed to loot the house more thoroughly, Meg replied disdainfully that the Sûreté should capture them and then pose the questions. Asked how anyone could have mistaken her for Marthe, Meg replied imperiously that before she had been left to rot in prison for 353 days, many regularly mistook her for her daughter, although rarely Marthe for her. It was Meg herself who brought up the question of the stolen costumes and the invitation and greeting card found in the Métro. De Valles called these a "puzzle," and this admission seemed to strike the jury. But the jury also took notice of Meg's one slip of the day, on the question of the ink spot. Why was there only the single mark on her knee? Meg had always explained it by suggesting that one of the murderers had soiled her with his dirty hands as he tied her to the bed. But then there should have been multiple spots: the image of a fastidious murderer was hardly credible. Meg seemed confused by the question and unready for it. She could only reply several times, vehemently but as if by rote, that she had not killed her mother. She did not mention Steinheil.[28]

De Valles concluded his *interrogatoire* on November 5, the third day of the trial. As on the two previous days, Meg responded to each precise question with a diffuse speech. She was indefatigable, refusing any chance to rest. De Valles began with more questions about the night of the crime, asking particularly about the clock with its pendulum mysteriously stopped at 12:10. In a vague comment, Meg replied that she could have no idea why anyone would want to stop the clock but that she did recall having heard it strike midnight as she was awakened by the murderers. Nothing more was made of the question of time as the presiding justice turned to other issues. Nevertheless, there was a nagging sense within the courtroom that the prosecution either had overlooked a critical matter or did not know how to develop it properly. Whoever committed the crime, Meg and the individual whose

28. *Ibid.*, November 5, 1909.

unknown fingerprint halted the movement of the pendulum wanted all to believe that the murders took place around midnight.

Perhaps De Valles merely felt on safer ground with two other topics, the amount of money and jewels allegedly taken by the murderers. During her many interrogations prior to the trial, Meg had offered conflicting answers to both. Now she insisted that a total of Fr 7,500 had been stolen, the money in two envelopes, one with Fr 5,000 the other with Fr 2,500. De Valles asked, with false innocence in his voice, how she could have given the Sûreté such different answers earlier. He added that an analysis of the Steinheil accounts at the Crédit Lyonnais revealed that the household did not even possess such a sum. Meg replied without evasion that she had not wanted anyone to realize how much money her lovers gave her. She readily admitted that Steinheil would not have wanted so much money around the house, as he was extraordinarily careless about currency. He frittered it away so easily that Meg had had to limit the amount in his hands. She added for good measure that her husband's inability to manage accounts had often forced her to make her own clothes. This admission, Meg said defiantly, would bring down upon her the contempt of the *femmes du monde*, the women of society, but she did not care. Those women, she claimed, had already revealed their quality by flocking to her salon when she had been considered chic and then deserting her after the murders.

The presiding justice waited patiently for her to finish this denunciation and then asked about the jewels. This was a difficult subject for Meg. Despite some efforts at investigation, the Sûreté had not been able to determine exactly how much money Meg could have had in the house on the night of the crime. The questions posed by de Valles about the money could only demonstrate that Meg lied copiously and frequently to the Sûreté and therefore might be supposed to be lying at her trial. For the jewels, however, there was a great deal of evidence to indicate that Meg attempted to shift suspicion to Rémy Couillard and might even have planned the crime. She was unable to deny that she had sent her best jewels to the villa on May 18 with Mariette Wolff. On May 31, after the crime, Meg claimed that five of the jewels in Mariette's keeping had been stolen. It was possible that Meg was confused, as she claimed, about which jewels were where, but this could no longer serve as an excuse after June 10, when Mariette brought the jewels back to Paris. Yet, on the following day, Meg formalized the list of jewels she claimed had been stolen and even advertised their theft at the Azur agency. De Valles related these events and asked Meg to account for them. To the surprise of the prosecution, she acted as if there was an entirely simple explanation to this vexing problem. To have changed the list and admitted to having been mistaken about the jewels might have brought suspicion upon her. An investigation into her jewelry would reveal how much of it had been gifts of lovers. Her daughter would learn the sordid truth about her mother. It seemed, Meg concluded, such a little lie. To maintain it, she had taken the jewels that she had claimed were stolen but were actually in her hands to Souloy to be remounted. She used the pearl from the art nouveau ring to frame Couillard.

The subject of the jewels led directly to the accusation of Couillard. De Valles insisted that Meg explain why she had placed the pearl in the valet's wallet. Here Meg took on again the role of the tormented woman. Waving her handkerchief and sobbing frequently, she admitted that she had lied in accusing Couillard and now repented of having done so. She swore that she would never have let him be convicted of the murders and only wanted to punish him for having stolen Marthe's letter to Pierre Buisson. De Valles then reminded her that it had not been she who had absolved Couillard. Indeed, she had continually declared his guilt and gone so far as to pretend to find a diamond brilliant in his room during the police search. This kind of conduct he called "abominable." But Meg would not accept this label. "I have been punished enough for that!" she cried. "I have been in prison a year for having placed Couillard there for a day!" What she had done, "any mother" would understand and approve, she claimed! As she finished, she and the presiding justice were glaring at each other ferociously.

De Valles broke the silence with the demand that Meg continue by explaining the confusing night of November 25–26, 1908, when she left the Quai des Orfèvres convinced that no one any longer believed in her accusation of Couillard. Hutin, Labruyère, and Barby had been at the Impasse Ronsin and pressed her to tell the truth. She had then accused Alexander Wolff. There followed the requests for poison and finally the decision about 4 A.M. to make her accusation before Hamard. As soon as Meg was aware that de Valles was insisting on her version of that night, she began to dab her eyes with her handkerchief. It was all true, she nodded, all true what he said about the journalists, the accusation, the decision to see Hamard, even the desire for poison. But she did no more than confirm the justice's bare outline of the night and offered no comments of her own. Remarkably, de Valles did not press her for more.

These questions completed the *interrogatoire*. To most observers, Meg seemed to have escaped unscathed. Neither de Valles nor Trouard-Riolle had cut short her passionate soliloquies with which she softened the blow of the most damaging questions and established her image as a woman driven by her fears and desperation into foolish accusations but hardly a murderess. She appeared more victim than criminal. De Valles showed himself either unwilling or unable to present the case for the prosecution with great rigor. He allowed Meg to equivocate and to answer questions obliquely, if at all. Where she stumbled, he failed to capitalize on her blunder. He seemed under her spell. His most critical failure was allowing Meg to establish her version of the case before the prosecution could present its own. De Valles and Trouard-Riolle would be left having to challenge her point by point, in essence reversing the roles of prosecution and defense to Meg's benefit.[29]

During the last hour of the session of November 5 and during the next four sessions, Trouard-Riolle called his witnesses, the first of a total of eighty during the trial. The testimony of Sûreté agents Buchotte, Pouce, and Debacq merely established the physical details of the scene of the crime. The appearance after them of Rémy Couillard raised the drama level much higher. He had begun his compulsory military service earlier in the fall and was dressed in the uniform of the dragoons of Provins. Blond, pale, his hair cropped short in the military manner, looking very sympathetic, he had apparently weathered quite well his travail before the law and seemed to delight in the publicity and fame it had brought him. He was even the subject of picture postcards. Before the court, he recounted his version of the dinner and rum toddies the night before the murders and insisted that he had heard nothing

29. *Ibid.*, November 6, 1909.

during his sleep. When he went downstairs in the morning, he heard Meg call his name and found her tied up in Marthe's bed, her arms across her stomach, the covers over most of her body. He untied her, called for help from the window, and only afterward discovered the bodies.

De Valles listened to these seemingly innocuous words with consternation. For Couillard directly contradicted a sworn deposition made by him to the Sûreté. In it he claimed to have heard only moans from Meg and to have found her hands tied above her head and the covers so removed from the bed that she was almost naked. Couillard's testimony also contradicted an affidavit from Lecoq, the neighbor who rushed to help when he heard the valet's call. Lecoq could not be called as a witness, as he had undertaken an engineering project in the United States, but in his affidavit he had sworn that Couillard untied Meg's hands and feet only after he arrived and that Meg's body was "undraped." Couillard coolly denied Lecoq's version and contended that the original deposition he had signed was in error.

This controversy cast some doubt on the remainder of his testimony. He asserted that on the day following the murders Meg told him that he should not worry about what had happened or talk about the crime to anyone because she, as mistress of the house, should tend to it. He also recalled seeing the supposedly prostrate Meg bound out of bed to answer the telephone the same day. Meg energetically denied these accusations and insisted that Couillard was lying in revenge for her having accused him of complicity in the crime. Almost haughtily, he rejected such a base contention. He admitted keeping the letter found in his wallet but explained that by claiming to have forgotten to mail it when he was supposed to do so and then to have been afraid to mail it later. Finally, he added that Meg had told him to lie to the police that a number of tapestries had been stolen on the night of the crime. Actually, the tapestries had never existed. With that, and in the midst of another heated denial from Meg, he left the witness bar.

Next up before the court were Jean Geoffroy and his wife. She was the daughter of Mariette Wolff and with her husband owned the watchdog Turc. Geoffroy asserted that Turc barked at anything that moved and that Meg had sent the dog back to them because it smelled of mud. His wife contended that the dog would bark at nothing and had been banished because it had soiled one of Steinheil's sketches. Here were more contradictions, but Geoffroy did add that he had awakened at 12:30 on the night of the crime and seen a lone man running away from the Steinheil house.

There followed three witnesses describing the world of Adolphe Steinheil, his brothers-in-law, Adolphe Geffroy and Albert Bonnot, both artists, and Steinheil's favorite model, Blaise Antemzio. Their depiction was of a man deep in depression who had thought of divorce from Meg in 1898 after the horrid finish of the affair with President Faure but who could not overcome his desperate love for her and for his daughter Marthe. Antemzio claimed that Steinheil had told him in April, 1908, that Meg was now the one wanting a divorce. Geffroy and Bonnot added more details about a loving husband with an unloving wife and denounced Meg as cruel and scheming. It had been Geffroy who had found and brought to the Sûreté the letter Steinheil had written to Meg about Borderel.

When Geffroy had finished, Meg eyed him with cold fury. Her voice laden with venom, she charged him with sullying her dead husband's name by proving him a willing cuckold. She herself had lied to protect his memory. Once again, the spectators in the courtroom seemed to take her side. The impact of the deeply pathetic depiction of Steinheil was dissipated by her single phrase.

The remaining witnesses on November 6 dealt with technical topics. Dr. Bertillon, the fingerprint expert of the Sûreté, admitted that of the ninety-one prints found at the scene of the crime, only fifteen or sixteen had been clear enough for use. These were the prints of Steinheil, Meg, Mme Japy, Mariette Wolff, Rémy Couillard, and persons unknown. In particular, there was a single, and unidentified, fingerprint on the pendulum of the clock. Dr. Lefèvre and Dr. Peuch, physicians under retainer for the Sûreté who had been called to the murder scene, followed. Both testified that they had seen only one piece of cotton wool that could have been the gag from Meg's mouth and that this piece of cotton wool had been taken to the police laboratory for examination. Finally, David Fineburg, an actor from the Hebrew Theater, provided some routine details about the disappearance of the black robe costumes so similar to those Meg had described as worn by the murderers.[30]

The fifth day of the trial, November 8, was the day of the experts. Dr. Maurice Courtois-Suffit, a well-known physician who often worked on retainer for the Sûreté, described the autopsies on the bodies of Steinheil and Mme Japy immediately after the crime. To protect himself against accusations of any type, he had insisted on the presence of Drs. Peuch and Lefèvre, as well as that of several medical students, while he carried out his examination. There was no evidence of trauma on Steinheil's body except for two furrows in the neck caused by the cord that strangled him. When opened, the stomach had a strong smell of alcohol. It had proved impossible to fix the exact time of death. The body of Mme Japy likewise bore strangulation marks, but less clearly. She had actually died of asphyxiation caused when a piece of cotton wool forced into her mouth broke her dental plate and pushed it deep into her throat. Courtois-Suffit had examined Meg on the day following the crime. The traces left by the cords binding her were very faint, indicating that she had not been tied tightly. The ink spot on her leg, he thought, could have been made by either a finger or a splash. There was no trace of any other injury to her.

Courtois-Suffit was followed by Dr. Victor Balthazard, the celebrated director of the Sûreté's medical staff. He had performed the second autopsies on the bodies of Steinheil and Mme Japy, after they were disinterred. He confirmed the results of the first autopsies and then began to examine various hypotheses about the crime. Steinheil, he felt certain, had not been killed in his bed, because there were no marks on his body to indicate that it had been moved or lifted. In addition, the position of the night tables near Steinheil's bed would have made the task of killing him there very difficult. There was no reason to assume that the painter had been drugged: narcotics were notoriously slow and unpredictable, and there was no trace of any narcotic in the body. Thus, Steinheil was probably killed where he was found, out of his bed. Mme Japy, on the other hand, had died of suffocation where she lay in bed, and Balthazard suggested that she had been killed first, perhaps by accident. The murderers might have tried to silence her

30. *Ibid.*, November 6–7, 1909.

while they dealt with Steinheil only to come back later and find her dead from the gag. One very intriguing fact was the lack of any struggle from either victim. The bedclothes were hardly ruffled about Mme Japy, and not a single button on Steinheil's nightshirt had been pulled loose.

Balthazard then speculated about Meg. He had proved that the gloves found in Meg's bedroom and identified by her as worn by the murderers had actually been hers, a gift from Chouanard. Much more serious, there was not a trace of saliva on the cotton wool that had supposedly been in Meg's mouth throughout the night. Finally, the spot of ink on Meg's leg was blue-black, but the ink on the carpet violet-black! What this revelation might mean he could not say. Finally, he suggested that it would have been physically possible, but unlikely, for a single woman to have committed the two murders.

The third physician of the day, Dr. François Acheray, took his place at the witness bar after Balthazard. Tall, slender, and elegant, a friend of Steinheil and a neighbor, he had often joined Meg and her husband for music after dinner. His opening statement was arresting: that any discrepancy between his present testimony and previous declarations would be the result of the Sûreté's failure to understand his remarks. He described Steinheil as gentle and melancholy but not unhappy, and particularly not unhappy on May 30 when Acheray greeted him after examining Mme Japy's ailing legs. On May 31, he had rushed to the Steinheil house in response to a call from Rémy Couillard and had found Meg in a state of profound distress and shock. De Valles questioned him about the Steinheil marriage. Acheray replied that Meg had told him of anonymous letters claiming that her husband took opium and had been surprised in his studio making love to a female model. Frowning, the presiding justice reminded him that in an earlier declaration he had spoken not of anonymous letters but of fact and had said that Meg and her husband lived apart, although under the same roof. Acheray repeated his assertion that he had been misunderstood earlier. He ended his testimony by describing his care of Meg after the crime and his certainty that she had not fabricated her illness and hallucinations.

The string of expert witnesses then reached almost ludicrous proportions. A clock repairman, M. Fournier, took the stand to testify to the sole fact that the pendulum of the clock in the Steinheil house had been stopped deliberately at 12:10. Next, an "expert on cord," a M. Chaffaroux, swore that the cord discovered about the necks of Steinheil and Mme Japy definitely came from a longer length of cord found in a cabinet of the Steinheil kitchen. Another physician, François-Jules Ogier, supported Balthazard's conclusion that no trace of narcotic could be found in the viscera of the victims. Brigadier Dechet of the Sûreté explained that all of the rumors and leads about the case had been dutifully followed and that there was, in the Sûreté's opinion, no credible witness other than Geoffroy who had seen any strange faces near the Impasse Ronsin on the night of the murders.

Mme Jane Mazeline, the artist whose card had been found on the Métro on May 31, finally broke the series of experts. She could offer no explanation for her greeting card's appearance with an invitation that she insisted never having received. Indeed, she had not seen Steinheil in years, had not ridden the Métro on May 31, and could not have written the costumer's name on the reverse of the invitation, since the handwriting did not even resemble hers. This entire issue was not made clearer by the testimony of Guibert, the costumer, Mlle Juliette Rallay, his assistant, and Fineburg and Goldstein of the Hebrew Theater. No one was quite certain when the costumes could have disappeared, and the actors mentioned that they had seen someone who was almost the double of their friend Burlingham, the American artist whom Meg had identified as one of the murderers.

Finally, on this day when a long series of witnesses had managed to make the case even more confusing, Burlingham himself took the witness bar at the close of the session. He was tall and elegant with a long blond beard, but his clothes were shabby. He spoke such miserable French that Trouard-Riolle offered him an interpreter. Burlingham angrily refused, deeply offended that he had been briefly charged with murder by the French police and intent on exacting a public apology at the trial. The Sûreté had managed to confuse most of the facts about him, claiming that his mistress was a red-haired Mlle Noretti whereas she was actually the brown-haired Mlle Crozette, and mistaking his address in Montmartre for a similar street name in Montparnasse. He left the bar little satisfied with the excuses offered him. His real impact was on many in the courtroom who now wondered to what extent they could believe in any assertion from a Sûreté that had failed to verify information and had apparently taken little care with sworn declarations during the investigation of the case.[31]

By the time of the court session of November 9, it was clear that Meg had conquered her public and that to win a conviction, the prosecution would have to mount a much stronger case in the closing days of the trial. To that end, Trouard-Riolle called as a witness Souloy, the jeweler to whom Meg had taken her allegedly stolen jewelry in mid-June of 1908 for resetting. Souloy told how he had remounted the stones and then in November learned that one of the pearls he had worked on had been found in Rémy Couillard's wallet and that Meg was claiming that it had been stolen the night of the murders. It had been Souloy who through his deposition had cleared Couillard of any suspicion. Meg's reply to this testimony was to repeat her desire to conceal the gifts of her lovers and to allege genuine mistakes in determining what had been missing after the murders.

The most exciting witnesses of the day were Meg's cousins, the Chabriers, and journalists Hutin of *L'Echo de Paris* and Barby and Labruyère of *Le Matin*. All testified about the night of November 25–26. Their stories, almost a word-for-word recital of previous statements to the Sûreté, were the first really damaging evidence Meg had faced. There could no longer be any doubt that Meg and Mariette Wolff had both contemplated suicide that night. Barby remembered Meg's saying cryptically that if she were arrested, Mariette would "deny everything." Barby had been uncertain whom Meg expected to be arrested, Mariette or herself. De Valles turned from him to confront Meg. Was it true that she had contemplated suicide and that she had told Barby that Mariette would "deny everything"? Meg turned unusually pale and hesitant; her fingers clenched her handkerchief, and perspiration dripped from her brow and upper lip. She could only murmur that she could not remember. It was the worst impression she had produced. With Mariette Wolff due to testify the next day, it was possible to wonder whether the trial was about to swing away from Meg.[32]

When the following day's session was ruled in order, Mariette walked quickly from the waiting room and took her place at the witness bar. She had acquired a well-deserved reputation as Meg Steinheil's con-

31. *Ibid.*, November 9, 1909.
32. *Ibid.*, November 10, 1909.

fidant, and she probably knew more than anyone else about the guilt or innocence of her mistress. Small and round, she looked much like a peasant woman from one of Balzac's novels. She was nearly fifty years old, her few gray hairs brushed back from a wrinkled forehead, her eyes suspicious, her lower jaw protruding so that she had an almost bestial appearance. She was dressed completely in black and wore an unusual bonnet with ribbons that fell to her shoulders. Her husband had died in 1894, and she had joined Meg's service that year. They had formed an immediate bond that had been broken only slightly and briefly when Meg accused Alexander Wolff, Mariette's son, of the murders. When asked about her mistress's life, the response from the chambermaid had almost always been: "When one is a domestic, one must see everything but say nothing."

It was quickly apparent that Mariette would not be forthcoming before the court. She claimed to have knowledge of only three of Meg's lovers, Chouanard, Balincourt, and Borderel, although she was willing to speculate that there might have been more. She denied that Meg treated her husband roughly or that after the murders she had said, "Enfin je suis libre" (Finally, I am free). Instead, Meg had said, "Me voilà libre" (So now I'm free). There were aspects of the case about which she claimed to know nothing: whether Steinheil had an opium habit, whether Meg had sent her jewels to Bellevue in mid-May. Mariette admitted carrying a package to the villa then but denied having opened it.

De Valles at this point began a series of questions about the night of the murders. Who had slept at the villa in Bellevue? Had Louis Buisson stopped by to provide protection for Marthe? Why had Meg made a trip from Paris to Bellevue on the afternoon before the murders? Had she already decided to spend the night in Paris? Was it decided then that Buisson should check the Vert-Logis that night? Had Meg called late in the evening from Paris, as she claimed, to tell Mariette about the plan to remain at the Impasse Ronsin? To each of these questions Mariette repeated a refrain of "I do not remember." But de Valles was tightening his noose. He cited telephone records to prove that there was no telephone call from the house at the Impasse Ronsin to the villa at Bellevue during the evening. Meg must have told Mariette early in the afternoon that she, her husband, and her mother would spend the night in Paris—in spite of Meg's assertions to the contrary. De Valles noted that the train ride from the Bellevue station to Paris was only forty-five minutes and that the walk from the Montparnasse station to the Impasse Ronsin took only fifteen minutes more. What de Valles wanted to know was exactly when Mariette returned to Paris from Bellevue. This the chambermaid could answer: she returned as soon as she received a telephone call around 7:15 A.M. from Dr. Acheray on May 31 alerting her to the tragedy. She claimed to have raced to be with her mistress in order to give what comfort she could. De Valles seemed to feel that he had made a point of some sort, because he changed the direction of his questions to ask Mariette's reaction to the bodies of Steinheil and Mme Japy and whether she knew much about cords and knots, since her husband had been a coachman and her son was a horse dealer.

It was difficult to comprehend exactly what de Valles thought to accomplish through this questioning of Meg's chambermaid that lasted two full hours. It seemed almost as if Mariette Wolff had become the defendant. Certainly she had not acquitted herself as well as Meg had. Her persistent refusal to answer questions raised the darkest suspicions, and because she was reputed to be so closely linked to Meg, those suspicions inevitably shadowed her also. Mariette's replies to questions about the night of November 25–26 were no improvement as she flatly contradicted the testimony of all previous witnesses on the episode. She denied having threatened to commit suicide; she denied having talked to any journalists; she even denied having been told by anyone that Meg had accused her son Alexander of the murders. These responses made it clear that it was pointless to ask further questions, and Mariette was excused.

Her son, Alexander Wolff, followed her at the bar. A solid man, robust, rough-looking, with a small blond moustache, large nose, and beady eyes, he walked with the rocking gait of a horseman. Despite his prominence in the case, his testimony was extremely brief. He recalled that Meg had seldom been informal with him: she had addressed him familiarly once on his birthday and once at a New Year's celebration. He agreed with Meg that Turc was a bad watchdog: that had been the reason he had given the dog away to his sister and her husband. Finally, he said cheerfully that he bore Meg no animus for accusing him, as it had led to an amusing adventure. As he left the witness bar, it was impossible not to remark the dramatic difference between mother and son, one silent, sullen, surly, her physiognomy hard, her face bony; and other jovial, smiling, large, fat, cordial.

There followed next the witnesses for whom scandalmongers had waited long. They were disappointed in the performance of Mme Prévost, in whose name Meg had rented the Vert-Logis. Mme Prévost had actually believed in the story of Aunt Lily and had broken with Meg when she realized how Meg had exploited her. She knew no other details. Emmanuel de Balincourt came next, young, rigid, well-turned-out. He was discreet and refused to say exactly how many times he had stayed at the villa with Meg. He was not ashamed of his liaison with this older woman, but he had broken it off because he found Steinheil sympathetic. The Count d'Arlon added some detail about Meg's retreat to his townhouse to recover after the crime and scotched any rumors that he might have been numbered among her lovers. Chouanard had departed on a round-the-world trip and would not appear. By now the spectators were growing restless. Where were the salacious details? Where was the passion? They were waiting.

At last, Borderel emerged from the witness room and made his way to the bar. He looked his part, pastoral, sentimental, almost a poet. When he turned toward Meg at the defendant's rail, it was impossible not to see that he had loved her, that he loved her still. His life was broken, his family appalled at him. He had come to fulfill a debt of honor, to defend the woman he had loved. He told the story of their affair simply and affectingly. He had met Meg at the end of February, 1908, and began his intimacy with her in early March. They had made five or six visits to the Vert-Logis. In the beginning, he had found the freedom she enjoyed astounding, but he soon grew used to it. He had never intended marriage because he refused to present his children with a stepmother. Perhaps after ten years, when he would be about sixty and his children would be married and settled, he might reconsider. He had told Meg this and insisted that she must expect nothing from him. In late May he had even decided to break off the relationship because his son suspected the trips to Paris. He had learned of the murders through a letter from Count d'Arlon and had at first feared that Meg had killed Steinheil in a quarrel. He had hurried to Paris to offer his condolences and then resolved to see her no more. He had been shocked when his name was revealed in the newspapers as her lover, but he had done his duty and cooperated with the investigation.[33]

Borderel's testimony concluded the case for the prosecution, and Meg's attorney, Aubin, began his defense on the following day, November 11. It would be remarkable for its brevity in a capital trial, only a few hours. His first witness was Eugène Bornèque, one of Meg's uncles. He revealed that of the four Japy children, only Meg had never asked for an advance on her anticipated inheritance. He also testified that the whole of the Japy family believed Meg to be innocent and were convinced of her love for her mother. Louis Buisson and Meg's brother-in-law, Frédéric Herr, echoed these sentiments. Aubin next produced an accountant, Guillaume Vial, whose figures indicated that while the funds available to the Steinheil household were in decline during a period of inflation, there was by no means a crisis. The implication was that Meg had no reason to act immediately to improve her financial condition.

Then, in an act of bravery and genius, Aubin presented two final witnesses. The first was Scheffer, now a captain. He described his love affair with Meg at Beaumont when she was hardly more than an adolescent and he a newly commissioned lieutenant. When he turned toward Meg, it was clear that he recalled this early love only too well. After a moment of silence, he described her touchingly as "charming, well-reared, an artist in temperament, gentle and good, not seeking any fortune as I had none." The emotional impact of these words on Meg and on the whole court was great, but Aubin was not yet satisfied with the depth of that feeling. For his last witness, he called André Paisant, an attorney who had been a close family friend both of Meg and of Adolphe Steinheil. In broad strokes, Paisant sketched the essential portrait of their marriage. He called Steinheil "honest, simple, almost childlike, passing his life in his studio, discouraged before his canvas, dreaming his vague dreams in the blue smoke of his eternal cigarette, and melancholic, disappointed, beaten, sitting in his big armchair, watching the fall of night." But Meg "brightened him, made him

33. *Ibid.*, November 11, 1909.

young, made him talk, gave him courage, was his inspiration, pawned her jewelry to pay for his extravagances, granted him life." Paisant concluded, "I judged her severely at first [for her weakness and her lovers], then more humanely, and I experienced for her an immense pity." Around the courtroom, there were many tears.[34]

Solicitor General Trouard-Riolle could not have been happy to begin his summation, the *réquisitoire*, after Paisant's performance, but he commenced manfully. The entire trial had been difficult for him because it revived rumors of how his own attractive wife had been a favorite of Félix Faure and had sped his promotion in unusual ways. His was a careful, well-argued summary, but Trouard-Riolle was not a brilliant speaker and lacked the voice and gestures to compete with the drama of the defense. He attempted to explain too much of the evidence in a trial where there was too much that could not be explained. He also spoke too long and confused the vital elements of his case with the unimportant. He began with a resumé of Meg's life: intrigues with the son of a grocer, a hopeless affair with a penniless lieutenant, an unhappy marriage, a succession of lovers, and finally the dream of marrying Borderel, becoming a chatelaine and not having to worry about "debts to the grocer, butcher, baker, of having to borrow ten francs from Mme Prévost." Here was the motive for the murder of Steinheil. To general surprise, he admitted that the prosecution had not and could not prove a motive for parricide. Mme Japy had probably suffocated herself on the gag while Meg and an accomplice killed Steinheil. But who was the accomplice? That revelation had to wait for the next session, and *tout* Paris wondered through the night.

Trouard-Riolle was not coy. Very early during the session of November 12 he made it clear that he thought Mariette Wolff the accomplice. He refused, however, to name her, because there was not sufficient evidence even to indict her. But he described someone who could only be Mariette, someone recruited to serve Meg personally, a woman who knew the house at the Impasse Ronsin well. Together, Meg and this woman set up the crime, planning to tie and gag Mme Japy, strangle Steinheil, and finally bind Meg. Mme Japy could be Meg's corroborating witness because she would not be allowed to learn the

34. *Ibid.*, November 12, 1909.

identity of those who attacked her, but she choked and died as the gag broke her dentures. When Meg and Mariette returned after murdering Steinheil, their witness was a corpse. If Trouard-Riolle was correct, Mariette had managed to escape an immense investigation, two examining magistrates, and a year of work subsumed in the thousands of pages in the dossier of *instruction*.

The solicitor general dismissed all of Meg's arguments. Robbery could not have been a motive because Steinheil's watch and the money in his pockets were left untouched. There was no sign of a serious search of the house. He characterized Meg's story of three men and a woman as an invention. She was poorly tied to the bed; she never had a gag in her mouth; the ink spot was a splash from the overturned inkstand—overturned in the haste of the murders; the cord about Mme Japy's neck was placed there to make her death resemble Steinheil's. Because she could have identified them, true murderers would not have spared Meg: "One kills everyone or no one. If Mme Steinheil is alive, it is because she played a role in the drama and knows the assassins." The pendulum was stopped because "in this night of horror, the pendulum made noise. Nervous as she is, Mme Steinheil heard the tic-toc. She could not stop the course of hours; she could at least stop the sound."

Trouard-Riolle explained that when the original inquest led to no suspects, Mariette Wolff was watched, with no result. All manner of trails were followed. Five hundred anonymous letters arrived, some from abandoned lovers denouncing those who had abandoned them. The only aspect of the case that could not be fitted into this reconstruction was the theft of the costumes from the Hebrew Theater. It had to be dismissed as a coincidence, he argued. Meg's attitude was proof enough of her guilt: lie first, accuse later. Her lies began with the description of the crime and moved through the question of the jewels and tapestries. After her lies came the accusations—against anyone who could lead suspicion away from her. If Souloy had not identified the pearl, Couillard would have been convicted. If Alexander Wolff's alibi had not held, he would have been brought to trial at least. Every act of Meg Steinheil since the crime, the solicitor general emphasized, reinforced the impression of her guilt. And the irony of it all was that by May, 1908, the poor Steinheil was contemplating a suicide that would have made Meg's murders unnecessary. On May 10, he had sealed a letter in an envelope marked "To be opened in case of death," a death he evidently expected soon. He called for the simplest possible funeral: a common grave, no flowers, no ceremony, no guests. Clearly, he was in deep despair. Yet the letter concluded, "May Marthe and Pierre [Buisson] keep the memory of their father, who loves them with all of his soul; I address them a last farewell, and also one to my wife, my sisters, and cousins for whom I have not ceased to have a profound affection." It took a cruel and calculating woman, it took a Meg Steinheil, Trouard-Riolle perorated, to murder such a man.[35]

After the solicitor general returned to his place, the court recessed, and Aubin was able to present the summation for the defense, the *plaidoirie*, with everyone fresh on November 13. Speaking warmly if too slowly at first, he reminded the jury that the Sûreté's belief in Meg's guilt had come late in the case and that the solicitor general had just been compelled to admit that the charge of parricide would have to be dropped for want of a motive. He continued by asserting that there was likewise no motive and insufficient evidence to accuse Meg of the murder of her husband. How could the upbringing she had received have prepared her for murder, especially for the murder of the innocent man whom she had married, for whom she was the guardian, guide, and stay? Steinheil had loved to work in the dim cathedrals; "away from the shadows, he was frightened and seemed to want to put his hands in front of his eyes." He gave Meg flowers, for "she was his idol—alas, the idol also of others . . . she was radiant and adorned with all the charms, a bouquet of smiles. Everyone wanted to pluck from the bouquet. So, she was unfaithful." But she was an emotional woman from an emotional and nervous family—witness her father's reaction to the affair with Scheffer. What motive could Meg have had to kill Steinheil? She knew that Borderel would not marry her. She also knew that the death of Steinheil would deprive her daughter of a father, the daughter Meg loved deeply and could not want to injure.

Aubin next ridiculed the evidence ranged against Meg by the prosecution. The watchdog Turc was sent away because he was useless, as his original owner, Alexander Wolff, had testified. Mme Japy stayed

35. *Ibid.*, November 12–13, 1909. See also Floriot's assessment of Trouard-Riolle's summation, *Deux femmes*, 64–68.

overnight at the Impasse Ronsin because she felt ill and her legs hurt, as Dr. Acheray testified. How could Mme Japy have possibly acted as a witness *for* Meg and Mariette when she would certainly have recognized one of them tying and gagging her? The best explanation for the crime, he argued, remained that of thieves interrupted at their work. They had entered through a door that Rémy Couillard probably forgot to lock and then looked for a cord in the kitchen to tie together the loot they expected to carry away. Because jewels are normally to be found near bedrooms, the thieves went first to the second floor before ransacking the rest of the house. There, they had to kill to avoid capture, but they very cleverly left Meg alive. Suspicion would inevitably fall on her—as it did. It was she who was on trial while they were free. The evidence against Meg from the scene of the crime was very controversial: the experts disagreed about the famous ink spot, witnesses conflicted on how, and how tightly, Meg was tied, and the experiments indicating that the cotton wool had never been in Meg's mouth proved nothing if the wrong piece of cotton wool had been tested.

Aubin brushed quickly over the weakest parts of his case. Meg, he said, had made false statements about her jewels first out of confusion and then out of a natural desire to conceal the gifts of her lovers. She had made the false accusations only after nearly suffering a nervous breakdown from the pressure of rumors, anonymous letters, the constant questions of journalists, and the failure of the police to find the murderers. Much more important than these lapses, he insisted, was the sighting by Geoffroy of a man fleeing the Impasse Ronsin near the time of the crime and the disappearance of the costumes from the Hebrew Theater on May 30, hours before the murders, costumes that matched perfectly the description given by Meg of the clothes worn by the murderers. There had also been the invitation and the calling card found in the Métro. All of this could not have been coincidence!

In his conclusion to this brilliant summation, Aubin enlisted French patriotism by evoking Meg's origin in Alsace and through an oblique reference to Faure, who was left tactfully unmentioned by name throughout the trial: "Let the one to whom I make allusion rest tranquilly in the thankful memory of those who know that he loved and served his country." Once more, he described Meg as the only light in Steinheil's gloomy existence. And finally, he referred to Marthe, who had been kept away from the previous sessions of the trial in order to provide maximum impact for the summation. Now, she sat directly behind her mother. Aubin beckoned to her: "I call to my side this pure and noble child. I want her close to me, stretching her arms appealingly toward you and defending her mother! These two unfortunate beings, how many tears they have already shed, how many tears they will still shed! Ah, gentlemen of the jury, give them the means to console one another and to forget together . . . while blessing your justice."[36]

As Aubin sat down, de Valles asked Meg whether she had anything to add as a final statement to the jury. She replied with not a single word or gesture. Dramatic to the end, she merely bent double in tears and anguish. Her fate was in the hands of the jurymen: Sporck, Legendre, Marlot, Palloc, Caucasson, Grosbois, Gillet, Klein, Autin, Goyard, Naveau, and Goumain. The last, originally the alternate, had taken the place of Poupart during the final arguments when he suddenly became ill. De Valles charged them with deciding Meg's guilt or innocence in the questions of the premeditated murder of her husband and the parricide of her mother. In an effort to complete its work, the court had sat late into the night, and the jury received the case at 10:30 P.M. Most of those who had followed the trial from the beginning predicted a close decision, 6–6 for acquittal or 7–5 for condemnation. When the jury did not reach a verdict by midnight, Meg's supporters grew much more pessimistic. Another ominous sign was that after they retired, the jury three separate times asked de Valles to explain the penalties Meg would undergo depending upon how each question was answered. More time passed until at 1:30 A.M. all of the parties were summoned to the courtroom to hear the verdict. The foreman stood and swore before "God and men" that the jury had reached a decision: the defendant was innocent of all charges. There were cheers from most of the spectators and jubilation from Aubin. But Meg Steinheil did not join in the triumph because she had fainted dead away.

Revived, Meg was barely able to escape the press of reporters in the company of Aubin, who had been so uncertain of acquittal that he had

36. *Le Figaro* and *Gazette des Tribunaux*, November 14, 1909. Floriot admired Aubin's summation greatly, and it still serves as a model in French law schools: *Deux femmes*, 68–70.

made no plans for hiding Meg. After an automobile chase through Paris, the pair managed to elude their pursuit and checked into separate rooms at the Hotel Terminus. By morning, the reporters had found them, but neither was in any mood to grant interviews. Aubin considered his reputation made, as indeed it was, although he was never again to defend such a celebrated client. Meg wanted to recover from a nightmarish eighteen months. She made a second attempt to hide, this time on the western outskirts of Paris in Le Vésinet, registered under the name "Mme Dupont" at the rest home run by Dr. Emile Raffegeau. This ruse was also penetrated, and on November 23, Meg left France for England. Aubin urged her not to return, because both Couillard and Burlingham had begun preparations to sue her for false accusation, Couillard demanding Fr 50,000, Burlingham Fr 20,000. The suits were never heard, for in the end Meg settled out of court with them after the sale at auction of Steinheil's last paintings and effects for Fr 25,295.[37]

When Meg left France for England, she left without Marthe. During the year of her mother's imprisonment and the trial, she had come under the influence of Steinheil's cousin, Edouard Chabrier, and her fiancé's father, Louis Buisson. She was made to feel deeply ashamed of her mother's life and told bluntly that Pierre Buisson would not be allowed to marry her unless she promised never to see Meg again. Confused and uncertain, Marthe agreed to this condition and moved into the house at the Impasse Ronsin with the Chabriers to plan her wedding. Even Meg's sudden descent incognito upon Paris in March, 1910, failed to sway her. But the wedding never took place. The Buissons began to think of Marthe as an embarrassment whose name would constantly remind of scandal, and they broke off the engagement in late 1910. Marthe then fell in love with a young Italian artist, Raphael del Perugia. She married him on July 26, 1911, at Saint-Jean Baptiste de la Salle, and the two joined Meg in London the following June.

A few weeks after Meg first fled to England, *Le Matin* announced with much fanfare that it would publish her "revelations" in serial. The second installment concluded with the tantalizing words: "I know who

37. Reports of November 11, 12, 18, 19, 21, 1909; March 13, 1912, APP, B A/1584, Affaire Steinheil; *Le Figaro*, November 14–15, 17, 1909; Steinheil, *Memoirs*, 456–60; Chrestien, *Steinheil*, 152, 169; Dudley, *Widow*, 180–85; Tavernier, *Steinheil*, 166–68.

the guilty are. Justice protects them." No third installment appeared. Instead, in 1912, Eveleigh Nash Publishers brought out Meg's *My Memoirs*, a highly sanitized and romanticized version of her life ghosted by the free-lance journalist Roger de Chateleux. Meg no longer claimed to know who the murderers were and merely appended a few speculations and not a single name.[38]

Five years later on June 26, 1917, during the worst year of World War I for the Entente powers, Meg married Baron Robert Brooke Campbell Scarlett-Abinger. She was forty-eight and still beautiful. Undaunted by her past, she put on the ostrich plumes of a peeress and marched, head held high, into Buckingham Palace. Together, she and her new husband restored the family home, Inverlochy Castle, in Scotland after the war. When he died on June 10, 1927, Meg retired to a flat in the posh suburb of Hove on the Sussex coast to live out her life on an allowance from the new Baron Scarlett-Abinger. The French journalist Jean Hamlin found her there in April, 1947. Nearly eighty years old, she appeared to be no more than sixty. Hamlin asked her whether now, forty years later, she might provide the "solution" to the Steinheil affair. He was surprised by the vehemence of her refusal, a refusal that seemed backed by a fear of what could still happen if she were to reveal more than she had at the trial: "I want nothing but to be left alone! Forget me, that's all I ask. I don't want to see my name printed in the newspapers. No one has the right to trouble my retirement!" She died at Hove on July 20, 1954, apparently leaving no posthumous confidences. Whatever her secrets, they died with her.[39]

There is a curious footnote to Meg Steinheil's extraordinary life. In her prime in the late 1890s, she posed for a nude statue, *La Source*, by Jean Hugues. Life-size in black marble, it portrays her as she was, a nymph, youthful and lascivious, her breasts lush and full, her legs parted. It rests today in the Luxembourg palace, where the French

38. For Marthe Steinheil, see reports of November 19, 26, 1909; March 8, October 11, 1910; January 19, May 5, July 24–25, 1911; for Meg's memoirs, see reports of January 14, February 5, 15, 1910, APP, B A/1584, Affaire Steinheil. The two installments in *Le Matin* appeared November 29, 30, 1909. See also Steinheil, *Memoirs*, 460–73; Lanoux, "Mystérieuse affaire," 292–95; Chrestien, *Steinheil*, 169.

39. Report of June 26, 1917, APP, B A/1584, Affaire Steinheil. See also Dudley, *Widow*, 189–91; Lanoux, "Mystérieuse affaire," 296–99. Jean Hamlin's interview appeared in *Ici Paris*, April 15, 1947.

Senate meets. As they file into the assembly, senators who pass by the statue touch the left breast: it is said to bring happiness.[40]

III

Even more to outsiders than to the French, the Steinheil case was baffling and paradoxical. Much of the evidence pointed clearly to Meg, but enough of it pointed just as clearly the other way for there to be more than a mere reasonable doubt of her guilt. There were too many coincidences, too many errors by the police, too much incompetence—real or feigned—in the conduct of this important investigation, too much testimony from important principals during the trial that varied from sworn depositions given before it. In November, 1909, it was simply impossible to tell where the truth lay. Trouard-Riolle's reconstruction of the crime was remarkable and suggestive, but hardly the only possible interpretation of the evidence. Meg's life was a tissue of dreams and nymphomania—perhaps the result of an early and forced marriage to a man nearly her father's age who could hardly satisfy her physically—but nothing in her life, as Aubin said very well at the trial, equipped her for murder.

In Great Britain or the United States, under Anglo-Saxon rules of law and constitutional guarantees against self-incrimination, Meg would probably never have been brought to trial. A writ of habeas corpus would have freed her from jail almost immediately, as there was insufficient evidence to hold her. The right to a speedy trial would have denied Examining Magistrate André or his predecessor Leydet the time to compile such a lengthy *instruction*. During the trial, if it had come to that, Meg would have been immune from the *interrogatoire*. For that matter, she would not have had to answer the questions put to her during the pretrial investigation. The presiding justice would not have been able to show such partiality against her and thus would have been less likely to influence the decision of the jury. Meg's only handicap in an English courtroom would have been less freedom to comment on the testimony of other witnesses. She would have had less opportunity to play the Sarah Bernhardt of the Assises. But she would have

---

40. Chrestien, *Steinheil*, 84; Lanoux, "Mystérieuse affaire," 304; Dudley, *Widow*, facing 177.

more surely been acquitted, especially since the decision of the jury would have had to be unanimous. That she was acquitted in France does not prove that she was rendered justice or that society was either.

What was the truth of the Steinheil affair? Innocent or not, Meg lied throughout the investigation and the trial. Her tale of the three men dressed in long black vestments and a red-haired woman was merely a tale. If it had been more than that, some new proof would have come to light. There would have been credible rumors of the murders in the criminal underworld. Someone would have bragged of doing the deed. The stolen jewels would have reappeared even after many years. The crime would have been the source of blackmail of some variety. But there has been nothing with even the slightest taint of truth to it. Even at the trial, the prosecution did quite an efficient job of demolishing the theory that the murderers were thieves caught in the act.

Perhaps because she understood the weakness of her only defense, Meg embellished the tale in her memoirs. She claimed, for the first time, that while President Faure's mistress she was entrusted by him with the manuscript of *his* memoirs. She also insisted that he had presented her with a magnificent pearl necklace, the provenance of which could not be revealed without precipitating an enormous scandal or even an international incident. It was to steal the manuscript and the necklace that the thieves entered the Steinheil house—so Meg would have all believe. Under the cover of an ordinary robbery, the theft of these highly sensitive items could be accomplished. This revised version of the tale has obvious appeal. The lure of conspiracy is great. The first half of the Third Republic was a time par excellence of conspiracies and of scandal. The rules were different: public idealism in government was less and cynicism correspondingly much higher. It was enough to think of the disgrace of President Grévy, whose son-in-law, himself a deputy, sold public decorations and offices through correspondence on the presidential letterhead; of the Panama Canal scandal, in which a large number of French legislators were bribed to overlook how the lack of progress on a canal through Panama was defrauding several million French stockholders in the company; and of the Dreyfus affair, in which the army and the government managed to convict the wrong traitor and then deny their mistake. It was enough to remember that cabinet ministers and legislators blithely loaned documents of great sensitivity to friends and routinely carted away all incriminating papers upon leaving office, the files standing empty for their successors. Meg's embellished version of the tale is highly appealing, but it must be dismissed as a fabrication. Not a single detail of it has ever been proved.[41]

If Meg lied during the investigation and the trial, the prosecution erred. Trouard-Riolle's imaginative reconstruction explains too little. Nothing in the character of either Meg Steinheil or Mariette Wolff portrays them as cold-blooded murderesses. More important, the prosecution's reconstruction is belied by the evidence. If Meg and Mariette planned and carried out the murders, they were extremely sloppy in their execution. Too many clues pointed to someone in the Steinheil household. But for many years both Meg and Mariette had proved themselves extremely adept at handling compromising situations. The parade of lovers to the villa at Bellevue, the story of Aunt Lily, the concealment of these arrangements from Marthe, all were possible only with precise planning and careful attention to detail. It is impossible to believe that Meg and Mariette would leave the scene of their crime in such disarray. Trouard-Riolle himself admitted that there was no evidence against the woman he alleged to be Meg's accomplice, a woman who could only be Mariette. In addition, the solicitor general was forced to fall back on coincidence to explain the theft of the costumes from the Hebrew Theater, the discovery of the invitation and the greeting card in the Métro, and the unknown figure seen by Geoffroy. Aubin could be certain of the jury's agreement when he ridiculed this attribution of such critical evidence.

There was never a lack of alternative explanations. A great deal of loose speculation went on in the Paris press throughout the Steinheil affair, with each newspaper floating any possible rumor about its particular bête noire. Deputies Eugène Etienne and Gaston Thomson and Examining Magistrate Joseph Lemercier were the most frequent targets of insinuations ranging from being the sole murderer to being Meg's accomplice. Few took this nonsense seriously, and none should have.[42]

---

41. Steinheil, *Memoirs*, 474–79.
42. Chrestien, *Steinheil*, 170–73, reviews some of the rumors, but there are more in the reports of December 12, 14, 1908; November 23, 1909; July 5, 1910, APP, B A/1584, Affaire Steinheil.

What is left as an explanation of the crime is conjecture, but conjecture that has gained in stature through the years and is tantalizing in its ability to explain the complexities of the case. It is obvious that Meg lied, but why did she lie? She might have been lying to cover her own guilt, but she was never a likely candidate for murderess. She was probably lying to protect someone else, and this hypothesis has the advantage of portraying her as she portrayed herself at the trial, innocent but not telling the whole truth. She could have lied because of love, but this would have been even more out of character for her than committing murder. Perhaps Meg loved young Lieutenant Scheffer; certainly she never loved any other man. It would seem clear, then, that she lied out of fear, a fear so great that she spent a year in prison and suffered through a trial for her life rather than reveal the truth. Even in her old age, the fear remained.

It was a fear that made her seek refuge in England. It was a fear that may have halted the publication of her revelations in *Le Matin* and that made her adopt a disguise for her return to Paris when she tried to persuade her daughter to join her in London. But whatever the fear and her role in the murders, these did not prevent her from marrying a peer of the realm or from being received by King George V at Buckingham Palace after 1917. It might be recalled that in 1913 George V's mother refused to be included in photographs with the wife of the French president, because Mme Poincaré had been divorced and her second marriage had not been consecrated by the church. It might also be recalled that George V's son, Edward, would marry Wallis Warfield Simpson, who would not be received at Buckingham Palace until the funeral of her husband thirty-five years later. It is hardly convincing to argue that accused murderesses are more palatable to the British royalty than divorcées. For some reason, Meg Steinheil was counted acceptable to the throne.

Dr. Edmond Locard was France's most distinguished contribution to the field of criminology. Superbly prepared by degrees in both medicine and law, he was for two generations the director of the crime and forensic laboratory at Lyon. His *Manuel de Technique policière*, published in 1923, was translated into English, Italian, Dutch, and Greek by 1925. In one of his many books, *Le Crime et les criminelles*, he offered his own reconstruction of the Steinheil affair as if there were no question of his being disproved. Meg, he explained, had exhausted her finances and was faced with extremely pressing liabilities. She telephoned a lover who had never refused her money before, and he came to the house at the Impasse Ronsin late in the evening on May 30 expecting to renew their affair. Meg met him alone and explained that this night it was a question only of money. He became furious, and there was a scene. Fearing the worst, Steinheil burst into the room. The lover, afraid of some ambush that would result in scandal, grabbed the artist by the throat, but too hard. Steinheil fell dead, his larynx broken. Mme Japy, coming upon the scene, gasped in horror, somehow swallowed her dentures, and suffocated. The whole tragedy took place in but a few seconds. Horror-stricken, Meg and her lover called "a very high official"—almost surely Leydet—who rushed to the house, quickly helped to stage-manage some of the evidence, and then departed. Locard probably knew more than he was willing to say, because he referred to Meg's lover as a "very noble foreigner" and her "Boyar friend," implying that he was a titled Russian. After his retirement, Locard enlarged upon his cryptic phrase in 1947 and 1959 to call this Boyar "a grand-duke, a close relative of the Tsar, to whom she turned on this occasion when in need of money." There is a measure of independent confirmation for this theory in the statement of a Dr. D——, a student of the famous forensic surgeon Henri Léon Thoinot and later a director of the Institut Médico-légal after World War I. He claimed to have observed the first autopsies of Steinheil and Mme Japy, and he charged that from the beginning of the case the medical service of the Sûreté were aware of a police cover-up. The autopsies indicated that Steinheil's larynx had been crushed by a hand, not by a cord, and that Mme Japy had died from shock and heart failure—the story of the swallowed dentures was a fabrication. The entire subterfuge was mounted, he contended, because the killer enjoyed diplomatic immunity and came from one of the embassies, most probably the British.[43]

43. Locard, *Crime*, 239–42. Lanoux, "Mystérieuse affaire," 300–303, takes up Locard's 1947 statements and the deposition of Dr. D——, which was contained in a letter to Lanoux in 1947 from a Dr. F. L——, who in turn had worked under Dr. D——. Dud-

There is contradiction and inconsistency here, but a common core. If any credence may be placed in this version—and Locard, for one, was in a position to learn sensitive information—the Steinheil affair becomes striking testimony to the failure of justice to operate. The scene of accidental death was transformed, through Leydet's intervention, into a scene of murder and Meg from a helpless onlooker to victim. The titled foreigner ceased to play any further part. The drama for everyone else was only beginning. Leydet and Meg had the most difficult roles to play, and to ensure that all went well, Leydet made certain that he was assigned to the case. Perhaps he insinuated part or all of the secret to Hamard, who took the unusual steps of convoking a massive force at the Impasse Ronsin on the following morning and of taking personal charge of the investigation. All seemed well by the end of the summer, with Leydet ready to file the case as unsolved. But Meg finally realized that she was free from Steinheil. She would not have killed him, and she would not have put Marthe through a divorce, but Steinheil's death gave her the chance to marry Borderel. When she learned that he would not see her again unless the case were solved and all suspicion removed from her name, she broke under the emotional strain of the preceding six months and went into a panic. Searching desperately for a victim, she accused first Rémy Couillard and then Alexander Wolff. It seems likely that Leydet and Hamard would have let either of these men stand trial for his life, just as they were willing to trump up charges against Burlingham, when they were well aware that neither was guilty.

The case took an awkward turn when it became clear that Couillard and Wolff were innocent. All suspicion now rested on Meg. Leydet was forced to step down as examining magistrate. Hamard's role after this also decreased drastically. Magistrate André knew nothing of the true events of May 30–31. In his dogged manner, he believed Meg guilty and set out to prove it. That he could not provides additional confirmation that she was indeed innocent, at least of murder. At her trial, Meg could count only on herself. Neither Leydet nor Hamard ap-

ley, *Widow*, 192–95, takes up Locard's 1959 statements. See also Chrestien, *Steinheil*, 173–76; Tavernier, *Steinheil*, 170–75. Lanoux, Chrestien, and Tavernier find Locard's thesis credible. Dudley, who has an antipathy for Meg surpassing even that held by magistrate André, does not.

peared. She could not claim that the crime had been a ruse, because she would not have been believed. She put up the best defense she could with the original story agreed upon with Leydet. She was aided by the theft of the costumes and the discovery of the invitation and greeting card, both so convenient that it may be assumed that Leydet arranged for them. The man Geoffroy saw at the Impasse Ronsin near midnight was probably Leydet himself, leaving after arranging the house. The rather haphazard job he did may be easily explained by noting that he had little time and no advance warning. Meg and her nobleman were probably useless because of paranoia or hysteria.

To accept Locard uncritically places the analysis of the Steinheil affair on the steepest slope of conjecture. Locard does not name the Russian grand duke or explain why Meg's sacrifices to avoid scandal to his name would allow her entrance to Buckingham Palace. The statement of Dr. D—— only expands the number of suspects, and Meg's circle of admirers was large. Yet it would have been decidedly out of character for the tousle-haired criminologist Locard to have fabricated this version of the case. If the ring of truth is not clear, it does explain more of the evidence than can any other reconstruction. The attitude of Mariette Wolff, in whom Meg would certainly have confided, becomes clear: she wanted to defend her mistress from an undeserved fate. Locard's reconstruction leaves a minimum of loose ends. And if it is reasonably accurate, it condemns the system of criminal justice in Third Republic France just as surely as the Dreyfus affair condemns the system of military justice.

Nevertheless, Locard may have been wrong, misinformed, or merely speculating. The explanation to the mysteries of the case may be absurdly simple. The striking incompetence of so much of the police work in this case need not be ascribed to underhand motives. Incompetence is often simply incompetence. The wrong gag could have been picked up. Depositions could have been carelessly drawn. Evidence could have been lost. Evidence could have been fabricated: Burlingham was almost the victim of the last. When Trouard-Riolle made his closing summary, he was admitting that French justice could find neither Meg's four intruders nor Meg's accomplice. Whatever the decision of the jury, some of the guilty would have escaped. Should incompetence be at the root of many of the mysteries, there is no way to solve the case if by solving it is meant to explain the role of each principal and apportion the guilt. It may be sufficient to note the degree to which the French judicial system failed to function, the degree to which justice was hypocritical. It may be unfair and unrealistic to expect perfection of any system. But it is manifestly proper to demand that a critical criminal investigation and trial not be shot through with errors of judgment and incompetence of craft.

Chapter 2

THE HUMBERT AFFAIR
Fraud as a Fine Art

Qui n'est que juste est dur.
Voltaire, Letter to the King of Prussia, 1740

I

In late February, 1902, the Paris press began to take note of a curious judicial process, the contest waged during twenty years for control of an inheritance estimated to be worth 100 million francs. It seemed that on his death in Nice in 1877, a certain mysterious American, Robert-Henri Crawford, had left two wills, each dated September 6 of that year. One left his entire fortune to Thérèse Daurignac, subsequently the daughter-in-law of Senator Gustave Humbert, one of the founders of the Third Republic, former minister of justice and, until his death in 1894, presiding justice of the Cour des Comptes. The other will divided the fortune, leaving it in equal parts to Crawford's two nephews, Robert and Henri, and to Maria Daurignac, Thérèse's sister. A court battle inevitably developed, and during the proceedings, the French 3 percent bonds (*rente*) that constituted the inheritance were placed in Thérèse's hands for safekeeping. From the beginning of the legal struggle, the Humberts won every court decision, but the Crawford nephews always appealed or initiated new litigation on obscure points of law.

Although the Humbert-Crawford process had bumped back and forth among the levels of French civil justice, there was every reason to believe that Thérèse would eventually receive the bulk of the inheritance if not all of it. While waiting for this nearly inevitable victory, she needed money to meet household expenses and to pay the mounting fees of her attorneys. It proved absurdly easy to find speculators who, in return for high interest rates, would advance loans against the projected inheritance. But after twenty years of pettifogging litigation, some of them sensed trouble and could not be put off any longer by the promises that came easily to Thérèse's mouth or even by the reputation of the Humbert name. They called for a sober accounting of the bonds and an early termination of the court battle by compromise between the opposing parties. Their easy confidence shaken, the creditors of the Humberts realized that some of the most elementary precautions had never been taken to assure their loans, that neither of the Crawfords had ever appeared before a French court, and that not even the attorneys retained by the Crawfords could supply an address for them. As a beginning to a thorough investigation, they sought from Henry Ditte, presiding justice of the Tribunal des Référés, a decree ordering an inventory of the bonds at the Humbert residence on the Avenue de la Grande Armée.

Justice in France moves slowly. On May 6, the decree was finally issued, setting the inventory for three days later. At 1 P.M. on May 9, attorneys for the Humberts, attorneys for the Crawfords, Jules Herbaux, the public prosecutor, Joseph Leydet, an examining magistrate, Armand Cochefert, the chief of the Sûreté, Edouard Demonts, the president of the notaries of Paris, and a crowd of assistants, reporters, and nervous creditors gathered at the door of the Humbert house. They were admitted by the servants, who told them that none of the Humbert family was at home. The chest where the bonds were thought to be held was locked. A pale Demonts called for locksmiths. When the strongbox was finally opened, there were no bonds, only an old newspaper, an Italian penny, and a trouser button. The Humbert affair had begun.[1]

1. There have been few accounts of the Humbert affair since its conclusion in 1903. Paul Guimard, "Thérèse Humbert," in Gilbert Guilleminault (ed.), *Le Roman vrai de la Troisième République: Prélude à la Belle Epoque* (Paris, 1956), 293–328, provides a less than satisfying introduction. René Floriot, a famous member of the Paris bar, composed a brief reconstruction of the case for his *Au banc de la défense* (Paris, 1959) and mentioned it in a section entitled "False Reasoning by the Law on the Basis of Sound Evidence" in his *Les Erreurs judiciaries* (Paris, 1968). The Humberts are also the subject of an unreliable popular book by Henri Varenne [Henri Vonoven], *La Belle Affaire* (Paris, 1925). Otherwise, the case has been so neglected that it hardly appears even in the standard political and social histories of the period. The *instruction* of the examining magistrate is closed until 2003, and many of the relevant documents are missing from the Humbert file at the Paris Prefecture of Police, APP, E A/118. These documents probably provided the basis for the

La Grande Thérèse at the height of
her success in the late 1890s

Frédéric Humbert enjoys the leisure
and wealth his swindle has provided.

The empty strongbox is removed from the Humbert *hôtel* at 65 Avenue de la Grande-Armée and taken into police custody, May 9, 1902.

A sketch of the Humbert family during the courtroom proceedings, drawn by P. Renouard

Thérèse's family, the Daurignacs, had an uncertain origin. Her father, Guillaume Auguste, had been found abandoned in 1801 in the tower of Notre Dame de la Garde in Toulouse. He had no surname until 1839, when a woman named Daurignac went through the legal process of recognizing him as her son while at the same time insisting that Auguste's real mother had been Mme de Montmalette de Castel, who had died before being able to give her name to this natural child. On the strength of this story, Auguste Daurignac began to put on airs. Although his station was at best demibourgeois, he changed his name to d'Aurignac and called himself a count. He and his family lived little better than peasants in a stone farmhouse twelve kilometers from Toulouse in the village of Aussonne, but he named the house the Château Oeillet. The new tastes he cultivated to match his pretentions could not be met by his previous occupations as indifferent vintner and operator of a bizarre *agence matrimoniale*—through which he claimed to link suitors. The bills piled higher. To meet them, he devised the tale of a legacy from his true mother, but a legacy unfortunately blocked by court proceedings. If the creditors would only be patient, they would be paid, for the d'Aurignacs were to be rich.[2]

Auguste Daurignac and his wife had five children, Emile (born 1852), Thérèse (born September 10, 1855), Romain (born 1857), Louis (born 1865), and Maria (born 1869). The eldest three inherited their father's skill at fraud and deceit, with Thérèse the most blessed. In contrast to the pretentious air of so many of her type, she seemed simple and hardworking. Without her father for an example, she would probably have wound up as a servant girl in Toulouse. She was able to inspire confidence. She seemed guileless and innocent, and a pronounced lisp completed this portrait of simplicity. From her childhood, she was capable of telling outrageous lies and convincing others to believe them. At the age of thirteen, she began to forge her father's signature. She

---

lengthy inquest in the *Journal Officiel*, Chambre des Députés (hereinafter cited as JOC), Documents, 1905, No. 2535, and were never returned. To a great extent, therefore, the remarkable story of the Humberts must be reconstructed from contemporary press reports. *Le Figaro* and *Le Matin*, in particular, provide excellent coverage of the case, and the semiofficial *Gazette des Tribunaux* adds a verbatim transcript of the trial and significant information about the investigation from informed sources at the Palais de Justice.

2. For general background, see the politically sanitized report, JOC, Documents, 1905, No. 2535, pp. 1–42, as well as *Le Figaro* and *Le Matin*, May 9, 1902, August 4–6, 1903. For Auguste Daurignac see *Le Figaro*, May 26, June 1, December 22, 1902, January 14, 1903.

had a friend who played the piano well and agreed to assist Thérèse in a hoax. Throughout one summer, Thérèse claimed to be an accomplished pianist but insisted that she could not play with anyone else in the room. After everyone but Thérèse withdrew, her friend came out of hiding and played in her stead. Thérèse took the credit. At seventeen, she went into Toulouse and arranged to buy a wardrobe of fine clothes on credit, explaining that she was to marry a wealthy young man from Bordeaux. The marriage never took place because no marriage had been arranged. Auguste Daurignac made vague promises about restitution upon final settlement of his legacy, but the merchants took him to court and expropriated a portion of his property.

This experience taught Thérèse that fiction based on inheritance is far easier to maintain than fiction based on marriages. Marriages are not likely to be held up by legal proceedings, and their completion is public record. Among contentious Frenchmen, litigation over an inheritance is almost expected, and a will is a private document that is almost never made public. From this lesson, Thérèse concocted a number of stories. For a while, she told neighbors that the forture of her godmother—she had none—would come to her on her majority. There were, alas, legal complications, but she was certain of winning. Within several months, however, she had settled upon a different tale. Because of an unexplained "family connection," she would inherit the "important fortune" of a Mme Bellac, who owned the Château de Marcotte. There would be some delay because a Mme La Trémoillière had the usufruct of the inheritance during her lifetime. Thérèse spread this version of her fortune widely and found a sufficient number of merchants willing to advance her credit to purchase the accoutrements of a young bourgeoise. The story even fit reasonably well with that of her father—the wealthy Mme Bellac could have been a relative of his mother—and with the story of her godmother's fortune—since no one seemed to know that she did not have one and assumed that it was perhaps Mme La Trémoillière. Certainly, any credibility accorded this tale is testimony to Thérèse's talent at spreading her lies and to the gullibility of Toulousain merchants.[3]

In 1878, when Thérèse was twenty-three, she met Frédéric Hum-

3. Thérèse's early life is well described in *Le Figaro*, May 17, 1902, January 9, 12, 1903.

bert, whose father, Gustave Humbert, had been an early and ardent republican and had achieved a success in which any Jacobin could delight. Born the youngest son of a relatively poor wine merchant who had been a volunteer in 1792, Gustave Humbert studied jurisprudence, became a member of the law faculty at Toulouse, entered republican politics, and in 1875 was made irremovable senator for Haute Garonne. Two years later, he was appointed prosecutor for the Cour des Comptes, the court which supervised government audits. Humbert was rigorously moral, indeed an emblem of integrity, but he was a poor judge of human nature. He had a small piece of property at Beauzelles, just across the fields from Aussonne, and bought wine from Auguste Daurignac. He came to like the marriage broker and vintner, and in the best republican manner, he even invited the Daurignac family to socialize with the Humberts. After all, while there was an enormous breach between the two in culture and station, the Humberts were not much wealthier than the Daurignacs. Humbert had barely survived on his salary as a professor of law, and his integrity forbade him to traffic in political influence now that he had reached a position of power.

Frédéric Humbert was in almost every way different from his father. His hook-nosed, thin, and withdrawn appearance contrasted greatly with that of the broad, expansive senator. The father lived for the law, the son for art, although he completed a law degree at his father's request. In 1878, the sessions of the Cour des Comptes required Senator Humbert to be in Paris almost all year. In his absence, Frédéric spent less and less time at the University of Toulouse and much more time with Thérèse. She was two years his elder, but she had won him with her tales of fortune that would allow him to fulfill his dreams of art and luxury. It was hardly a relationship built on trust: the Château de Marcotte that was to be the fulcrum of his new wealth did not exist. Like others, he believed the lies Thérèse spoke with her childlike lisp. By the early summer of 1878, he was writing his father for advice on the intricacies of an inheritance such as the one she described. By the end of the summer, he had asked and received permission from his father to marry her.

Were they in love? It seems very doubtful. This was par excellence a *mariage de convenance*. Thérèse saw in this taciturn and studious young man her complement: he would be the administrator of her schemes. He knew the law, even if it was distasteful to him, and in his name he bore the cachet of respectability. Seeing in him such a combination of attributes, she must have pressed him toward marriage as hard as possible. For him, she was the promise—albeit false—of fortune and an escape from his father's standards and way of life. She was older than he and never pretty, but she was willing. Irresolute, he allowed her to persuade him. They were married on September 7, 1878. Characteristically, Thérèse managed to avoid paying for the wedding flowers. Talleyrand's epigram fit her perfectly: "Pour faire fortune ce n'est pas du talent qu'il faut, c'est de la délicatesse qu'il ne faut pas."[4]

What was the reaction of Frédéric Humbert when his new bride told him that the Château de Marcotte was a myth? He may have succumbed to anger, despair, disillusionment, perhaps ironical laughter. His second reaction is certain: he comforted himself that his wife's talents could be utilized very effectively on others. The pair moved to Paris, set up housekeeping in a modest apartment at 68 Rue Monge in the shabby district near the Ecole Polytechnique, and began plotting. Thérèse found a victim immediately, the widow Delattre, who lived just down the street. The gregarious Thérèse had visited nearly everyone in the neighborhood but kept coming back to see Mme Delattre after the old woman let slip that her husband had left her some shares in the Malfidano mines. One morning, Thérèse came in with the information that her father-in-law, the senator, "with so many connections," had told her that the mines were about to declare bankruptcy. The old woman was horrified, but Thérèse restored calm by promising to sell the shares for her. A few days later, Mme Delattre learned that instead of heading toward bankruptcy, the Malfidano mines were prospering. Confronting Thérèse with this, she demanded at least the value of the shares. Thérèse only laughed, promised to repay the widow at some future date, and then never returned. Frédéric was almost as successful, obtaining a "loan"—never to be repaid—from an engineer working with the French railroad concession in Tonkin. The reimbursement of these eight thousand francs was to come from an inheritance that Thérèse was certain to receive. When the engineer was

4. For the progress of young love and marriage, see *ibid.*, January 22, 28, 1903.

reluctant, Thérèse accompanied Frédéric on his next visit and osten-
tatiously displayed Senator Humbert's card. The name promised integrity but also the political power that could extend or cancel economic
concessions in French spheres of influence.[5]

These swindles were not the major occupation for Thérèse and Frédéric. They were in the process of conceiving and polishing a plan that
would utilize all of their advantages and be proof against exposure. By
the end of 1881, they were ready with the fictitious story of Crawford.
According to it, Robert-Henri Crawford was a strange and reclusive
American millionaire who through some unexplained circumstance
happened to meet the Daurignac family in 1853. During each of the next
six years, he returned to Aussonne to spend time with them, ultimately becoming the lover of Mme Daurignac and the natural father of
Thérèse. He had died on September 7, 1877, leaving the two identi-
cally dated wills. There was no internal evidence to indicate which had
been the latter, but that presented no difficulty to French justice because there was a law providing that in such cases, the will naming the
closest relatives would be honored. Any claim by Thérèse would
thereby be disallowed, although her sister, Maria, would receive one-
third of the estate, the two nephews receiving the other two-thirds. But
nothing was simple and clear-cut about the case. The nephews, millionaires themselves, saw no reason to cut out Thérèse completely and
offered to come to a compromise. She seemed certain to receive something. In the meantime, there might be those who would advance her
money against what she would eventually gain. Not just anyone could
borrow under these uncertain circumstances, but the daughter-in-law
of Senator Humbert could do so. This was even truer in January, 1882,
when Thérèse and Frédéric began to spread the story of Crawford, because Gustave Humbert had just become minister of justice in the cabinet of Charles de Freycinet and had named Frédéric as his chef de
cabinet.

This triumph was only one of three for the Humbert household. January, 1882, also brought the birth of Thérèse's only child, Eve, and a
move from the dingy Rue Monge to a smart *hôtel* at 10 Rue Fortuny,
only two blocks from the chic Parc Monceau. Now, they had a carriage

5. *Ibid.*, June 10, 1902, and *Le Matin*, May 25, 1902.

and horses; Thérèse opened a salon. Senator Humbert listened to the story of Crawford with care and then told everyone he knew of his children's extraordinary luck. As an old theoretician of the law, he delighted in being asked to help plot strategy and even consulted one of the justices on the Cour de Cassation about procedures in contested legacies. He believed everything Thérèse and Frédéric told him and never thought to question the honesty of those he loved. This unexpected blessing was some recompense for the privations he had condemned his family to suffer for the republican faith. Beyond this, he did not bother to inquire. From January to August, 1882, he was preoccupied by the task of directing the Ministry of Justice at the Place Vendôme. Soon thereafter, he assumed the important and time-consuming positions of vice-president of the Senate and presiding justice of the Cour des Comptes.[6]

The new honors for Senator Humbert and his endorsement of the inheritance were grist for the mill Thérèse and Frédéric were turning. They were about to take steps that would provide official documents attesting to the imaginary inheritance and transform a merely clever fraud into high art. By early 1883, the Crawford brothers, they claimed, had decided after more than five years of amicable negotiations that the ultimate disposition of the fortune had to await the attainment of Maria Daurignac's majority in 1884. During the interim, they proposed that Thérèse agree to a protocol that they presented to her on March 14. The terms were highly unusual: Thérèse was to act as depositor for the entire fortune, 100 million francs in French 3 percent *rente*, and assume responsibility for clipping the coupons of the bearer bonds each trimester and purchasing additional bonds of the *rente* with the proceeds. She was not to sell any of the bonds, not to alter any aspect of their investment, and above all, not to allow anyone else other than the Crawfords or their legal representatives to count or even to view the bonds. If she failed in even the slightest regard to fulfill these duties, she was to forfeit any claim to the inheritance but would be granted an annual life annuity of thirty thousand francs.

The terms of the protocol were out of the ordinary and designed to trap Thérèse and Frédéric, but they were willing to sign, because they expected to conclude a final settlement within another year or two and

6. *Le Figaro*, June 18, 1902, April 1, 1903.

because they wanted to remain on the best possible terms with the Crawfords during the final negotiations. It seemed to work well, as both sides rapidly reached an agreement signed on December 11, 1884. By this, the two brothers promised not to contest Thérèse's right to the fortune of their uncle if, in return, she would make over to them the lump sum of six million francs. What seemed the final understanding, however, would be the basis for all future misunderstandings. With this document in hand, Thérèse had no difficulty borrowing the amount of the lump sum, but the Crawfords would not accept it, declaring that the agreement presupposed the arrangement of a marriage between Maria Daurignac and the son of Robert Crawford. French law did not recognize this variety of convention, but that, they insisted, had been clearly their intention in signing away their rights. Thérèse responded by refusing to recognize their claims and by insisting on the enforcement of the agreement as drawn. But unless she could compel the Crawfords to accept the six million francs, she could not touch the inheritance without violating the 1883 protocol and providing the brothers with the legal justification to seize the entire 100 million.[7]

Very angry—as she would recall in telling this part of the story—she consulted an attorney, Armand Labat, who directed a bailiff, M. Lecomte, to serve papers upon the Crawfords naming them in a suit for breach of contract. The Crawfords were not easy to locate, but in April, 1885, Thérèse reported meeting them at the Hôtel du Louvre, and Lecomte went there immediately. He found two elegantly dressed gentlemen of apparent middle age in a magnificently furnished apartment. Each had a beard and a moustache, and each spoke French with what Lecomte described as a "sterling American accent." The brothers received the bailiff with exceedingly bad grace and professed to be astonished that Thérèse would threaten them with a suit or that in the France that was known as the land of hospitality they could be disturbed by such vulgar plebeians as Lecomte. After a half hour of discussion, they consented to accept the papers, but they declared themselves so disgusted by this episode that they would leave France immediately, never to return.[8]

The scene had been a master stroke for Thérèse and Frédéric. No one

7. For the details of these early agreements, see the background articles in *ibid.*, and *Le Matin*, May 9–10, 1902.
8. *Le Figaro*, May 22, 1902.

knew that the Crawfords were played by her brothers, Romain and Emile, and now no one could be surprised that the Crawfords were seen seldom or never. She was prepared for her most audacious move, actually referring the broken contract to the first chamber of the Civil Tribunal of the Seine on October 31, 1885. The Humbert-Daurignac marriage of convenience had provided exactly the proper combination of talents. Thérèse had the daring and the imagination to conceive the Crawford story; Frédéric contributed his father's reputation among the magistrature and a shrewd appreciation of the limits of civil justice. As would anyone trained in the law, Frédéric understood that the jurisdiction of the civil tribunal extended only to the question posed before it. If the Humberts presented the court with the contract of December, 1884, the court could rule upon its provisions but make no inquiry into the inheritance at all. At the same time, the court's decision, ultimately rendered in favor of the Humberts on October 27, 1886, would refer to the right of Thérèse to take possession of the 100-million-franc fortune. She and Frédéric were bringing a forged contract involving two nonexistent nephews of a nonexistent American millionaire and a nonexistent inheritance before French civil justice in order to create legal documents lending credence to all they claimed.

It would have been difficult for Romain and Emile Daurignac actually to appear at the trial masquerading as the Crawford brothers, but they were quite ably represented by attorneys. Here was another brilliant ploy by Thérèse and Frédéric. In late April, 1885, Romain Daurignac appeared at the office of attorney Emile Parmentier in Le Havre. The Normans had a reputation for producing the most litigious and tenacious lawyers, and Parmentier was counted a master at delaying tactics. Claiming to be Robert Crawford, Romain charged Parmentier with the direction of the brothers' cause against the Humberts. Parmentier was told to spare no expense and to choose whichever Parisian associates he judged best qualified. The Havrais attorney may be faulted for accepting this client's story on good faith, but few in the legal profession demand identity cards before proceeding with a case, especially when the prospective fees appear lucrative. During the succeeding seventeen years, Parmentier would have several meetings with the Crawfords, receive numerous letters from them with suggestions for the conduct of the case, and be paid Fr 350,000 in fees—

on schedule. If he had no reason to doubt, how could his colleagues in Paris be expected to doubt the Crawfords? These clients were protected by the excellent reputation of their principal attorney. Along with the slowly mounting legal decisions based on the fictitious inheritance, there was now the testimony of respected attorneys to the existence of the Crawfords and their fortune.

Parmentier, as expected, found room to appeal the decision by the civil tribunal to the Cour d'Appel of Paris. It rendered a verdict on January 3, 1890, again in favor of Thérèse. This time, Parmentier appealed to the Cour de Cassation, which two years later, on January 11, 1892, came to the same conclusion as the lower courts. But Parmentier was hardly stymied. With the brilliant assistance of Paul Poujaud, Eugène Bazille, Antoine Auzoux, and briefly, Eugène Pouillet, he challenged the rulings on obscure points of law, the last of which, the absence in any ruling of an address for the Crawfords, would eventually bring down the entire scheme, hoist by its own petard.[9]

The sensational news of a court battle over so immense a fortune spread the myth of the Crawford inheritance. The presence at Thérèse's side of eminent attorneys and the mounting legal decisions in her favor combined with the reputation and authority of Senator Humbert to ease the doubts of any who suspected the bizarre elements of the case. So did the lives of Frédéric and Thérèse. In early 1886, they purchased a sumptuous *hôtel* at 65 Avenue de la Grande Armée from Count Amédée Branicki, an unrepentant Bonapartist who was president of the Comité centrale imperialiste, and proceeded to furnish it with plush, overstuffed furniture, some undistinguished examples of mid-nineteenth-century art, and a horde of servants. The salon that Thérèse transferred from the Rue Fortuny now attracted the luminaries of the Paris political world. Three future presidents of the Republic, Jean Casimir-Périer, Félix Faure, and Paul Deschanel, came frequently, as did a pretender to that office, the minister of war, General Georges Boulanger. Following close behind came Charles de Freycinet, Louis Barthou, Camille Pelletan, and the prefect of the Paris police, Louis Lépine. There were also ministers plenipotentiary like Fernand Gavarry,

9. For details of Parmentier's relationship with the Humberts through the early litigation, see *ibid.*, May 9, June 17, 1902; and the reports of May–July, 1902, APP, E A/118, Affaire Humbert.

important magistrates like Frédéric Périvier, a presiding justice of the Paris Cour d'Appel, and high permanent officials like Etienne Jacquin, a conseiller d'état directing personnel at the Ministry of Justice. The Humbert daughter, Eve, who was only fourteen but because of her height looked twenty, was much sought after for her supposed dowry. Before 1890, Thérèse and Frédéric also purchased the Château de Vives Eaux near Melum, the large estate of Celeyran near Bordeaux, a farm at Orsonval, and several more properties in Paris and the suburbs. In 1885, Frédéric won election to the Chamber of Deputies from Seine-et-Marne. With this brilliant facade, who could doubt the Humberts and their story? Who indeed, for by 1890, Paris society spoke of "la grande Thérèse."

Attorneys and notaries swarmed about the house on the Avenue de la Grande Armée, hoping to tap some of the large sums the Humberts were paying in legal expenses. They were joined by a near mob of bankers and speculators wanting to loan the pair almost any amount of money against the day that the inheritance would be freed by the courts. Each time Frédéric and Thérèse borrowed successfully from one, it became that much easier to borrow from another. They created a self-accelerating circle. Each loan made them richer and an apparently better risk on which to exact an eventual profit. No financier wanted to lose the opportunity to benefit from a couple determined to live well in the present by mortgaging a seemingly assured future. This was especially true because Thérèse offered the best terms in France. Creditors were allowed 5 percent annual interest on their loans and participation in the final settlement up to 50 percent of the loan. On a loan of Fr 1,000,000, speculation on the Crawford story would bring an annual income of Fr 50,000 and an eventual return of capital of perhaps Fr 1,500,000! To ensure that the harvest of the loans was bounteous, Thérèse offered a commission equal to 10 percent of the loan negotiated to notaries and brokers who brought their clients to her. To meet these enormous charges for debt service, the Humberts required an ever-increasing number of new loans, but their pose was so convincing that there was no shortage of those willing to invest in their honesty, and many were eager to increase initial loans.[10]

10. A description of the Humbert social life and alliances, based on the testimony of many witnesses, can be found in *Le Figaro*, May 10, 17–18, June 2, 16, 18, 1902.

Even so, there were some doubters, and there were always the attorneys and notaries whose belief in the Crawfords had to be maintained. Thérèse, Frédéric, and Romain, Emile, and Maria Daurignac came to feel constantly on stage—in retrospect, it seems that their lives were perfect for the Comédie-Française. They came to glory in their roles, although probably only Thérèse was wholly equipped for her part. The charade they carried on for twenty years rivals even the conception of the Crawford fortune itself as an accomplishment. A glimpse of a Crawford or of the bonds constituting the inheritance or of the coupons clipped from them—this was all any of the doubters required to be converted. They wanted to believe, and with a little assistance, they did.

Parmentier came in for the closest attention because his role as director of the Crawford brothers' litigation was critical. From 1885 to 1902, he received approximately 3,500 letters from one or another of the brothers or from the Crawfords' chef de cabinet, a Robert Muller. All of the letters were typed and contained explicit suggestions for Parmentier's conduct of the case. He carefully kept every one, filing the correspondence by year in folders that eventually occupied an important portion of his office. Ultimately, he would learn that the signatures of Robert and Henri Crawford bore a suspicious resemblance to the writing of Romain and Emile Daurignac, while the signature of Robert Muller was close to the writing of Frédéric Humbert. When he was finally introduced to the Daurignac brothers, he would find resemblances between them and the Crawford brothers he had met rarely in his office. Parmentier was never alerted in advance of these visits and had to content himself with conducting almost all of the business of the case by mail. As the Crawfords seemed to have no settled residence, there were difficulties that should have alerted Parmentier to investigate his clients more thoroughly. Some of the Crawford correspondence was directed to a New York address, 1202 Broadway, necessitating a delay of several months for transatlantic delivery and reply—an ideal tactic for the Humberts. Other mail went to various luxury hotels throughout Europe, but particularly in London. Most of it, however, was to be sent addressed either "H. C." or "R. C." to poste restante at the Louvre station in Paris. The explanation the Crawfords gave for this variety of addresses was that they wanted to make it impossible for French justice to identify their "true domicile," the only location where official papers could legally be served upon them by a bailiff.

Parmentier clearly believed all the Crawfords told or wrote him, although it does not appear that he had any confidence in the ultimate outcome of the litigation, as he personally loaned a substantial sum to Thérèse Humbert. He had more than the letters and the visits from the brothers as proof. At the end of March, 1894, he received instructions from them to act as their representative on April 4, when Thérèse clipped the trimester coupons. As requested, he journeyed to Paris and received from her Fr 587,000 of coupons, placed them in an envelope, and rode a carriage the few blocks to the Bourse. There he purchased that amount of 3 percent *rente* bearer bonds and returned with them to the Avenue de la Grande Armée. His only thought as he handed the newly purchased bonds to Thérèse to add to the others was that in order to have a trimester's clipping of Fr 587,000, there had to be bearer bonds worth Fr 78,266,666 in the strongbox already. It was effortless to believe that the remainder of the hundred million must be in registered bonds, the interest on which was mailed out each quarter by the state treasury. Until the strongbox was found empty on May 9, 1902, Parmentier would never doubt the story of the Crawfords.[11]

Another one who would trust until the end was a notary from Rouen, Louis Dumort. He met the Humberts in 1889 in his office and was so impressed by their references and documents that he loaned them Fr 1,300,000 of his own money. Later, he recommended so many of his clients to the Humberts that he was responsible for a total of Fr 8,000,000 in loans to them. A small, thin, dry man, he was an authentic provincial who went to Paris rarely, but Thérèse made these visits memorable. In 1889, Dumort came to see the famous exhibition of that year, which featured the new Eiffel Tower. Thérèse invited him to the house on the Avenue de la Grande Armée, where she sneaked him upstairs. Warned not to make any noise, he was led to a hall from which he could see into Frédéric Humbert's study. Across from Frédéric, with his back to the door, sat a well-dressed man speaking French with a pronounced accent as he counted what appeared to be an immense for-

11. *Ibid.*, May 12, 18, 24, 30, June 20, 1902, January 21, 25, 28, 1903; reports of May–July, 1902, APP, E A/118, Affaire Humbert.

tune in bonds. After Thérèse led him away, she told him that the man was Robert Crawford verifying that the fortune had been maintained as stipulated in the 1883 protocol.

Dumort returned to Rouen very pleased with his good sense in loaning money to the Humberts. He was even more impressed in January, 1894, when business brought him back to Paris. It was time to clip the trimester coupons, and Thérèse, insisting that he must never reveal this breach of the 1883 protocol, invited him to help her with the cutting. He set to work delighted at this opportunity to touch the millions with his own hands, but he clipped only a very few of the coupons. For a small man, Dumort had large hands with thick fingers. Thérèse could find only embroidery scissors for him to use, and these hurt him. He left early but convinced that no doubts could be raised against the Crawford fortune.[12]

Other notaries received similar, if less elaborate, treatment. The office of Etienne Dupuy in out-of-the-way Bayonne became the favorite spot for the Daurignac brothers, posing as Crawfords, to file and notarize official papers. They would appear in elegant clothes, spend money freely, and speak a gibberish considered in Bayonne to be "New York English." Dupuy and his clerk, Jean-Baptiste Delsez, would later identify Emile and Romain Daurignac as the Crawfords who had come so regularly to file their documents. Dupuy never questioned why the two should have chosen Bayonne for their business: foreigners were so strange, he thought. Notary Elie Langlois of Paris was convinced of the millions after he attended a court session where the Crawford case was defended by the distinguished attorney Pouillet and where Thérèse pointed out a man in the audience as "a Crawford." Louis Delacherie, a notary at Lille who in return for exorbitant commissions lured many loans to the Humberts—including 3,500,000 from the textile family Schotsmans alone—also believed Thérèse and Frédéric implicitly. He brought a few of his wealthiest clients to Paris to discuss loans personally with the Humberts. When any of the clients appeared reluctant, it often occurred that one of the Crawford brothers unexpectedly rang at the door to harangue Thérèse. There would be a brief scene, and after the American left, she would denounce him as a "crude barbarian."

12. Reports of May–July, 1902, APP, E A/118, Affaire Humbert; *Le Figaro*, May 22, 1902, February 22, August 6, 1903.

This performance usually ensured that she received her loan, but Delacherie never suspected that it had been somehow contrived.[13]

Once convinced, attorneys and notaries rarely questioned their faith in the Crawford millions no matter what rumors were passed around. A number of the creditors were more easily shaken, forcing Thérèse to devote much care to reassuring them by all possible means. To some, she pointed out "the Crawfords" from a distance; to others, she showed letters from the Crawfords, sealed with an enigmatic Minerva signet. Always, there was a great show of mystery and the sense of sharing a confidence. Creditors who thought of calling in their debts were telephoned by a man calling himself Robert Crawford and asking to purchase the debt held by the creditor. The plan, he said, was to buy up Thérèse Humbert's debts and suddenly call them all at once to ruin her. Each time, the creditor ended the conversation by refusing to sell: any debt that someone wanted to take over was worth retaining. For the creditors with the largest balances, there were more elaborate precautions. In December, 1901, Jean Schotsmans grew worried at the bon mot he heard repeated at a soirée: "In the famous Humbert strongbox, the bonds are not from the French treasury but from that of Sainte Farce." Thérèse arranged for him to meet her at the Avenue de la Grande Armée on December 17 and also invited her attorney, Labat, and two attorneys for the Crawfords, Parmentier and Auzoux. In front of Schotsmans, she discussed a proposal to offer the Crawfords a lump-sum settlement of twenty million francs to halt their legal proceedings. Parmentier promised to submit the proposition to his clients, and Schotsmans left thinking that the inheritance would quickly fall into Thérèse's hands.[14]

It was not always that easy. By the middle 1890s, the Humberts had built such a tower of loans, purchased so much property, and begun to spend so lavishly that they required a constant infusion of new loans and renewal of old ones. There were inevitably moments when they were unable to make prompt interest payments, and the calling in of a large loan presented embarrassing difficulties. This danger pressed Thérèse's dramatic skills to the limit. One creditor, no longer willing

13. *Le Figaro*, May 17, 27, June 1, 4, 1902, January 13, 16, February 1, 1903; reports of May–July, 1902, APP, E A/118, Affaire Humbert.
14. *Le Figaro*, June 7, 11, 1902, August 6, 1903.

to be palliated by excuses, obtained a writ empowering the bailiff who accompanied him to the Humbert house to seize property equal to the debt if Thérèse could not pay him in currency. As was customary, the writ was to expire at 5 P.M. that same day, but the creditor and the bailiff arrived in midafternoon with what they considered plenty of time to accomplish their task. When she was told why they had come, Thérèse became enraged that anyone would question her honor, ripped a magnificent pearl necklace from her throat, and threw it at them. She screamed that it was worth fifty thousand francs, more than the debt, and that they should take it and leave. But the gesture, in breaking the necklace cord, allowed the pearls to scatter across the room in all directions. The creditor, the bailiff, and Thérèse crawled around the floor trying to find all of them. When they finally did so, the clock had long past rung 5 P.M., and the creditor had no right to seize the necklace. He did not return with a new writ because the performance had won his confidence.[15]

The reaction of Thérèse in the case of the necklace was not entirely acting. Perhaps because she realized that the prestige and wealth of the Humberts was a species of cloud castle, she was preoccupied with her public image. She was a near-peasant girl who had reached the social heights of Paris with the mighty in her salon, but that was not enough. She pretended to be in close relations with officials she did not know even by sight, once claiming to her dinner guests that they were of an odd number because a noted conseiller d'état had declined her invitation at the last possible moment. There was general consternation at the table because the man had been dead for three months. Probably most of the guests dismissed this incident as a slip of her tongue or a lapse of memory. But dinner at the Humbert house was always a strange affair. Until they were acutally seated at table, the guests were kept apart as much as possible by the servants and the Daurignac brothers. During dinner, Thérèse dominated the conversation and prevented any talk of the Crawford inheritance or the legal proceedings. When alone with each guest, Thérèse had one question on her mind: whether the Humberts were thought to be *honnête*—respectable and honest.[16]

15. *Ibid.*, May 26, 1902.
16. *Ibid.*, June 16, 18, 1902.

The qualms, rages, and questioning grew out of a feeling that came in the early 1890s that the scheme could not be sustained forever. The reputation of Senator Humbert, who would die in 1894, could be stretched only so far to cover his son and daughter-in-law. In spite of the fertility of Parmentier's strategies, even French civil justice had to complete the details of the Crawford case eventually. Every year, the pyramided loans became more and more difficult to manipulate. What was needed, Thérèse decided, was a *legal* means of consolidating their *illegal* fortune for the future, one that would allow all of the loans to be repaid and yet preserve the wealth already acquired. Thus came the idea of the Rente Viagère.

Ostensibly, the Rente Viagère was another of the many companies providing a home for the savings of thrifty bourgeois Frenchmen. In return for their investment, the Rente Viagère would pay a life annuity. But none of the Humbert financial schemes was ever exactly what it seemed. Under the auspices of Parisian notary Victor Lanquest, the Rente Viagère was constituted on May 17, 1893, by seven men whose capital amounted to Fr 10,000,000: Romain Daurignac (Fr 9,750,000), Emile Daurignac (Fr 120,000), Louis Daurignac (Fr 50,000), Armand Parayre (Fr 50,000), Alexandre Parayre (Fr 10,000), Emile Thenier (Fr 10,000), and Jacques Boutiq (Fr 10,000). Lanquest had met none of them previously, and not all of the seven were present for the constitution of the company. They were a curious lot. Romain, Emile, and Louis Daurignac were the three brothers of Thérèse, but they could hardly have been more different. Romain was an ebullient womanizer, while Emile was a dour misanthrope; both had played major roles in the Crawford fraud. Louis, the youngest brother, had never been close to his sisters and other brothers, and they had contrived to have him first sent to a Trappist monastery, then enrolled in the army, and finally dispatched to Tunisia. He learned of his position as a founder of the Rente Viagère only in 1902. Alexandre Parayre ran a fashion shop on the Boulevard Saint-Denis. Armand Parayre and his wife lived with the Humberts and were entrusted with numerous delicate operations to maintain confidence among the Humbert creditors. Thenier and Boutiq were the managers of Humbert property at Vives Eaux and Celeyran, respectively. With the exception of Alexandre Parayre, none of the founders could possibly have possessed the capital attributed to him.

Actually, all of the capital came from the Humberts, who went to some pains to conceal their participation. The formal address of the company's offices was 15–17 Rue Auber, in the Chaussée-d'Antin district, but the founders would have their meetings at 16 Rue Pergolèse, the back entrance to the Humbert *hôtel*. The administrator of the company would be Paul Girard, long one of the Humbert minions, and the actual direction would come from Thérèse and Frédéric, with some advice from Romain and Emile Daurignac. The minutes, signed by Armand Parayre as secretary, pretended that six of the seven founders always attended company meetings—Louis Daurignac was "excused" because he was in Tunisia—and concealed the presence of the Humberts.

These irregularities were quite secret, and no one suspected the new Rente Viagère of questionable activity. From the beginning, there were many investors. The Humberts spared little expense in creating handsome offices and brochures and were not above listing the names of Lanquest and Henri Du Buit, one of the Humbert attorneys, in the advertising as endorsing the company, although this act violated the canons of the Paris bar. The initial ten-million-franc capital increased steadily and was used to purchase property first in Paris and later in the provinces. The return on the investments was generous, and each year after 1894 the company was able to point to a 4 percent return. The dividend was never distributed, however, because annually the founders voted to reinvest it. The plan was for the company to function legally but for the Humberts to skim the profits, leaving just enough for the Rente Viagère to meet its obligations and to attract new investors and capital. Thérèse and Frédéric would slowly pay off their loans with the income it produced. Both in theory and in fact, the plan worked as envisioned. The Rente Viagère prospered, and if the Humberts could have avoided detection for another decade or two, they might have become legitimate millionaires.[17]

The Humberts did not have that decade or two because the manip-

17. For the Rente Viagère, see *ibid.*, May 10, 11, 13, 31, 1902, January 14, 15, 17, 21, 23, February 5, August 6, 1903.

ulations of maintaining the myth of the Crawford inheritance were becoming more and more complicated. In January, 1892, after the decision of the Cour de Cassation on the 1884 agreement, Thérèse had asked that the lump sum of six million francs to be turned over to the Crawfords be simply deducted from the rest of the inheritance. At the insistence of the Crawfords, who were determined to cause difficulties, Parmentier refused and went before the civil tribunal to prevent her doing so. Thérèse pretended to be immobilized in her finances by this suit, but finally, in May, 1896, the tribunal found in her favor. Parmentier appealed, and the case disappeared into the Cour d'Appel. By then, after more than eleven years of litigation, there began to appear some public speculation that the Crawfords were a myth and la grande Thérèse a fraud. These had been stimulated partly by a short campaign against the Humberts in *La Libre Parole* by Hervé Breton in 1895, although that could be attributed to the antirepublican bias of the newspaper's editor, Edouard Drumont.[18] Most of all, the speculation had grown out of the suicide of Etienne Girard.

Girard's bank in Elbeuf had made substantial loans to Thérèse Humbert in the late 1880s and early 1890s. In 1896, it experienced a series of losses on other obligations, and Girard went to Thérèse to call in the loans he had made to her, pleading that he would be bankrupt without them. She had heard all manner of excuses before and made them herself: his bankruptcy meant little to her. Certainly she never displayed any grief that he shot himself rather than face his failure. Alexandre Duret, the receiver appointed for the Girard bank, engaged as his attorney René Waldeck-Rousseau, one of the most distinguished members of the Paris bar and a republican politician who had been a close associate of Léon Gambetta in the early stages of the Third Republic. Waldeck-Rousseau conducted the effort to collect the largest of the outstanding accounts, and it was in this way that he came to know the Humberts.

When Waldeck-Rousseau opened inquiries into the debts owed by the Humberts to the Girard bank, he had heard of the Crawford fortune but had taken no interest in it or developed any suspicions. As his inquiries spread, however, he began to feel doubts. Thérèse claimed

18. See *La Libre Parole*, March–May, 1895, *passim*.

to have borrowed far less money from Girard than the account books of the bank indicated, and she called in Henri Du Buit to represent her, while Eugène Pouillet spoke for the interest of the Crawford brothers. Here was an error on Thérèse's part. Waldeck-Rousseau's rigorously Cartesian mind required absolute order in all of his undertakings, and the entrance of Pouillet led him to investigate the Crawfords. Quite naturally, there was little to discover other than what Thérèse could tell. In order to serve a writ upon them, he was compelled to ask Thérèse to invite them to dinner and have the bailiff break in upon them, in itself a breach of procedure that could invalidate the writ. When the case came to trial at Elbeuf in December, 1898, no Crawfords appeared in court, and the arguments of Thérèse's attorneys could not overcome the well-audited figures in Girard's account books.

But the doubts Waldeck-Rousseau had come to feel were as important to him as the decision in his client's favor. In his closing summary, he called the very existence of the Crawfords into question—and by extension labeled Thérèse a fraud. What surprised him, he said, was that men called millionaires could "promenade about the world without having, I will not say a domicile, I will not even say a 'home' in pronouncing the word dear to the English, but even a refuge, a resting place, where a bailiff may come when he has a process to serve. For in effect, the first act of procedure that has taken place in this suit was the serving of a copy of it upon the Crawford brothers. And where did this take place? At the house of the Humberts, at a dinner to which the Crawfords willingly came! And even this act did not take place in conditions of regularity." These words were spoken in open court, but no one else seemed to take them seriously. In particular, the magistrates at Elbeuf acted as if they had never heard the Waldeck-Rousseau summation, obeying the Talleyrand injunction: "Pas trop de zèle!" Etienne Jacquin, the close Humbert friend and director of personnel at the Ministry of Justice, had been in the audience throughout the suit. Every magistrate knew that Gustave Humbert had been minister of justice and that his son had been his chef de cabinet and later a deputy. Thérèse's salon attracted the cabinet ministers of the past, present, and future. Du Buit, by now her most important attorney, had just been elected president of the Paris bar. Only a Waldeck-Rousseau could afford to take on defenses so powerfully arrayed, and even he did not press for a thorough investigation. He was increasingly preoccupied by the dangerous political crisis engendered by the Dreyfus affair, and in June, 1899, he would become premier. He had no more time to devote to the Humberts personally. Perhaps curiously, he did not order his subordinates to take any action after he became premier.[19]

The most interesting result of Waldeck-Rousseau's intervention was the reaction of the Humbert creditors. Some were frightened, but most saw only an opportunity for greater gain. They willingly believed that Waldeck-Rousseau had simply failed to understand the complexities of the Crawford-Humbert dispute. Because he had made his doubts public, the creditors could claim to Thérèse that loaning money to her was extraordinarily speculative and thus require even higher rates of interest than she had previously promised. And so the charade continued until Parmentier's 1896 appeal to the Cour d'Appel came up for a hearing in February, 1902.

After the numerous delays that normally afflicted civil justice, Presiding Justice Emile Forichon was ready to rule in favor of the Humberts. But on April 30, as he prepared to hand down his ruling, he asked what was the actual address of the Crawford brothers. Certainly it could not be the hotels to which letters had been mailed; it could not be the post office on the Rue du Louvre; it could not be 1202 Broadway in New York because inquiries had revealed that to be a public square with a post office opposite. The attorneys for the Humberts had no reply. Neither did the attorneys for the Crawfords. Vexed, Forichon invited the counselors to meet with him in his chambers. A few minutes later, they emerged, and the presiding justice declared that he would issue no ruling until an address for the Crawfords could be obtained for the court.[20]

This new pressure from the magistrature came at an awkward moment for the Humberts. During March and April, *Le Matin's* best reporter, F. I. Mouthon, had conducted a press campaign against them, using information and documents obtained from Duret, the receiver for the Girard bank, and from Elie Cattauï, president of the French Exploration Company and the Anglo-Egyptian Bank. Cattauï had loaned

19. For the Elbeuf case, see *Gazette des Tribunaux*, June 15, 1898; *Le Figaro*, May 11, 1902, August 5, 18, 22, 1903.
20. *Gazette des Tribunaux*, February 12, May 1, 1902.

large amounts of money to the Humberts at high rates of interest and with exorbitant commission charges. When he tried to recall the loans, Thérèse had offered her usual excuses. He had refused to accept them, threatened legal action, and hinted at even worse. In an access of fear combined with arrogance, Thérèse then committed the error of charging him with usury on October 1, 1901, expecting to bargain the lifting of the complaint for his silence. But in doing so, she failed to reckon properly two factors: Cattauï was an implacable foe, a much more dangerous enemy than she had faced previously, and in taking a complaint of usury to the Palais de Justice, she was for the first time submitting the Crawford myth to the inspection of *criminal* justice, which was charged with discovering the truth in a case, not merely adjudicating the matters presented before it.[21]

The campaign in *Le Matin* and the declaration of Justice Forichon precipitated real fear among the Humbert creditors. One of the most frightened, Emile-Léon Morel, hastened before the Tribunal des Référés, which could issue emergency civil decrees, to demand that Thérèse Humbert be replaced as official depositor for the inheritance. Speaking for the Humberts, Du Buit objected, and Azoux read a letter from the Crawford brothers opposing any alteration in the 1883 protocol. Nevertheless, there was clearly a panic among the creditors, and Du Buit told the court that the Humberts proposed to end all speculation about the fortune. They would ask for an official inventory, by whomever the court might appoint, of the bonds constituting the inheritance. Morel and his attorneys professed to be entirely satisfied by this proposal. Presiding Justice Henri Ditte then issued a decree (on May 6, 1902) calling for an inventory of the Humbert strongbox at 1 P.M. on May 9, 1902, by Edouard Demonts, president of the notaries of Paris, with Lanquest, the notary for the Rente Viagère, as his assistant.[22]

These developments called forth ever greater press coverage, with *Le Figaro* now taking the lead through a long, detailed article on May 9 examining the thesis that the Humbert millions were a fraud. The publicity ensured that a large crowd would gather in front of the Humbert *hôtel* on the Avenue de la Grande Armée. *Le Figaro* assigned one of its

21. Mouthon's excellent articles represented the best in investigative reporting. See *Le Matin*, April 23–30, May 1, 1902.
22. *Gazette des Tribunaux*, April 23, May 1, 7, 1902.

best reporters, Jules Huret, to the inventory, but although he had carefully researched the background to the story, he was as astonished as the rest of the crowd when the notaries were accompanied by important representatives of the criminal justice system, Herbaux and Leydet of the Paris parquet and Cochefert of the Sûreté. They were to learn only later that on May 8 Cattauï had revenged himself on Thérèse by charging her with criminal fraud, thereby providing the parquet with the first opportunity to open an *instruction* against her.[23]

Huret was fascinated by the handsome dwelling of three storeys built of cut stone with high windows, a large porte cochere of polished oak, and an escutcheon above the front door reading—ironically—*Pro Fide et Patria*. At 2 P.M, fearing the worst from the absence of the Humberts, the notaries emerged to send for the locksmiths. Huret found Cattauï in the crowd and persuaded the banker to allow him to pose as his representative at the opening of the strongbox. This ruse permitted Huret to enter the house while the rest of the press was kept outside. During the wait for the locksmiths, he wandered around the rooms, ignored in the general confusion. Everything was sumptuous. There was marble throughout, a paneled billiards room, tableaux on every wall, paintings by Edouard Manet and Ferdinand Roybet, heavy sofas and armchairs covered in silk, tapestries, a portrait of Senator Humbert by Frédéric, and a gilt harp. Finally, he heard the sound of tools and moved toward the noise on the third floor, passing Cochefert, the chief of the Sûreté, who was asking the servants for photographs of the Humberts and the Daurignac brothers. Huret reached the room containing the strongbox just as it was opened. At that moment, he was recognized by a Sûreté agent and led back outside.[24]

As it became clear that the Humberts and their supposed millions, as well as the real millions they had borrowed over twenty years, had disappeared, there was frantic activity at the Palais de Justice. There were four critical issues. First, with the Humberts gone, there had to be immediate provisions to limit as much as possible any further losses by those who had entrusted money to them. Second, there would have to be a massive hunt for the Humberts before the trail became cold. Third, there would have to be explanations of how this fraud had con-

23. *Le Figaro*, May 9, 1902.
24. Report of May 9, 1902, APP, E A/118, Affaire Humbert; *Le Figaro*, May 10, 1902.

tinued undetected for twenty years while the civil justice system had been used as its accomplice. Finally, the most conspicuous of those attorneys and notaries who had been the perhaps unwitting assistants of the Humberts would have to be arrested, if only to gratify a public opinion bound to be thoroughly shocked by the laxity of the Ministry of Justice.

On May 14, the Tribunal de Commerce declared the fraudulent bankruptcy of the Humberts and the Rente Viagère. François Bonneau was named liquidator for the property of the Humberts, Henri Vacher liquidator for the property of the Rente Viagère. There was a full-scale search of the house on the Avenue de la Grande Armée, and that turned up the titles to numerous properties, most notably the Château de Vives Eaux, the estate of Celeyran, and the farm at Orsonval. Bonneau called in Georges Petit and Arthur Bloche, who conducted posh auction sales at the Hôtel Drouot, to help with the appraisal and inventory of the houses. The task was enormous. From the Grande Armée house alone, there were 379 paintings—far more than Huret had noticed—by such artists as Gustave Moreau, Jean Louis Meisonnier, Jean Baptiste Corot, Charles François Daubigny, Henri Rousseau, and Paul Baudry, as well as Edouard Manet and Ferdinand Roybet. The worth of these paintings was estimated to be Fr 1,200,000. In addition, there was sculpture by Antonio Canova, precious tapestries, valuable furniture, old silver, furs, clothes, boots, shoes, and books. Petit planned a titanic auction for mid-June, and Bonneau made preparations to sell the Humbert real estate over the next six months.[25]

Because Thérèse and Frédéric left no records behind, Bonneau also had the difficult task of identifying who had loaned money to them. He announced through the newspapers that there would be a mass meeting of all the creditors on May 27 at the Tribunal de Commerce. As expected, however, only a handful of the estimated number appeared. Public opinion had already divided the Humbert creditors into two not necessarily exclusive groups: those who had speculated on the Crawford story in return for usurious interest and those who had been negligent and obtuse in their investments; all deserved to lose their money. Those creditors willing to endure this raillery learned that they

25. *Gazette des Tribunaux*, May 15, 1902; *Le Figaro*, May 10, 15–16, 18–19, 23, 1902.

had until June 21 to produce records substantiating their claims against the Humbert estate. Few had any hope of recovering more than a fraction of their loans. When one creditor learned that Eve Humbert had marked her linen with an embroidered apple, he immediately ordered twelve dozen handkerchiefs marked with a pear—French slang for a simpleton—to symbolize his stupidity. Cafe poets celebrated the Humberts and their dupes in songs and broadsides:

> Bonnes gens de la Provence
> De Paris et autres lieux.
> Ouissez, c'est merveilleux
> L'histoire d'un lapin immense
> Qu'était dans le coffre-fort
> De l'affaire Humbert-Crawford.
> Les Humberts avaient un grand homme,
> Qui fut Gustav', le garde des sceaux.
> Crions: "Vive la République!"
> En méditant cett' moralité
> Qu' les Gros ont toute liberté![26]

> [Good people of Provence,
> Of Paris, and other places.
> Listen to the marvelous tale
> Of a great fraud
> That was the strongbox
> In the Humbert-Crawford affair.
> The Humberts claimed a great man,
> Who was Gustave, the minister of justice.
> Let us cry: "The Republic forever!"
> While meditating on this morality
> Where the great have all liberty!]

Those who stood to lose money on the bankruptcy of the Rente Viagère were a completely different sort, approximately 1,100 small investors who had accumulated capital to invest in an annuity for their old age. The public sympathy that was distinctly lacking for the creditors of the Humberts was very much present for them. All was not lost for these rentiers, however, for the assets of the Rente Viagère—in real

26. Reports of May–July, 1902, APP, E A/118, Affaire Humbert; *Le Figaro*, May 28, June 1–5, 21, July 9, 1902, the broadside from June 5.

estate—covered all but approximately five million francs of the capital invested by them. Liquidator Vacher and several of the investors thought to recover the outstanding balance by suing De Buit and Lanquest. Their names had appeared on the prospectus of the Rente Viagère, and Lanquest had, in addition, served as the notary to the company. De Buit was quickly able to prove his ignorance of the misuse of his name in the prospectus, but Lanquest was in a more difficult position. It took only a brief inquiry to demonstrate that the seven founders of the Rente Viagère had been a mere facade for Thérèse and Frédéric Humbert, and while there was no indication that Lanquest had been a participant in the fraud, he had been grossly negligent in failing more properly to investigate the company for which he was providing the official documentation. If Lanquest protested his innocence of fraud, he was still liable for suit and probably would lose. If he admitted guilt, the Paris association of notaries would assume the liabilities he had caused, but he would go to prison. He resolved his dilemma by voluntarily turning over to the Rente Viagère the bulk of his personal fortune, Fr 3,700,000, thereby striking a tacit deal with the investors of the company and the magistrature to avoid any prosecution or litigation. Vacher was ultimately able to return almost every franc invested in the Rente Viagère to those who had purchased its annuities.[27]

While the Tribunal de Commerce sorted out the possessions of the Humberts and the Rente Viagère, the Sûreté attempted to find Frédéric, Thérèse, her sister Maria, and her brothers Romain and Emile. All of them but Emile had lived at 65 Avenue de la Grande Armée, and his residence had been a block away at number 22. Both houses were thoroughly searched, as were all of the other properties known to belong to the Humberts or Daurignacs. While none of the fugitives was found, the Sûreté was able to report intriguing details. It had not been generally known that Emile Daurignac had married the youngest daughter of Senator Humbert, making the intermarriage between the two families double, or that the widow of the senator lived with her daughter and son-in-law. Both women defended Emile and Frédéric, laying any blame for the flight on Thérèse, whom both professed to hate. The searches also revealed that Frédéric Humbert passed much of his time

27. *Le Figaro*, May 11, 13–16, 18–19, 31, June 2–3, 5–6, 1902.

in an apartment at 11 Place de Vintimille, on the edge of Montmartre, where he painted indifferently and was known as M. Lelong.

The Sûreté did learn that Thérèse and her family left Paris on the afternoon of May 7 after withdrawing Fr 40,000 from her bank account, "borrowing" Fr 42,000 from the Rente Viagère, and pawning the magnificent pearl necklace that she had once ripped from her throat for Fr 43,000 at the state pawnshop. Before her departure, she gave the servants Fr 7,000 in wages and made a special trip to her dressmaker's shop, where she paid Fr 3,000 for dresses she had ordered as gifts for Du Buit's two daughters—probably fearing that he would be asked to pay for them if she did not. Emile Daurignac did not leave with the others because he was to appear that night with his wife in the Humbert box at the opera in order to give the impression that the family had not fled Paris. Where the Humbert-Daurignac fugitives went after leaving the city and how Emile joined up with them remained unknown despite the assignment of forty-five agents to the case—at the rate of three francs a day, the newspapers reported. During the first two months of the search, there were over seven hundred sightings of the Humberts. Not a single one could be verified. At first, the Sûreté was convinced that the family would head north and even asked the Belgian police to watch for them. Late in May, there was circumstantial evidence that they had managed to reach England, had traveled to Liverpool, and were making arrangements to charter a boat to Argentina, which had no extradition treaty with France. Scotland Yard assigned one of its best men, Inspector Richard H. P. Matthews, to the case. The Sûreté sent its deputy chief, Octave Hamard, across the Channel. The newspapers made much of an imminent arrest, and many witnesses claimed to have had fleeting glimpses of the Humberts or Daurignacs. In the end, Matthews went back to London and Hamard to Paris because the Humberts had never been to England.

Having speculated on flight to the north and to the west, the Sûreté now decided to look to the south. As soon as this intelligence was reported, there were sightings in Bordeaux and the Gard and eventually the rumor, spread by Henry Rochefort in *L'Intransigeant*, that the Humberts and Daurignacs had escaped across the Pyrenees into Spain and were arranging for passage from Lisbon to Panama or Argentina or Brazil. Various of the Humbert hangers-on had been left behind, such as Armand Parayre and his wife and Paul Girard, but they knew nothing more than the details of their relatively minor roles in the drama. One lead that seemed promising was to follow the mistresses of Romain Daurignac in hope that he might attempt to contact one of them. The Sûreté finally learned that Andrée d'Alaza, the twenty-four-year-old woman whom Romain called his "Blondinette," had booked passage for Buenos Aires in late November. A possible conclusion was that she was going to join him there, but the Sûreté planned to learn the details not through classic detective work but through the assignment to the ship of a handsome inspector with the task of seducing Blondinette. This evidence of inept leadership was reinforced when it became known that the Paris parquet and the Sûreté had competed to determine which could capture the Humberts first instead of working together. One examining magistrate, Joseph Lemercier, had gone so far as to employ a private detective to assist the parquet in besting the Sûreté. Ironically, Thérèse had utilized the same detective on several occasions. It was not surprising that in mid-November Lemercier was relieved of his duties and Cochefert was promoted to the powerless post of controller general of the Paris police. Hamard was made the new chief of the Sûreté.[28]

While the Sûreté searched futilely for the Humberts and Daurignacs, the Ministry of Justice attempted to explain how Thérèse and Frédéric had practiced their frauds and swindles undetected for twenty years. There was much shrugging of shoulders and reference to "narrowly worded suits" and the "limitations of civil justice" in these explanations, as well as a defensive attitude that impressed no one. It was difficult to justify court decisions such as that in 1900 by Presiding Justice Manuel Achille Baudouin of the Tribunal de la Seine. A prominent creditor, Edouard Tronsens, had brought suit against the Humberts to regain money that he had loaned them at the rate of 6 percent. Baudouin, a frequent visitor to Thérèse's salon, treated Tronsens as a usurer in dismissing the case and commented that there was no risk inherent in the loan because even if the Crawfords were to win the inheritance,

28. The futility of the Sûreté search was recounted with increasing sarcasm in *ibid.*, May 10–31, June 17–18, July 8, 27, November 9, 23–24, 1902. The details about Lemercier, Cochefort, and Hamard are in the November 23–24 issues. See the reports of May–July, November, 1902, APP, E A/118, Affaire Humbert; and Lemercier's personnel file: AN BB 6 II, 1009.

Maria Daurignac would receive a third of the total. There was a similar attitude toward criticism at the Ministry of Finance when the civil servants charged with registering wills and imposing succession taxes were asked why they had never mounted an inquiry into the Crawford legacy. Marcel Fournier, the director of the section, replied imperiously that the treasury took no note of newspaper articles or even of the decisions of the courts, that it composed its lists of wills entirely from the names of the deceased reported quarterly by the mayors. He also refused to accept any responsibility for the dispositions made by a man who "was not French."[29]

It was inevitable that because a swarm of politicians had surrounded the Humberts there would be charges that corruption and favoritism had charmed the lives and the frauds led by Thérèse and Frédéric. Some of the most brilliant attorneys of the Paris bar, Félix Decori, Emile de Saint-Auban, Maurice Tézenas, Henri Robert, Charles Chenu, and Raymond Poincaré, himself a former minister of justice, agreed in print that "politics is the plague of justice" and that the Palais de Justice was "too close" to the Palais Bourbon, where the Chamber of Deputies sat. Jean Cruppi, another attorney and deputy for Haute Garonne, was less discreet in a statement to *Le Temps*: he called the magistrature plainly corrupt. The mounting criticism caused Etienne Jacquin's resignation on May 20, and there was pressure for a thorough purge of the Ministry of Justice. The difficulty of that course for the government of newly named premier Emile Combes, who had assumed office only on June 7, 1902, was that the Humberts were a republican scandal par excellence. Combes was the most blatantly partisan premier of the Third Republic, determined to do nothing that would compromise the radical republicanism that counted Gustave Humbert in its pantheon. His majority was instructed to cease comment on the scandal, ensuring that those who criticized the conduct of the Ministry of Justice could be labeled "antirepublican." Gabriel Syveton, the violent leader of the Ligue de la Patrie Française, spoke the thoughts of many deputies on June 27, when he argued: "In this Humbert affair, there has been a swindle that could not have been perpetuated without accomplices in the po-

29. *Le Figaro*, May 10–12, 17, 21, 25, June 9, 1902. See also Baudouin's personnel file: AN, BB 6 II, 650.

litical and judicial world. The magistrates who have protected knaves are knaves themselves. It belongs to the government to search them out." But given Combes's attitude, he could win little support.[30]

Combes did not have the same power outside the Chamber of Deputies, and the criticism in the press of the magistrates and politicians eventually came to encompass Senator Humbert. Initially, there were only the complaints by creditors that they had feared to engage Thérèse in litigation because the elder Humbert's influence and friends would put them at the mercy of justice in France. At the end of May, however, Léopold Sée, whose Comptoir d'Alsace was an important regional bank, directly challenged the republican saint's reputation for virtue. Sée charged that Humbert had been a significant force in provoking the disastrous collapse of the Union Générale, a so-called Catholic bank formed to compete with the Rothschilds and Pereires, which had attracted the savings of many old monarchist families. Sée claimed that Humbert, for his part in the conspiracy, had received half a million francs, which he had deposited in the Comptoir d'Alsace. Humbert's widow angrily denied the story and charged *Le Gaulois*, which first published it, with defamation. But Sée's denunciation had found a ready audience.[31]

To mollify public opinion, French justice took revenge for its humiliation on those it could reach, arresting attorney Parmentier, notaries Dumort, Langlois, and Delacherie, and Humbert aides Girard and Parayre. The charge in each instance was fraud, but the interrogations carried out by examining magistrates Joseph Leydet and Louis André revealed that there was insufficient evidence to bring any of them to trial. Parmentier was the worst treated of the six. A stout, balding father of eight children, he was held in high regard in his native Le Havre. He was also a diabetic. The police agents sent to arrest him, however, cared little for his social standing or his physical condition. They hustled him away from his house without his medicine and with as little discretion as they would reserve for a pickpocket. Because Parmentier

30. *Le Figaro*, June 22–24, 26, 30, 1902; JOC, Débats parlementaires, June 27, 1902. For the general tone of the Combes administration, see Malcolm Overstreet Partin, *Waldeck-Rousseau, Combes and the Church: The Politics of Anti-Clericalism, 1899–1905* (Durham, 1969). See also Jacquin's personnel file: AN, BB 6 II, 951.

31. *Le Figaro*, May 30, June 1, 15, 19, 21, 1902.

had been the legal adviser to the Crawfords from the beginning of the litigation over the inheritance, Leydet thought it likely that he had at some point penetrated the charade. A close scrutiny of Parmentier's meticulous records proved the examining magistrate incorrect. The attorney had been credulous, perhaps incautious, but not guilty of fraud. He had faithfully carried out his instructions to prolong the life of the case in the courts, and he had believed so thoroughly in the Crawfords, although not in their ultimate victory, that he had himself made loans to Thérèse. Parmentier proved his innocence, but by mid-June the experience of interrogation and prison had so undermined his already shaky health that he had to be hospitalized.[32]

The three notaries fared little better. The short, bearded, bespectacled Dumort appeared devastated by his arrest. He had not yet recovered from the shock of the empty strongbox and the realization that the Fr 1,300,000 he had personally loaned the Humberts was lost. He produced his records and, like Parmentier, told of his experiences seeing the Crawfords and clipping coupons with Thérèse. He also explained why there were so few records at the Humbert residence: "Mme Humbert pushed prudence to the most extreme limits; she never wrote *anything.*" Langlois, who was known as Thérèse's *rabbateur* (beater) because he had arranged so many of her loans, was also shocked to be arrested. His white whiskers bristling but his voice as slack as chiffon, he protested that his only relationship to the Humberts had been to draw up loan requests. He admitted recommending to his clients that they make these loans, but he argued that the Humberts had repaid their debts in the past and that he had had every reason to expect that they would continue to meet their obligations. After all, he had been among Thérèse's creditors himself. Dumort and Langlois were arrested in mid-May, and by the end of the month, Delacherie was expecting the same treatment because he had also arranged several large loans, including those of the Schotsmans family. Leydet did not disappoint him, and he joined his fellow notaries and Parmentier in prison. Like Langlois, Delacherie claimed that the Humberts had appeared to be a reasonable risk because they had never defaulted on previous loans—although repayment had occasionally been delayed—and seemed certain of winning their case in the courts. Delacherie was also

32. *Ibid.,* May 11, 14–15, 18, 25, 29, June 6–7, 15, 17, July 11, 13, 1902; reports of May–July, 1902, APP, E A/118, Affaire Humbert.

able to produce witnesses among his clients who had loaned money to the Humberts willing to swear that he had always warned them personally to investigate the Humberts before making the loans. It was clear that all three of the notaries had taken some precautions against possible deception, and this relieved them of the accusation of fraud. But the arrest and publicity ruined their reputations forever.[33]

It was also impossible to maintain the arrests of Girard and Parayre. The records of the Rente Viagère clearly bore out their protestations that they had known nothing of the true operations of the company. Girard, as administrator, had received a minimal salary for carrying on the day-to-day procedures of the Rente Viagère, collecting the investments and arranging for the payment of annuity checks. Parayre was genuinely shocked to learn that he should have been present at meetings of the founders instead of merely signing the minutes when they were presented to him by Thérèse. Both were straw men whose loyalty to the Humberts had led them to be Thérèse's dupes. With Parmentier, Dumort, Langlois, and Delacherie, they were released in mid-July. The parquet had proved that it could take action even though that action led nowhere.[34] The scandal moved to the back pages of the Paris newspapers until the editions of December 21 announced the sensational capture of the Humberts and Daurignacs in Madrid the previous day.

The arrest had been relatively simple. An anonymous letter to the French ambassador to Madrid, Louis Patenôtre, had denounced the hiding place of the fugitives, the first floor of a modest house in one of the better neighborhoods of Madrid, 33 Calle Ferraz. A squad of Spanish police under the lead of an Inspecter Caro surrounded the house and then forced the door. The three Humberts—Thérèse, Frédéric, and Eve—and the three Daurignacs—Romain, Emile, and Maria—were there. When the police broke in, there was no attempt to escape, but Eve fainted and Thérèse began to cry. A search of the rooms produced stacks of Parisian newspapers, the remains of some burned documents in the fireplace, a few minor jewels, a fine necklace of sixty pearls, several thousand francs in currency, and 410 francs in gold.

---

33. *Le Figaro*, May 11, 14–15, 18, 22–24, 27, 29, June 4, 7–8, 20, July 13, 1902; reports of May–July, 1902, APP, E A/118, Affaire Humbert.
34. *Le Figaro*, May 14, 22, 23, June 5, 8, 17, July 13, 1902; reports of May–July, 1902, APP, E A/118, Affaire Humbert.

In Paris, the minister of justice, Ernest Vallé, was radiant and eagerly explained to reporters that extradition procedures based on an agreement of December 14, 1877, would probably have the Humberts in Paris within ten days. But as details about the escape of the Humbert family from France and their life in Madrid for seven months became available, there were new and embarrassing questions to which the Ministry of Justice refused to reply. The Humberts and Daurignacs did not seem to have taken extraordinary precautions, having left Paris on May 7 and proceeded directly to Madrid within two days. After some time in hotels, they decided to rent the portion of the house in which they were captured. Romain Daurignac was fluent in Spanish and made most of the arrangements. Once installed, each assumed a Spanish name: Frédéric posed as Carlos Blanco, Thérèse as Marthe Blanco, Eve as Julia Blanco, Romain as Leon Marquez, Emile as Pedro Duval, and Maria as Rita Marquez. Because Eve was strikingly tall, she was rarely allowed to venture out, but the other five wandered freely around Madrid without adopting any disguise. They had subscribed to six Parisian newspapers—*Le Figaro, Le Gaulois, L'Echo de Paris, Le Temps, Le Matin,* and *Le Petit Parisien*—and received mail! At the Spanish banks, they had changed large amounts of French currency. In comparison to the Crawford myth, the escape of the Humberts was simplicity itself. Why, then, had the Sûreté failed to find them when by July it had already decided that they had fled south? Patenôtre had been alerted and had spread their descriptions and photographs throughout Spain. The French government had even advertised a reward of twenty-five thousand francs for information leading to their capture. Nevertheless, it had required seven months and an anonymous letter from a Spanish attorney (a Señor Cotarello) to capture them. As they awaited extradition, it is little wonder that the Humberts and Daurignacs recounted how much they had enjoyed reading in the Paris press about the frantic and futile efforts of the Sûreté to find them.[35]

II

The inefficient government of Spanish King Alphonso XIII complicated the process of extradition, but the six prisoners were finally placed

35. *Le Figaro,* December 21, 1902, devoted several pages to the details of the arrest.

aboard a train in Madrid on December 27 and arrived in Paris soon after dawn two days later on December 29. By 10 A.M. all were placed in cells at the Conciergerie prison except for Eve, who was universally considered innocent of any part in her parents' schemes and was released to the custody of her grandmother, the widow of Senator Humbert. When the keys turned on Thérèse and Maria Daurignac, it was the first time in more than a century that women had been housed in the Conciergerie. The Palais de Justice had also prepared for their arrival, with examining magistrates Leydet and André cutting short the *instructions* of other cases in their charge to concentrate on the Humberts. After a long discussion with Vallé, the minister of justice, they had already made the important decision to charge the five—Thérèse, Frédéric, Romain, Emile and Maria—not only with swindles (*escroqueries*), which could be tried in the Magistrate's Court (Tribunal Correctionnel) and carried a maximum penalty of five years in prison, but fraud (*faux*), which would be heard before a jury in criminal court (Cour d'Assises), where conviction meant a minimum sentence of five years' imprisonment at hard labor and the possibility of a twenty-year sentence. The distinction between swindling and fraud is not absolutely clear in French law, and the blurring allowed for some degree of bargaining between the state and the defendant, especially the first-time offender. In the case of the Humberts, it was clear that some elements at the Palais de Justice still wanted to handle them gently. The decision to try them before the Cour d'Assises indicated that political necessity and public opinion now required the magistrates to be stern.

Despite seven months of flight, hiding, arrest, extradition, and the threat of a harsh future in French prisons, the Humbert family were unbowed. Even before they left Madrid, they indicated that their defense would be a combination of denial, diversion, and unrestrained attacks upon their opponents. On December 21, the day after the arrest, Thérèse was allowed to meet with reporters from Paris. She told them that her family wanted to return to Paris as quickly as possible in order to prove themselves innocent and insisted that their borrowings had been wholly legal but vastly exaggerated by the press. All of their difficulties, she claimed, had arisen as the result of a complicated scheme of revenge by the banker Cattauï, whom everyone knew to be a usurer. The French government had conspired with him against her family, allowing them to live in Madrid until there was a politically opportune moment to make the arrests. She and her husband had openly written friends in Paris and had even been greeted on the street by Ambassador Patenôtre, all months before the arrest. "We are honorable people," she concluded. "Gustave Humbert, my father-in-law, was the honor of France. My husband also is a man of honor." In the Spanish jail cell awaiting transportation to France, Thérèse dominated all of the other prisoners, leading the warder to say, "I have never seen such a woman; she has a heart of iron." Finally boarding the train with her daughter at her side, she commented fiercely about a reporter, "There is a man who looks at us as if we were curious beasts."[36]

This attitude carried over into the interrogations. At his first appearance before Leydet, Frédéric began by declaring, "I and my family are the victims of an odious machination, and I am able to affirm resolutely my innocence." When it came Thérèse's turn to face the magistrature, she prefaced all of her other statements with: "I do not know what you are going to ask me. But I insist on declaring to you above all else that all the members of my family are innocent of the shortcomings with which you reproach them." And having avowed this, she thought it proper that the Humberts and Daurignacs be immediately released. Emile sulked and refused to answer questions. Maria proved incapable of responding and, when tested, was shown to be of less than normal intelligence. Romain complained bitterly that Jane d'Arvalho and his children by her were not permitted to visit him regularly in prison and passed the remainder of his time making fun of Leydet's questions and singing, "Mon pauvre Romain Daurignac / Te voilà maintenant dans l' sac" (My poor Romain Daurignac / Now they've got you in the sack).[37]

When the Humbert family did deign to reply to questions, it was only to deny the evidence slowly building against them. Leydet confronted Romain with the testimony of two postal officials, Duhamet and Castel from the Rue du Louvre station, that he was the man who picked up

36. For the extradition and preparations in Paris, see *ibid.*, December 22–31, 1902, with the decision of the charges December 31, the quotations by Thérèse December 22 and 29, respectively, and the quotation by the Spanish warden December 24.
37. *Ibid.*, January 4, 9, 10, 1903.

mail sent to poste restante addressed "R. C." or "H. C." and with the deposition by the Humbert coachman, a certain Jacottet, that he had often taken Romain to that post office. Laughing, Romain replied that the coachman was mistaken and that the postal officials had confused him with another man, the son of the Crawfords' secretary, Muller. The resemblance was so close, Romain asserted, that they were often taken for brothers. Emile was less inventive but just as categorical in his denials. Handwriting experts claimed close similarities between Emile's script and the signature "Henri Crawford" on documents notarized in 1896, 1900, and 1901 at Dupuy's office in Narbonne. These dates were important because the statute of limitations on fraud (*faux*) was ten years, and if the Humbert family was to be charged in the Cour d'Assises, their guilt would have to be proved with documents dating from after 1892. Emile denied ever having been in Bayonne, declared handwriting experts to be little more accurate than fortune-tellers, and insisted that Dupuy was mistaken in identifying him as the man calling himself Henri Crawford. He had, he concluded, never taken a part in any of Thérèse's business ventures and had followed the progress of her litigation with little interest because his own brandy company occupied all of his time and provided him with sufficient income.[38]

Frédéric was no more forthcoming. The Sûreté had discovered a list of more than two hundred creditors in a notebook that he had carried to Spain. One well-known speculator, Emile Marchand, had advanced the family Fr 25,000,000, and the total of debts surpassed Fr 110,000,000. Very coolly, Frédéric declared the notebook a false clue contrived by the Sûreté, although it was clearly in his handwriting. He also denied having misappropriated funds from the Rente Viagère but admitted that the company had loaned him Fr 3,600,000. Examining Magistrate André immediately challenged this assertion, charging that Frédéric had used the company funds for his own benefit. Not at all ruffled, Humbert replied that he had signed a receipt for the money in the offices of the Rente Viagère and added acidly that if the receipt could not be located, he should not be held accountable for the Sûreté's incompetence. Whether before André or Leydet, Frédéric continued to insist

38. *Ibid.*, January 6, 13, 1903.

upon the regularity of the Rente Viagère's business conduct, the existence of the Crawfords and their fortune, and the innocence of his entire family of all the charges against them.[39]

It was left to Thérèse to provide the most heated moments of the first interrogations. Leydet, who had the responsibility for drawing up the *instruction*, considered that it would be impossible to understand completely the course of the Crawford swindles without extending his investigation as far back as Thérèse's childhood. Not unexpectedly, his subject was entirely uncooperative. She was also extremely sarcastic. When Leydet asked her to tell him the location of the famous Château de Marcotte, with which she had duped Frédéric when he was her fiancé, she replied: "It's not for me to tell the police. Look for it yourselves!" Leydet persisted, trying to unravel the connections between the Daurignac and Humbert families that led to a double intermarriage when the latter were far superior socially to the former. Thérèse provided an explanation that resolved nothing: "Among young people, when you fall in love, you marry." Other witnesses confirmed that Thérèse never spoke of her youth or the circumstances of her marriage. Yet she was inordinately proud of acquiring the Humbert name and was the most vocal defender of Senator Gustave Humbert's honor. Her possessiveness toward Frédéric was similar to a peasant's toward his land, and she often cited as her motto the phrase "One love, one bed, one tomb."

Leydet found it impossible to obtain useful information from Thérèse. As he became increasingly frustrated, their exchanges grew bitter and loud. Investigating her role in the Rente Viagère, André had no more success and finally warned her that the refusal to cooperate would turn back upon her when the case came up for trial. If she truly believed herself and her family innocent, these efforts to thwart the *instruction* were a poor means of demonstrating it. All that his words earned him was a concession by Thérèse that the Rente Viagère might have conducted some of its proceedings with minor irregularity "if you insist on the most literal interpretation of the law!" Other than this admission, Thérèse contented herself with the threat to tell all—but only when the trial began. She claimed that usurers, the government, and

39. *Ibid.*, January 1, 8, 15, 21, 1903.

unnamed forces had persecuted her and brought about her family's present disgrace. France would learn all at the Cour d'Assises.[40]

In February, 1903, the Humberts were still several months away from the Cour d'Assises. Certainly France learned almost nothing new during the first appearance of the Humberts in court, before the ninth chamber of the Cour Correctionnelle. On October 1, 1901, Thérèse had charged banker Elie Cattauï with usury, and in revenge, Cattauï had filed criminal complaints of fraud against the Humberts in May, 1902, the act that precipitated their flight. But even the satisfaction of seeing the Humberts in the Conciergerie was not sufficient for him. As soon as they were arrested in Madrid, he brought suit for defamation of character against Thérèse and Maria, who had signed the charge of usury at her sister's command. The parquet urged Cattauï not to press the suit, because it would interrupt the *instruction* of the Humberts for fraud. But the vindictive banker insisted, and hearings began on February 11.[41]

There was considerable interest in the suit because of the possibility of revelations by the Humberts and because it would mark the first opportunity for reporters and the public to view the master swindlers. Thérèse, at least, disappointed no one. After her performance on the first day, *Le Figaro*'s reporter Henri Varennes wondered how it would be possible for anyone *not* to believe her. She had an extraordinary ability to persuade, by turns menacing and discreet, sometimes amusing, sometimes ironic, sometimes pathetic. A judge would vote her acquittal, a millionaire would loan her his fortune, he said. Still, she was remarkably ugly for having married the son of a distinguished politician and having become an arbiter of Parisian society. Her eyes were too round, her nose brusque, her upper lip too long, her chin manlike and hard. Yet these very traits made her the mistress of the session. In comparison, Frédéric was much less prepossessing: hunchbacked, with a pointed bald head, his moustache too large for his face, he had the air of a pale young man entering middle age. Maria was clearly the Cinderella, dressed meanly, her skin sallow, looking at the court through gentle, fearful eyes.

Cattauï and his attorneys, Rodolphe Rousseau and Maurice Ber-

40. *Ibid.*, January 9, 10, 16, 17, 22, 23, February 5, 1903.
41. See the background article in *ibid.*, February 10, 1903.

nard, developed a weak case. The banker had first loaned money to the Humberts, approximately one million francs, in the early 1890s. When he was not repaid and was constantly presented with excuses, he demanded sureties and increased interest. In comparison with some of the Humbert borrowings, the loans from Cattauï were insignificant, and Thérèse did not take him seriously. Although she acceded to some of his demands, she eventually quieted him by threatening to use the influence of Etienne Jacquin at the Ministry of Justice. Cattauï understood that he could not afford to have French justice arrayed against him, and he had retreated, but only until he won powerful allies of his own, Senators Fernand Crémieux and Ernest Vallé. The wisdom of his choices was apparent now that Vallé was minister of justice. Cattauï renewed his demands, and Thérèse filed her charges of usury. She did have cause: an independent inquiry by court-appointed accountant Henri Vereeque revealed that the interest on Cattauï's loans to the Humberts, after all commissions were added, came to 63.14 percent. Indeed, he had known that Thérèse's charges would be substantiated and had therefore sent his personal account books to Egypt before the parquet could order their examination. His excuse was that they were needed for the operations of his Anglo-Egyptian Bank, but actually, it was to gain the time necessary to reorder them. One of the Humbert attorneys, Charles Chenu, capped the presentation for his clients by declaiming that there were two sorts of people who should not sue for defamation of character: those who were above calumny and those who were beneath it. He would leave it to the court to decide where to place Cattauï.[42]

After two days of this envenomed debate with its overtones of the abuse of political influence, the presiding justice, Paul Puget, declared a recess for a week. The parquet needed time to reflect upon two difficulties raised by Cattauï's insistence on bringing the suit. First, the notoriety of the case ensured wide publicity for the accusations by both parties that the Ministry of Justice was venal. Second, the Humbert attorneys, Chenu, Henri Robert, and André Hesse, had so clearly shown Cattauï to be a usurer that the parquet looked suspicious for having dropped the charges against him in the aftermath of the Humbert flight.

42. *Le Figaro* and *Gazette des Tribunaux*, February 12–13, 1903.

More important, Cattauï would certainly lose his suit when the five-judge panel of the Cour Correctionnelle rendered its verdict, and Thérèse's victory there might influence the jurors in the Cour d'Assises. When the court reconvened on February 19, Assistant Prosecutor Théodore Lescouvé appeared before it to argue a brief carefully composed during the preceding week. He denied that politics had played a role in the consideration of any cases concerning Cattauï or the Humberts. He assailed both parties: the Humberts for attacking the names of Vallé and Cattauï when it was they themselves who were on trial, not their accusers; Cattauï for seeking a vengeance that did not belong to him with the Humberts already in the cells of the Conciergerie. Lescouvé called on the justices to dismiss Cattauï's suit but to enter into their ruling the stipulation that this judgment of innocence for the Humberts applied only to the charge of defamation. On February 21, the justices obediently rendered exactly this verdict and ordered Cattauï to assume the expenses of the trial.[43]

There were few surprises in the interrogations that followed the completion of the Cattauï suit. Leydet lost the assistance of André, who was given charge of the cases brought against the religious congregations by the anticlerical Combes ministry, but Leydet seemed entirely capable of completing the *instruction* by himself. During March and April, he added many details about the Humbert household to his dossier of evidence. The final reports of the handwriting experts added even more bulk. To Leydet's questions, however, the Humberts paid little attention. They refused to answer anything about their personal expenses and travels and enjoyed mocking the conclusions of handwriting experts who had disagreed so fervently at the trials of Alfred Dreyfus. Only two topics ignited any reaction. When asked about her family's interlude in Madrid, Thérèse readily repeated her earlier charge that the French government had known of the Humberts' location within days of their flight, and she promised to prove this assertion at the trial. It was disturbing that they had openly received mail and newspapers from Paris and had gone frequently to the currency exchange. Yet, as Leydet reminded her, the family had altered their names and dress in order not to be recognized. Thérèse replied that

43. *Ibid.*, February 20, 22, 1903.

they had done so only in order not to embarrass the Ministry of Justice by being discovered by *canaille* before the proper moment. She concluded by insisting that they had been shadowed by four agents from their departure from Paris to their capture in Madrid.[44]

The only other question to provoke an extended response was the delicate issue of Gustave Humbert's role in the swindle, and Leydet posed it to Frédéric. Leydet treated the problem gingerly: the senator had died in 1894, but many of his associates were still alive, and the Combes ministry wanted no republican scandals. Still, the magistrate had compiled circumstantial evidence that could be interpreted in a fashion damaging to the senator's reputation in death. Three members of the parquet, François Accarias, Théodore Barthélemy, and Jules Amygues, recalled Gustave Humbert's speaking to them frequently of the Crawford inheritance and of how his children would be rich. Antoine François Grenier, an aide to the senator, remembered Humbert's showing him a copy of the 1886 civil tribunal decision. Most damaging, one handwriting expert had identified as Gustave Humbert's the marginal notes on a letter signed "Robert Crawford." Frédéric listened impassively and then in cold fury denied each charge in detail, concluding with the blunt declaration that his father had never interested himself in Thérèse's affairs. Leydet never raised the issue again.[45]

When Leydet completed his *instruction* in mid-May, he recommended that the government press no charges against Louis Daurignac, Maria Daurignac, and Eve Humbert, concluding that they had been essentially bystanders to the schemes of their relatives. Because they had been relatively innocent dupes, he asked that Parmentier, Dumort, Langlois, Delacherie, Parayre, and Girard be spared further pains from French justice. But for Thérèse and Frédéric Humbert and Romain and Emile Daurignac, the *instruction* called for their indictment on the charges of swindles (*escroqueries*), fraud before a notary (*faux en procuration*), fraud through impersonation (*faux par supposition de personnes*), and fraud in written documents (*faux en écriture*). If convicted on any charge of fraud, they would face a minimum penalty of

44. *Le Figaro*, March 6, 1903.
45. *Ibid.*, April 1, 1903. Other stories dealing with these later interrogations appeared in *Le Figaro* and most other Parisian daily newspapers; February 24, 27–28, March 1, 7, 12, 18, 22, 26, April 2–3, 22, May 5, 7–10, 13, 1903.

five years' imprisonment at hard labor. A conviction of swindling would mean only imprisonment. The indictment court, the Chambre des Mises en accusation, heard the case on May 28 and found Leydet's arguments impeccable. On June 9, it bound the four defendants over for trial before the Cour d'Assises beginning on August 8.[46]

In the midst of the deliberations of the indictment court, the issue of political corruption appeared again, this time involving the minister of the navy in Combes's cabinet, Camille Pelletan. The accusation came from *Le Figaro*, whose editor, Gaston Calmette, had aligned his newspaper with the premier's opponents and intensely disliked Pelletan, whom he considered the perfect symbol of Combes's Radical party: filthy in appearance, foul in language, and possessed with an air of venality. These charges were all true of Pelletan, and incapacity could be added, as he mismanaged the navy into near disaster. They were certainly not an accurate representation of the Radical party at large, however, and Pelletan owed his appointment to thirty years of party seniority and to the disinterest Combes felt toward the navy. Newspapers made allegations against their enemies every day, and this one, first appearing on May 25, would have been dismissed with little notice if *Le Figaro* had not boasted of holding a document proving Pelletan's involvement with the Humberts.[47]

The newspaper had acquired a copy of the letter sent by Armand Parayre to Pelletan on September 25, 1902, asking that the minister of the navy intercede with the minister of justice, Vallé, to ensure that Parayre would not be prosecuted. The letter reminded Pelletan that nearly thirteen years earlier, on December 24, 1889, Parayre had handed him "a considerable sum" as a reward for Pelletan's speech before the Chamber of Deputies the previous day praising the Humbert family for producing such excellent republicans as Gustave and Frédéric and labeling as false the rumors about the Humbert "finances." Pelletan published a rebuttal of these allegations in the May 29 *Le Figaro* but was

46. *Le Figaro* and *Gazette des Tribunaux*, May 20, 28, June 10, 1903. For "normal" treatment of fraud investigations, compare the cases in AN, BB 18, 2314 (1905), 2388 (1908), 2417 (1909), 2444 (1911), 2462 (1911), 2474 (1911), and 2475 (1911).

47. *Le Figaro*, May 25, 1903. For Pelletan, see John Raymond Walser, "France's Search for a Battlefleet: French Naval Policy, 1898–1914" (Ph.D. dissertation, University of North Carolina, 1976), 199–227; Tony Reveillon, *Camille Pelletan* (Paris, 1930); and Ernest Charles, "Camille Pelletan," *Revue politique et parlementaire*, June, 1900, pp. 625–54.

questioned about them that afternoon in the Chamber. He replied by denying that he had received any money in 1889 for his defense of the Humberts or that he had intervened on Parayre's behalf. He had not, he claimed, even received the letter cited by *Le Figaro* and did not believe that it had ever existed. Combes insisted that his majority support Pelletan, and it did so, giving him a vote of confidence.[48]

Even as the Chamber of Deputies accepted Pelletan's explanation, *Le Figaro* published the photostat of a registered-mail receipt for Parayre's letter, showing that it had been logged into the Ministry of the Navy on September 26, 1902, as document 706. *Le Figaro* called this receipt proof that Pelletan had received Parayre's letter and demanded to know why the navy minister had not charged Parayre with defamation of character if the details of accepting money in 1889 were untrue. An unnerved Pelletan replied briefly that the letter must have been lost at the office because he himself had never seen it. He refused any further comment even to newspapers such as *Le Radical* that were invariably his supporters. He waited two days, until May 31, to appear with his chef de cabinet, Théodore Richard Tissier, for interviews. Both conceded that Parayre's letter must have arrived but declared that it had somehow disappeared before it reached Pelletan. They were quite anxious to deny the allegation that Parayre had ever given Pelletan "any 30,000 FF" or that there had been any attempt to influence the Ministry of Justice not to prosecute him. *Le Figaro* was hardly the only newspaper to notice that Pelletan mentioned the figure of thirty thousand francs, while Parayre had written of "a considerable sum." Nevertheless, Pelletan and his Radical party colleagues refused to answer any more questions. As long as Combes and his majority were willing to support him, *Le Figaro* had to content itself with charging that Pelletan had to be either corrupt or negligent and in any case unfit for office.[49]

The Pelletan episode was a sensational aperitif to the Humbert trial. During June and July, 1903, when the Republic's president, Emile Loubet, was visiting London to further the arrangement of an Entente Cordiale with Great Britain and Catholics throughout the world were praying for Pope Leo XIII as he suffered in his final illness, Parisians

48. *Le Figaro*, May 28, 1903; JOC, Débats parlementaires, May 28, 1903.
49. *Le Figaro*, May 29–31, June 1, 1903.

were more concerned with the Humberts' decision to retain as attorney Fernand Labori, famous as the defender of Dreyfus at Rennes in 1899, and the request of Thérèse that she be allowed to purchase a corset to wear at the trial. François Gaston Bonnet, who had been named presiding justice for the case, made himself ridiculous by hesitating over this decision. Before he granted his permission, he even consulted a physician in order to learn whether the corset might enable Thérèse to claim fainting spells more readily. It would be foolish to grant her any means of eliciting sympathy from the jury, the parquet believed, but no one in the Palais de Justice could think of an acceptable reason for denying her vanity. The public snatched up this and other tidbits of gossip that clung to this case, such as Romain Daurignac's numerous love affairs and the absurd story that Thérèse had won Gustave Humbert's confidence by becoming his mistress. Yet what caused the greatest stir was that the Humbert affair laid open to observation a corner of society rarely seen subjected to close scrutiny and inaccessible to most Frenchmen, the complicated relationship between politics and wealth. Thérèse had moved through the world of the rich and the powerful with such sureness that it seemed reflex, using politicians, civil servants, businessmen, speculators, attorneys, notaries, and even the courts. She had played her role for twenty years—and in some sense from childhood; she had to play it one more time before the show closed.[50]

The fascination of the case, and the pervading sense that in certain trials the courtroom became a stage, created a great demand for seats at the sessions. There were more than four hundred places for spectators in the elegant room in the Palais de Justice, but many of the curious had to be turned away, as nearly half of the seats were reserved for journalists and their assistants, unofficial stenographers, cartoonists, and, as an innovation, two photographers. Even so, Mme Darthoux, the curious middle-aged woman nicknamed "la dame blanche" who had not missed a single session of the retrial of Dreyfus at Rennes, managed to find a place every day. In the wait for the first session to begin, there were animated discussions among reporters and the spectators, most of it absolute speculation. Would the Humberts be as crisp and impressive in their defense now as they had been in February

50. *Ibid.*, July 7, 12, August 1–2, 1903. See also Bonnet's personnel file: AN, BB 6 II, 690.

against Cattauï? How effective would the florid Labori be against the solicitor general, Louis Marie Blondel, a tall, austere man known to be severe. When would come the moment for Thérèse to reveal the secrets she had promised during her interrogations? The sense of anticipation grew as Presiding Justice Bonnet entered the courtroom with his two associate justices. Blondel and Labori were already at their tables. With a touch of drama, Bonnet hesitated a moment before ordering the defendants to be led into the court, and excitement reached its highest point during the trial.

For the astute, everything after Thérèse's entrance would be an anticlimax. She was much changed from February: despite the corset, she appeared ill and tired, visibly sagging. This woman had neither secrets nor hope. After seven months of life as a fugitive and seven more as a prisoner, after the desertion of her powerful friends, she had lost the flair that had been her success. Now she was less the artist than the mummer, less the chatelaine than the charlatan, her ripostes slower, her tirades tiresome. She camped herself across from the jury at the defendant's rail, her arms crossed, her big voice filling the room with ridiculous claptrap, proclaiming her innocence and promising to reveal the secrets "in my pocket." During the reading of the act of accusation, she interrupted to cry out, "They've spent fifteen months putting together this tissue of calumnies!" The gesture did not appear to win her sympathy.

During the *interrogatoire*, the direct examination by the presiding justice, Thérèse continued her poor impression. Like Leydet during the *instruction*, Bonnet went back to her childhood and her marriage to Frédéric. Thérèse roused herself to exclaim that love and nothing else had moved them to marry, but she sank back onto the defensive when he asked her to explain her claims to the Château de Marcotte. She promised to do so if Bonnet would have patience, but when he offered her all the time she needed, she replied only that she was ill and had been in prison for seven months without air and "without seeing the sky." After a long hesitation, she added conspiratorially that there were "strange things" about the Château de Marcotte, as there had been about her flight from Paris—but the latter was to go "where her duty lay." No one else seemed to have any notion of her meaning. Shaking his head, Bonnet pressed on, asking about her life with Frédéric on the

Rue Monge and the Rue Fortuny. Thérèse began to reply to these questions but suddenly shifted to a denunciation of Cattauï and obscure
references to her departure in May, 1902, to avoid "horrible danger."
Again, Bonnet ignored her words and began a series of questions about
the "contrived" fortune attributed to Crawford. Thérèse protested that
the fortune existed, that many had seen it, counted it, clipped coupons
from the bonds. When the presiding justice interrupted her to explain
to the jury how she had duped Parmentier, Dumort, and others with
her ruses, she waited with increasing impatience until he was finished
and then her words exploded furiously. No one, she insisted, should
doubt her word, for she was an honorable woman and had lived in
prison for months on only two eggs a day for food but still had her
strength and *was not crazy*. Before the trial, no one had suggested that
she might not be sane, but after this outburst, the suspicion was planted
and grew that she was mentally disturbed.

As the *interrogatoire* continued, Thérèse became stranger and
stranger. In response to questions from Bonnet about her life on the
Avenue de la Grande Armée, she denied absolutely having heavy expenses and, with almost complete irrelevance, claimed that she had
"worked constantly" throughout her life and that "there are few
women who are as strong and as courageous as I am." Bonnet then
informed the jury that Thérèse routinely employed a coachman, two
footmen, a butler, a valet, a chambermaid, and two other menser-
vants. By contacting the merchants she patronized, the Sûreté had
learned that in 1898, for example, she had spent Fr 130,000 for dresses,
Fr 16,000 for furs, and Fr 58,000 for hats. As a summary, he estimated
that the personal and household expenses for the Humberts had ex-
ceeded Fr 400,000 a year. Thérèse did not deny these figures but replied that she *now* had only the straw hat and black dress she was
wearing.

When the questions turned to the Rente Viagère, Thérèse brightened again. She bragged that the company had been her idea but conceded that her brothers had assisted in refining it. She was extremely
pleased with the Rente Viagère: in the style of a prospectus, she proudly
cited undisputed figures to demonstrate that by 1902 it was flourish-
ing. Bonnet reminded her that in this grand work she was claiming,
her name had not appeared as a founder and that she had, in fact, used

seven straw men as the founders. He also asked about the forty-two thousand francs the Humberts had "borrowed" from the company before fleeing Paris. After another hesitation, Thérèse promised again to explain her flight—but not before all the witnesses had spoken. Yes, she said, she had left France, but she had never wanted to do so, and in leaving France, she had headed for a rendezvous where she had been deceived. Bonnet had no more questions, but Thérèse turned once more to the jury to declare that she was honorable and not insane.

After she sat down, it was Frédéric's turn to face the *interrogatoire*. The months in prison since February had accentuated the sunken quality of his eyes and the paleness of his face. He glared at the court and replied to questions with an aggressive, insolent tone. His answers were no more revealing than those by Thérèse. Like the second-rate paintings he produced in the apartment on the Place de Vintimille, the portrait that he sketched of himself in his testimony was not the one he intended. Beginning by declaring that he had always been indifferent to money and that he had completed his law degree only to please his father, he described his life in Paris after 1878 as that of a gentleman artist and sometime politician. He had trusted his wife implicitly and had allowed her to conduct the family finances and contend for the Crawford inheritance. Only in the 1890s, when the creditors had their knives to Thérèse's throat, had he intervened personally. In an unusual metaphor, he argued: "You may sometimes see a cat swimming, but you do not infer from that that the cat is an aquatic animal. The cat swims because it has been placed in water in spite of itself: thus my role in this affair." It might well have been riposted that a cat would have sought the bank as soon as possible instead of staying in the current for so many years enjoying the millions Thérèse procured.[51]

After several more questions, Frédéric recognized that the defense of claiming ignorance and hiding behind Thérèse's broad skirts was not prepossessing to the court and jury. During the rest of his interrogation, which lasted into the second session on August 10, he adopted the familiar Humbert tactics of misdirection, denial, and abuse. Ac-

51. *Le Figaro* and *Gazette des Tribunaux*, August 9, 1903. See also Blondel's personnel file: AN, BB 6 II, 679.

cording to him, all who had loaned money to them were usurers, and he claimed that many of them were paid back twice what they were owed. He replied contemptuously to Bonnet's accusation that he planned the Humbert and Crawford legal strategies much as someone might play chess solo. He had been a mediocre law student, Frédéric reminded the court, and had not pursued the special studies that would have qualified him for the complicated litigation of legacies. The Sûreté had found no lawbooks at any of his houses. Perhaps the presiding justice believed the Holy Ghost had provided him with extraordinary powers, he asked facetiously. For good measure, he added an attack on Waldeck-Rousseau and Minister of Justice Vallé, who, he claimed, had conspired to make a mockery of the French judicial system by arresting an innocent family. A thoroughly aroused Bonnot struck back by accusing Frédéric of conduct that besmirched the reputation of an innocent and honorable man, his own father. After more heated words, the presiding justice challenged him to reveal the location of the Crawford millions, if they existed. Frédéric replied that he did not know where the millions were.

As soon as her husband had answered, Thérèse stood up and cried out that *she* did know and that she would tell the court. Insisting that the explanation was very complex, she began it by saying that her father had come to Paris soon after her marriage to Frédéric and had lived near them, first a few doors down from their apartment on the Rue Monge, then on the Rue de la Terrasse after the move to the Rue Fortuny, and finally on the Impasse Royer-Collard after they had settled on the Avenue de la Grande Armée. Dropping her voice conspiratorially, she said that her father had always rented a "double apartment." Without stopping to explain to a mystified court what significance that had, she went on to claim that the Crawford millions had always been stored in her father's apartment except when it was absolutely necessary to show some of the bonds to creditors. When Justice Forichon ordered the inventory, she went to the strongbox only to discover it empty! Her flight from Paris on May 7 was a desperate attempt to locate the Crawfords and regain the bonds before the May 9 deadline. But when she found the brothers, they refused to help and astounded her with a "terrible revelation." Declining to say more at this point in the trial, she concluded by insisting that while the name Crawford was an alias, the brothers were not a fantasy. When she sat down after this startling intervention, she had enlightened none of the mystery.

There was a noticeable relaxation of tension when Bonnet turned to interrogate Romain Daurignac. Unlike the other defendants, he seemed to be enjoying the trial, and during his testimony he smiled and laughed often, playing to the spectators and the jury. He was not handsome, but his fashionable clothes, his well-oiled black hair, and his carefully clipped vandyke beard made him seem more distinguished than he was. His life had been a series of adventures. Through a mistake, his name was not drawn for the military draft, but he had tried to enlist in the cavalry, only to be rejected for lacking a half centimeter in height. Determined to ride horses in battle, he went to Argentina and served with distinction as a mercenary. With several years of combat pay in his pocket, he set off to explore Africa. After some months in Madagascar, he changed his mind and came back to France, where he joined his sister and Frédéric in Paris. They made him a factotum in charge of bringing in investors, investigating anyone, particularly newspapers, that cast suspicion on her suit with the Crawfords, and generally supervising the operations of their scheme. Bonnet could not make him admit that he had played the role of Robert Crawford or picked up letters addressed "R. C." or "H. C." at the Rue du Louvre post office, but he did acknowledge that he had been only a fictitious founder of the Rente Viagère. He found questions of finance mystifying and preferred to talk about his mistresses.

If Romain was the comedian of the Daurignac brothers, Emile was the bore. Dour, balding, and gray-bearded, he answered questions disagreeably. He claimed never to have imitated anyone and certainly not a Crawford. When Bonnet charged that he, like Romain, had only been a fictitious founder of the Rente Viagère, Emile did not protest. But he snarled when Bonnet reproved him for appearing with his wife in Thérèse's opera box on the night of May 7 to reassure those who were afraid that the Humberts would disappear. Who had the right, Emile demanded, to tell him when to go to the opera or not? Despite his outbursts, he looked convinced that he would be found guilty and made a deplorable impression on the jury.[52]

52. *Le Figaro* and *Gazette des Tribunaux*, August 11, 1903.

The first important witnesses appeared during the third session, on August 11, a parade of the attorneys caught up in the affair, Parmentier, Auzoux, Labat, Du Buit, and Pouillet. Their reputations had been shattered by the revelations of the *instruction*, and they were eager to explain publicly their role in order to refute the rumors that they had participated in conspiracy with the Humberts. Before the first witness could be called, however, Frédéric Humbert was granted permission to expand on his previous testimony and took the opportunity to begin another violent attack on Vallé, whom he accused of dealing in political influence and the most open venality. Bonnet and Solicitor General Blondel allowed the tirade to run its course and then demanded to know how the Humberts could complain of political intrigue in their arrest when the famous strongbox had been found empty. The Humberts' attorney, Labori, answered that question by recalling that at the same time many newspapers were speculating that the strongbox would be empty, the Humberts were not prevented from boarding their train at the Gare d'Orléans, and Romain Daurignac openly dispatched a telegram to Jane d'Arvalho announcing his departure. Labori found it strange that this laxity transpired at a time when Waldeck-Rousseau was premier. The great Waldeck-Rousseau, he declaimed scornfully, who had denounced the Crawford millions as a fraud—did he actually believe in the millions until the strongbox was opened? Once in Madrid, the Humberts were not recognized by Ambassador Patenôtre, although he had once sought the hand of Maria Daurignac. For a second time, Bonnet and Blondel sat silently through an assault on government policy, but the attacks died for want of a response.

When Parmentier finally reached the witness bar, the session was an hour behind schedule and tempers were already heated. Suffering from laryngitis and barely audible at first, he began his testimony by trying to explain how he and the French courts had jointly been the dupes of a nefarious swindle. At that, Bonnet interrupted brusquely. He would not countenance this accusation of French justice, insisting that the civil courts had no responsibility to verify the documents carried before them. He went on to lecture Parmentier about a lack of prudence in dealing with the Crawfords and to declare that the attorney was very fortunate to be standing at the witness bar instead of the defendant's rail. Ill and cowed by Bonnet's rebuke, Parmentier still managed to defend himself with vigor. Occasionally waving his gold spectacles, he evoked an office full of letters from Crawfords, 3,500 in eighteen years, and a bank balance swollen by Fr 350,000 from their fees. There had been personal meetings. How could he not believe in their reality?

Parmentier's performance won him considerable sympathy, and it increased as the other witnesses recounted how thoroughly the Humberts had played their roles. Bailiff Lecomte told of serving papers in the Hôtel du Louvre. Attorney Auzoux, who assisted Parmentier from Paris, explained that he had never asked for the original of the Crawford will because it did not directly concern the topics under litigation. Labat, the first attorney retained by Thérèse, revealed that between 1897 and 1902, the Humberts reimbursed five million francs of their loans, with his office providing the receipts. How could he have been expected to doubt such clients? Du Buit added that when he joined the case for the Humberts, he found the dossiers in a state of completeness rarely to be seen. Finally, Pouillet, who had briefly collaborated with Parmentier and Auzoux, coolly told Bonnet and the court that he had pleaded the cases of several Americans and Englishmen before French justice without ever meeting his clients. Why should he have treated the Crawfords differently?[53]

It was clear from the attitude of the court that the Ministry of Justice would not turn the trial into a public morality tale emphasizing the laxity of institutions and individuals of the government, not least the parquet itself. The Humbert trial would encompass only swindlers and defrauders; French justice would discipline its own in private. Cattauï's unsuccessful suit publicized the fear of many creditors that their complaints would not be heard by the ministry that Thérèse's father-in-law had headed and where her powerful friend, Jacquin, sat in charge of personnel. Yet, when Jacquin testified on August 12, the prosecution did not challenge his assertion that he had never had any material interest with the Humbert family and allowed him to complain at length that the "rumors" about the case had besmirched his reputation. He had already resigned his position, and for the parquet, that was sufficient.

53. *Ibid.*, August 12, 1903.

Following Jacquin at the witness bar came a series of handwriting experts and postal officials who made an excellent case that Romain Daurignac was the author of letters signed "Robert Crawford" and the retriever of mail from Parmentier addressed to the Crawfords by their initials at poste restante. There was so little way of refuting them that Romain was reduced to claiming that he had a double.

The remainder of August 12 and all of August 13 were given over to testimony by notaries and their clients who had loaned money to the Humberts. For the most part, it was a sorry tale of frantic speculation and usurious interest that reminded many of Balzac's remark: not all notaries finish in convict prison—some are guillotined. Delacherie described the great incentive for speculators to make the loans—the return was 55 percent—and for notaries to lure their clients—they would receive a 10 percent commission on each loan. He had always warned his clients to be prudent and had never asked the Humberts for more than the usual commission. Langlois, the next notary to face the court, could claim less purity. He had arranged loans totaling Fr 17,000,000 and, when the Humberts had been particularly desperate for funds, had exacted 25 percent in commission charges. Only Dumort rescued the reputation of notaries, producing his records to show that when he loaned his own funds to the Humberts, Fr 1,300,000 between 1889 and 1898, he did so at 5 percent interest with no commission of any variety. After the revelation of the fraud, he had bankrupted himself in repaying as much of the capital lost by his clients as possible. But if Dumort proved that a notary could be honest, he proved himself, said the Paris press, surely speaking for many Frenchmen, a double fool—to have believed in Thérèse Humbert but not to have taken advantage of her.

The creditors were merely pathetic. The lure of great profits had overcome their caution at dangerous ventures and their scruples at usury. For every Marquis Albert de Cazaux, who could say proudly that he had never asked the Humberts for more than 5 percent on the Fr 1,171,800 he had loaned them and boast, "I eat neither the bread of swindle nor the bread of usury," there were twenty such as banker Benjamin Haas, who exacted interest and commissions surpassing 55 percent. The normally responsible became irresponsible at the thought of sharing in the Humbert wealth: a widow from Roubaix, Mme Joseph Rodière, loaned Fr 41,000; two industrialists, Jacques Grandischadten, Fr 900,000, and Antoine Prouvost, Fr 300,000; a notary, Georges Duchange, also from Roubaix, Fr 50,000; a brewer from Nîmes, Maurice Vandame, Fr 200,000; an industrialist from Lille, Jean Schotsmans, Fr 3,500,000; two bankers from Paris, Gustave Kann, Fr 1,400,000, and Jean Paul Roulina, Fr 10,000,000. Most were resigned to their losses: rage would do them no good, and little public sympathy followed them as the court recessed for the day.[54]

After five long sessions, the prosecution had presented its most interesting witnesses. The major task it had left was to examine the bankruptcy proceedings carried out for the Humberts and the Rente Viagère. Because his interests were involved, Elie Cattauï made a point of attending the session of August 14, and his presence in the courtroom excited Thérèse to absolute fury. Waving her arms and occasionally shouting, she called Cattauï "a liar, vampire, miserable lout, blackmailer, and cheat!" The court sat fascinated, and Cattauï impassive, as she continued her denunciation for twenty-five minutes with no thread of organization. She accused him of paying Vallé Fr 235,000 to bring about the Humberts' humiliation and of financing the campaign against her by Mouthon in *Le Matin*. He was her greatest enemy, but she had beaten him in February and would beat him again, for his wicked schemes would never triumph over her. At the end of this performance, Cattauï replied haughtily that the Humberts, and not he, were behind the defendants' rail.

With Thérèse seated again, the court heard a recital of figures by Bonneau, the receiver for the Humbert estate. The sale of property owned by Thérèse and Frédéric had produced receipts of Fr 5,367,000, and he estimated that what remained to sell would add approximately Fr 750,000, bringing assets to Fr 6,117,000. Creditors had submitted claims for debts of Fr 117,000,000, but Bonneau judged that only Fr 65,000,000 could be substantiated. Even so, that left a deficit of Fr 58,883,000 that would probably never be covered. When Bonnet asked Thérèse and Frédéric to comment on this report, they declared that the true question of the trial was not their affairs but the role of Vallé as minister of justice. Thérèse added that she had felt pity for Jean Schotsmans on the previous day when he recalled how his brother Paul, murdered mysteriously in 1899, had opposed the loans to the Hum-

54. *Ibid.*, August 13–14, 1903.

berts, but she insisted that "death is nothing compared to what my family suffered in Madrid and in the Conciergerie."

With an expression of disgust, the presiding justice interrupted her and moved on to the next witnesses, Armand Parayre and his wife, and Lanquest. Neither prosecution nor defense wanted to inquire into Parayre's relations with Camille Pelletan, and both seemed relieved when his testimony lasted an astonishingly brief four minutes. He admitted being a fictitious founder of the Rente Viagère and signing minutes of the company's meetings without having been present. Brushing over his other duties for the Humberts, he caused ironic laughter in the courtroom when he recalled that his habitual remark in introducing creditors to Thérèse was "Entrez les capitalistes." Parayre's wife spent not much more time before the court and added no essential information. Lanquest followed her and portrayed himself as the dupe of the Rente Viagère, as other notaries and attorneys had been the dupes of the Crawford inheritance. For a badge of his honesty, he produced documents proving that he had accepted only Fr 23,000 in fees from the Humberts, a figure that conformed to the recommended charges of the Paris association of notaries. In spite of his lack of complicity or guilt, he had willingly contributed Fr 3,700,000 of his own money to the Rente Viagère to maintain its solvency. The prosecution did not want to broach the question of whether the Ministry of Justice had struck a deal with Lanquest to refrain from prosecuting him in return for the deposit of the funds. Labori did ask the question, however, because he feared that the jury would otherwise draw what was indeed the proper conclusion from Lanquest's testimony: that the operations of the Rente Viagère were irregular and that the notary had pledged the Fr 3,700,000 to avoid facing trial. Labori gambled that neither Blondel nor Bonnet would admit that Lanquest had been saved from prosecution by his wealth, and he was correct. Bonnet ruled that Labori's question was out of order: there was no *instruction* against the witness. Quite pleased, the defense attorney was able to turn to the jury and explain that no irregularity of procedure had been charged against the Rente Viagère.[55]

After this technical exercise by the defense, the court adjourned for

55. *Ibid.*, August 15, 1903.

the weekend, reconvening on August 17 for its seventh session. At that time, Henri Vacher, the receiver for the Rente Viagère, testified that because of Lanquest's contribution to the capital of the company, it had assets of Fr 6,150,900 and obligations of Fr 6,000,150. All of the investors had been saved. Vacher had also concluded from his examination of the account books that the Rente Viagère's operations had been highly profitable and that within a decade the Humberts could have become legitimate millionaires. Although this admission was made grudgingly, Vacher could not entirely conceal his respect for the Humberts' direction of the company. For this reason, his testimony was probably more valuable to the defense than to the prosecution. It also meant that the government's case ended weakly, for Blondel had no further witnesses to call.

Labori's choice of witnesses for the defense was a curious combination. First he called Emile France, the special police commissioner sent to Madrid to arrange for the extradition of the Humberts and Daurignacs. The testimony provided Labori with an excuse to repeat his clients' claim that the French government had been aware of their existence in Madrid long before the arrest. Labori made no effort to explain the reasons for the delay, thus perpetuating the theory of a mysterious conspiracy against the Humberts. But Frédéric did interject that the agents who had followed them were easily recognized because one of them had a large birthmark on his right cheek. Thérèse continued her installment version of the flight from Paris: this time she added that the rendezvous had been to arrange for a "Crawford," whose real name was not Crawford, to make a telephone call to Paris to arrange for Thérèse to be given possession of the bonds. The rendezvous was supposed to be in Bordeaux but was suddenly changed to Madrid. That was why she and her family had gone to Spain, not to escape justice. Those who knew her well, Thérèse insisted, knew that she would not flee "even before a revolver."

There was considerable skepticism within the courtroom about this complicated tale, but Labori was determined to exploit to the full the suspicion that the fate of the Humberts was somehow connected to political intrigue. Even the newspapers most hostile to them acknowledged that there were many unexplained elements in the case, and these admissions reflected the traditional French mistrust of government. The individual most likely to have discovered the secret links in the whole affair was Joseph Leydet, who had drawn up the *instruction*, and Labori called him to the witness bar. The Ministry of Justice condemned this tactic because examining magistrates were, by tradition, never called to testify as witnesses. Any evidence uncovered by an examining magistrate but not included in his *instruction* was considered subject to "professional secrecy" because it might bear upon innocent parties. As Labori must have expected, Leydet exercised his prerogative to answer not a single question. This refusal increased the sense of conspiracy and secrecy in which Labori wished to cloak the Humberts.

As a final touch to the mystery, Labori called Duret, the receiver for the Girard bank from 1896 to 1898. He asked him to explain why Waldeck-Rousseau denounced the Humberts before the tribunal at Elbeuf but took no action after becoming premier less than a year later. Duret replied that he could not answer for Waldeck-Rousseau. But Labori would put no other questions, preferring to raise once more the issue of political intrigue in circumstances in which it could not be addressed and thus leave the jury in doubt. This task accomplished, he concluded his defense with several witnesses to the good character of the defendants, although the number was very few and their names almost unknown. Not many Frenchmen wanted to align themselves on the side of the Humberts now.

When Labori had finished his case, Bonnet called upon Thérèse to reveal her secrets, as she had promised to do when the final witness had testified. She replied that she was still not ready to do so but that she would tell all—eventually. Her answer seemed to have a very deleterious effect for the defendants on the jury. Their expressions indicated that this was one delay too many and that they no longer believed Thérèse to have any secrets. Much of the effect of Labori's defense was probably undone at that moment. Noticing her mistake, Thérèse tried to repair her image by embarking upon another passionate denunciation of Waldeck-Rousseau, Cattauï, and Vallé, becoming more incoherent by the minute. Labori finally stopped her, and Bonnet adjourned the session to allow prosecution and defense attorneys additional time to prepare final summaries.[56]

When Solicitor General Blondel began his *réquisitoire* on August 18,

56. *Ibid.*, August 18, 1903.

he had every reason to believe that the jury would return convictions against the defendants. He spoke with great confidence, his summation sober and clear. It was also long, requiring eight hours to deliver and running into a second session. Quick character sketches of Thérèse and Frédéric came first: Thérèse was described as an ambitious, intriguing child reared in a milieu of dreams and chimerical fortunes but beset by the harsh realities of debts, bills, and property seizures; Frédéric was called a dissembler, who hid behind the actions of his wife. Blondel then related the origins of the Crawford story, arguing persuasively that the elaborate details of this myth were the finished oil portrait for which the earlier swindles by Thérèse's father were the outline. Only the amount of the inheritance was significantly different, but it was greater because the Humbert needs were greater. Thérèse and Frédéric became accustomed to luxury, and they began to move in the world of high society. Their entrée was the Humbert name, which was sufficient to assure probity and republican rectitude.

Blondel admitted that the Crawford story was given additional substance by the legal processes invoked by the Humberts after 1884, but this misuse of the courts did not make French justice the accomplice of the Humberts and could not justify the outrageous accusations made against the magistrature. The system of criminal justice likewise bore no blame. No *instruction* could be opened until charges were made; no police action, and particularly no arrest, could occur until there was evidence that a crime had been committed. That evidence had come only when the strongbox was found empty and after the Humberts had escaped. If the Sûreté had arrested the Humberts and the strongbox been found full of bonds, there would have been cries of police tyranny—and rightly. He dismissed as beneath notice the charges of political influence in the administration of justice and called false the supposition that the Sûreté had known of the Humberts' presence in Madrid before the arrest.

Each of the defendants had played a specific role in the fraud, Blondel continued, and the responsibilities of each before justice varied similarly. He called Romain Daurignac the commissioner of the affair, carrying out the minutiae. For his sister, he had run from the Nord to the Midi, played Robert Crawford, written letters, signed transactions, made payments to Parmentier, and while doing so, cheated

Thérèse in order to have extra pocket money. Unable to stop herself, Thérèse gave Romain a deadly glance at these words. Blondel called Emile Daurignac the least guilty of the four. He had been the only one to work honestly, earning a modest income first as an administrative assistant to Gustave Humbert and later as an salesman for a brandy distiller. This income would have been sufficient for many, but not for Emile once he saw the luxurious life of his sister and heard her grandiose plans. He had joined her scheme, eventually participating in everything. As his last act, he covered his family's escape by appearing at the opera.

The solicitor general had much harsher words for Frédéric and Thérèse. This son of a republican immortal had posed as a sedentary man, detached and taciturn. Actually, he engaged in prodigious activity directing the details of the fraud's litigation. He did so in secret to avoid suspicion, but Blondel felt that Frédéric remained out of sight also because his upbringing must have made him feel ashamed of these activities. But Thérèse, he was certain, had never felt any embarrassment. The lie was her element. Her whole life was oriented toward the acquisition of luxury, grandeur, domination, and the attainment of an immense fortune. She was untiring: between a visit and dinner, between a reception and a soiree, she courted bankers, negotiated loans, obtained the renewal of old loans. She conducted business with such spirit, such sangfroid, such feminine grace. Mistress of herself, she always knew when to be violent, when tender, when imperious, when charming. She knew how to choose a role for herself: that of victim. She thought to realize her dream through intelligence and an infernal genius, and that had nearly been sufficient. Finally exposed, Thérèse and Frédéric had draped themselves during the *instruction* and the trial in a silence they portrayed as enigmatic and threatening. In doing so, they had proved only that they could not speak usefully in their own behalf. The jury, he concluded, understood this tactic for what it was and would do their duty.[57]

Throughout the solicitor general's summation, Thérèse sat quietly, almost inattentively, as if Blondel were speaking of someone else. Romain affected a smile of amusement at his alleged role. But Frédéric

57. *Ibid.*, August 19–20, 1903.

and Emile looked intensely anxious, sometimes pale, sometimes angry at the words they heard. They clearly understood that they had no chance for acquittal unless Labori's summation for the defense worked magic on the jury.

Labori had very little with which to work, but he produced an excellent *plaidoirie*. Always a warm and florid orator, gesticulating vehemently, commanding attention, he had the physical gifts for his major task, the obfuscation of the issues. His summation was even longer than Blondel's, and he delivered it with many calculated pauses, as if he were weighing whether or not to reveal sensational secrets. He would furrow his brow, touch his hand to his flowing blond moustache and vandyke beard, offer the tantalizing hints that seemed to prove that he knew more than he could tell, and then continue with another topic.

Labori began by declaring that if the story of the Crawfords was not true, the imagination of an Honoré de Balzac or an Edgar Allan Poe would have been required to conceive of it. Then he attacked the weakest element in the prosecution's case, the role of the magistrature in the affair from 1885 to 1902. There was Waldeck-Rousseau's warning in 1898, and there had been isolated rumors about the Humberts for years. But justice, assuming the same hauteur with which it had just denounced the alleged fraud of the Humberts, had ignored all. No warrants had been issued even during the press campaigns of *Le Matin* and *Le Figaro* in the spring of 1902. Now, in August, 1903, justice demanded a conviction. Labori rhetorically asked why and provided his own answer: first, the Humberts had been brought low and could be challenged with impunity; second, the empty strongbox required action. He would not speak of the first cause, for to do so would divert the path of justice by naming those who had conspired to destroy the Humberts. By this hint, he assured the jury that he had the information to prove a political scandal but that there were compelling reasons not to do so.

It was, instead, the empty strongbox Labori wished to explain. Suppose, he asked the jury, that the true name of the Crawfords was so odious that "it would create revulsion in your hearts as citizens and patriots." Suppose that Thérèse's father had concealed from her the source of the fortune and caused to disappear the testaments, which bore the trace of the origin, and maintained only the protocol making Thérèse the depositor of the bonds. Suppose that one day Thérèse violated a clause of the protocol and the Crawfords assumed control of the inheritance. And suppose, finally, that Thérèse went to the brothers on May 7 to request the return of the bonds if only for the inventory and that the Crawfords refused to do so for fear that the fortune would be seized and then told her the whole truth about themselves. Labori paused dramatically and then declared that all of these suppositions were fact but that he could not divulge the name of the Crawfords. Thérèse had told it to him in confidence; it would have to be she who would make the final revelation.

Labori had put together an explanation of the empty strongbox and the Humberts' flight that could be substantiated only by Thérèse, and she had forbidden him to disclose the true name of the Crawfords. Yet, in combination with the hints Labori dropped of a political conspiracy against the Humberts, the story had an appeal. In spite of all the evidence produced by the prosecution and the poor impression presented by the defendants, it was difficult to believe that so many people could have been fooled by Thérèse and Frédéric for so long unless there was some truth to the Crawfords. If there was reasonable doubt, there had to be an acquittal, and Labori used the rest of his summation to intensify the uncertainties he had skillfully created.

In a bold maneuver, the defense attorney exploited the prosecution's decision to assume Gustave Humbert innocent. The evidence that the former minister of justice had been aware of the fraud was slight and contradictory. It was also inopportune politically to sully Humbert's memory, and justice had no call on a man who had died in 1894. Understanding all of these factors, Labori insisted on combining the fate of the defendants with the reputation of Gustave Humbert, who had—no one could deny—boasted of his children's fortune. He also took up the question of the bankers and speculators who had loaned money to Thérèse and Frédéric. The trial, he declared, had revealed these men to be Shylocks, greedy usurers. But Shylocks are not stupid, and they are not prodigal. They earned their reputations by their determination always to profit. Such men would not loan money recklessly. They had seen some of the bonds and held the coupons. Where did these bonds come from? The prosecution could not say. Here was another reason, Labori argued, to doubt the government's case. He concluded by returning to the issue of political intrigue with which he had begun. Just as the Humberts had done, he attacked Waldeck-Rousseau, who, he claimed, had deserted the public interest by failing to resolve the doubts about the Humberts when he became premier. Implying that politics must have been behind the failure to act, he enlarged his attack to include Vallé, who he charged had acted so passionately against the Humberts that he seemed to be not the minister of justice but still the attorney of Elie Cattauï.

Almost as an afterthought, Labori requested that the jury disregard the attitude of the press, which was almost uniformly hostile to the Humbert family. He mentioned in particular the extraordinary decision by *Le Matin* to hold a referendum among its readers on the guilt or innocence of the defendants. He urged the jury to ignore the pressure of public opinion, whatever it might be, and to make its decision on the merits of the case. Blondel concurred with these sentiments and announced that the Ministry of Justice considered the *Le Matin* referendum a violation of the laws governing the press and would begin an investigation.[58]

After this brief exchange, there were two more short statements, one to close the session of August 21 by Edouard Clunet for Emile Daurignac, the other to open the session of August 22 by André Hesse for Romain Daurignac. Each attorney associated himself with the summary by Labori and asked special consideration for his client: for Emile because he had had only a tangential relationship to Thérèse's business, for Romain because he was a hail-fellow-well-met.[59] After Hesse sat down, there was nothing left in the procedure of the trial except for Presiding Justice Bonnet to ask whether any of the defendants had something to add. This was the moment for Thérèse to reveal her secret if she was to do so. The tension created a hush, and as everything became still, Thérèse stood up.

Speaking very calmly for the first time during the trial, Thérèse claimed that the threat of an inventory had frightened her. The Crawfords had taken back the bonds in 1898, when she breached one of the clauses of the 1883 protocol: she had loaned several hundred thou-

58. *Ibid.*, August 20–22, 1903.
59. *Ibid.*, August 22–23, 1903.

sand francs worth of the bonds for only a few hours to an old friend in desperate need of collateral to renew a loan. She could not say how the Crawfords had learned of her action. Yet, she hoped eventually to win the entire inheritance in spite of this mistake. On May 7 she asked the son—she supplied no name—of one of the Crawford brothers to allow her to take back the bonds for the inventory. His father was away, and on orders from his uncle, he refused, fearing that the inventory might end in a sequestration. At that point, Thérèse recalled, she became frantic and begged the young man to consult his father. He told her that to do so would serve no purpose but did not object when she offered to make her request in person. She was told to look for this Crawford in Bordeaux, and when he was not there, in Madrid. That was why she and her family had left France, to make this rendezvous. When she finally found him, Crawford refused to loan the bonds and told her the truth about the fortune. Here Thérèse hesitated before revealing the last of her secrets: that the real name of the Crawfords was Régnier and that the fortune had been made in 1870 during the Franco-Prussian War by purchasing large amounts of French bonds when France lay defeated. The price recovered later, producing an enormous profit.

When Thérèse sat down, Labori explained that in 1873 Edmond Régnier had been convicted in absentia of treason for having attempted to serve as a go-between for Prussian Chancellor Otto von Bismarck and French Marshal Achille Bazaine in September, 1870. His goal had been for Bazaine to save his troops to overturn the new Republic and restore Emperor Louis Napoleon to the French throne. The sentence was death, but Régnier had escaped to England after his unsuccessful attempt to save the Second Empire. He managed a laundry at Ramsgate until his death in 1886. Having offered this clarification, Labori also sat down. There was no great commotion in the court. Clearly, the revelation did not have the impact for which the defense had hoped. Before Thérèse named Régnier, the jury could have imagined the Crawfords to be anyone. In this trial, imagination was on the side of doubt and the defense; reality belonged to the prosecution. Yet, Thérèse had promised to reveal her secrets, and not to have done so would probably have been just as damaging.

By then, it was 2 P.M. The presiding justice charged the jury to do its duty to justice and handed the foreman a list of 247 questions to which they had to respond. The number was so great because each instance of fraud was made a separate question. As soon as Bonnet ruled the court in recess and the jury departed for their deliberations, there was immediate speculation about the verdict. Most of the guesses were for guilty, although a few suggested that Emile Daurignac would win acquittal. There was also some limited interest in Régnier, but almost no one knew more than what Labori had told the court. Eventually, Albert Danet, an attorney who had participated in the 1873 trial, came to the courtroom and entertained those waiting for the jury with details about Régnier, Bismarck, and Bazaine. Finally, at 6:30 P.M., after four and a half hours of deliberation, the jury returned.

When the court had reassembled, the foreman of the jury read the verdicts. Simply stated, Thérèse and Frédéric Humbert were found guilty of both swindles and fraud, and Romain and Emile Daurignac were guilty only of swindles. The jury considered that there had been extenuating circumstances in the cases of all four defendants. As the verdicts were read, Thérèse displayed no emotion; Frédéric and Emile appeared in despair; Romain finally lost his smile. The justices retired to determine the sentences and returned within fifteen minutes. Because the jury had found extenuating circumstances, the court sentenced Thérèse and Frédéric each to five years imprisonment at hard labor, Romain and Emile simply to prison, for three years and two years respectively. The four were collectively held liable for the expenses of the trial, Fr 130,000.[60]

Thérèse and Frédéric appealed their convictions to the Cour de Cassation. Pending the outcome of that appeal, they were held in the departmental prison at Fresnes, where Romain and Emile had been sent to serve their terms. Because the attorneys who presented cases before

60. *Ibid.*, August 23, 1903. For Régnier, see his memoirs: Edmond Régnier, *Quel est votre nom? N.   ou M.   ? Une étrange histoire dévoilée* (5th ed.; Brussels, 1870), and Michael Howard, *The Franco-Prussian War: The German Invasion of France, 1870–1871* (London, 1961), 269–71, 278. From 1901 through 1913, the French Ministry of Justice pursued 1,631 cases of *faux*. Of these, 49 were "major," involving large sums of money, with the Humbert case clearly the single most important. In each of the 49, the sentence handed down was for a term of imprisonment at hard labor, with five years the minimum. Under the circumstances, the Humberts appear to have escaped lightly. See the annual report of the Ministry of Justice, *Compte général*.

the Cour de Cassation were specialists, Labori transferred the dossiers of the case to Louis Emile Devin. There was very little basis for an appeal, but on November 5 Devin argued before the court that the act of taking the name Crawford—this was no longer denied—did not constitute *fraud* but only the preparation for *swindle*. As a secondary point, he challenged the right of postal officials to identify those to whom they delivered mail, insisting that they had a duty to maintain its secrecy. The parquet had justified the testimony of the officials on the ground of "public interest," but it was possible to see that position leading to tyranny. Even if successful, Devin's brief could only mitigate the penalties Thérèse and Frédéric faced. Although the Cour de Cassation could order a new trial, that was highly unlikely in view of the minor points Devin presented. Even if the court accepted both of his arguments and eliminated the conviction for fraud, there would still remain a prison term for swindles.

The Cour de Cassation actually had no difficulty in deciding that the Humbert appeal had no basis. It held that in taking the name Crawford, the Humberts had damaged the cause of justice through the falsification of documents, the very definition of fraud. As for the postal officials, their responsibility to justice outweighed their duty to maintain the secrecy of the mail. With that decision on November 5, there was no reason to delay the execution of the sentence imposed on the Humberts. Thérèse was moved to the state prison for women at Rennes on November 8 and there assigned duties in the prison laundry. Five days later on November 13, after a decision by the minister of justice himself not to send him to the penitentiary at Poissy, Frédéric was transported to the central prison for men at Melun. With fine irony, the train that carried him there passed within sight of the Château de Vives-Eaux. At the prison, he was ordered to the carpentry shop and placed under the surveillance of a guard who had once been one of his electors from Seine-et-Marne.[61]

61. *Gazette des Tribunaux*, November 6, 1903; *Le Figaro*, October 31, November 2, 5–6, 8, 13, 1903. The members of the Humbert family served their sentences with no reduction. After their release, Thérèse, Frédéric, and Romain disappeared so thoroughly that the standard biographical sources for parliamentarians lack a death date for Frédéric. Emile alone was to have a final moment of publicity. As an old man in 1935, he was arrested for shoplifting a pair of cheap bedroom slippers.

III

In concluding his brief reconstruction of the Humbert affair, René Floriot, one of France's most distinguished attorneys, wrote in 1959: "La grande Thérèse mystified magistrates, attorneys, prosecutors, notaries, the most suspicious bankers, and the most cunning businessmen. But at least, she did not exploit small savers, and I avow, for my part, that I have no pity for her victims: these creditors who, dazzled by the usurious interest she offered, did not dream of making the most elementary verifications."[62] With such light-hearted words, he dismissed losses of capital totaling more than a hundred million francs and, in a curious combination of caveat emptor and rugged individualism, blamed those who loaned money to the Humberts for failing to discover what eluded the most respected members of the French bar and the magistracy for twenty years. Fraud, it would seem for Floriot, was the proper reward of usury. This attitude was widely shared during the trial: the Humbert affair was an enormously funny joke on unpleasant financiers and speculators. Thérèse herself became the comedienne whose show finally folded because her lines risked ceasing to be funny. *Le Figaro*'s reporter Henri Varennes wrote that Thérèse's appeal was satiated for him after the first ten days of the trial, and he suggested that Frédéric deserved lenient treatment for tolerating twenty-five years of marriage to her.[63]

This spirit of fun and the depiction of the creditors as co-villains frivolously concealed the deeper implications of the trial, the most important of which were political corruption and the influence of politics on the administration of justice. It was easy to dismiss these issues, because they had been a portion of Labori's losing defense. The conviction of the Humberts discredited the allegations that they flung at the Ministry of Justice in general, and Waldeck-Rousseau and Vallé in particular. Because the reasons for the Humberts' success in the civil courts for twenty years, the ambiguous evidence against Gustave Humbert, and the much clearer evidence against Camille Pelletan constituted an embarrassment for both prosecution and defense, these topics were brushed over or omitted entirely from consideration during the trial.

62. Floriot, *Au banc*, 182.
63. *Le Figaro*, August 21, 1903.

Instead, they sat as ghosts in the court, incapable of walking but invulnerable to exorcism.

For, in point of fact, the justice of the Humbert affair was shaky justice. When Thérèse concocted her myth about the Crawfords and brought it before the civil courts, she could be certain that the Humbert name guaranteed her case the benefit of much doubt. Most of the magistrates would feel no need to question the word of the former minister's daughter-in-law. Those who did thought first of their careers, as they recalled the Humberts' friendship with Etienne Jacquin. Civil justice assumed Thérèse's honesty instead of requiring it to be proved. In its defense, it is fair to remember that the narrowly worded suits drawn up with great guile by Frédéric gave the courts only limited access to the overall controversy and, most important, jurisdiction over only a few documents. Nevertheless, the evidence of laxity is overwhelming, and the suspicion that the sins of omission were accompanied by those of commission cannot be eliminated.

Who could have committed those sins to aid the Humberts? Jacquin is an obvious suspect. So too is Gustave Humbert. Jacquin was the éminence grise of the Ministry of Justice and controlled the promotion list even before he was officially awarded that responsibility. As a member of the board of governors of the Légion d'Honneur, he was a keeper of the gate to that dignity. A mere word in the presence of a presiding justice with jurisdiction over the Humberts' latest litigation would have had immense influence, whether uttered in innocence or not. Despite his entrenched position, Jacquin did find it prudent to resign in 1902 after the Humbert strongbox was found empty. The ministry was obviously loath to prosecute him and considered his departure in disgrace sufficient punishment. What of Humbert *père*? He did not merely return to the Senate after the fall of the cabinet in which he was minister of justice. He became that assembly's vice-president, then vice-president of the High Court in 1889, and in 1890, the chief justice of the Cour des Comptes, the audit office of the government. He was a person of immense power in the judiciary. If he was even tacitly aware of the conspiracy, he could hardly have been better placed to aid it. If, as seems more likely, he merely believed Thérèse's stories of the Crawford legacy, the same is true. For his reputation, it is fortunate that he died at Beauzelles in September, 1894, at the age of seventy-two.

It is impossible now to learn whether compelling evidence existed against Jacquin or Humbert. The *instruction* against the Humbert family was drawn up by Joseph Leydet, an examining magistrate of much cleverness and discretion—qualities that would lead to his own disgrace five years later during the Steinheil affair. He approached the question of the responsibility of the Ministry of Justice with great delicacy. He alone had access to all of the evidence pulled together by the Sûreté, and he alone drew up the *instruction*, including only that material he felt to be germane. The rest he would have destroyed. It was not merely a case of the magistrature protecting its own: Emile Combes, the current premier, had decreed that there would be no republican scandal. The Humbert affair would not be written with a capital *A*.

The Humberts themselves made their tracks difficult to trace. By arranging to borrow money at usurious rates, they ensured, first, that there would always be someone eager to make the loans, and second, that these creditors would be unlikely to threaten legal action to regain their funds. Usury was a crime—as it remains today—and although rarely prosecuted, it could be charged against anyone sufficiently brave to send a bailiff to the Avenue de la Grande Armée to collect a debt. Bold, even foolhardy, with their money, the creditors were timid about the courts, especially when Thérèse surrounded herself with the most illustrious attorneys in Paris and boasted of her credit at the Ministry of Justice. These were useless against Cattauï, but he was a different sort, and Thérèse should have known it.

The Humberts also made use of their political contacts beyond the sphere of the Ministry of Justice. Although Frédéric was a deputy for only a single session of the legislature, 1885–1889, he had belonged to an exclusive club whose members had a reputation for protecting one another, within limits. Only the single deputy who confessed faced penalties during the Panama Canal scandal of the 1890s; Daniel Wilson was welcomed back in 1889 after having been disgraced two years earlier when it was discovered that he had sold entrance into the Légion d'Honneur. As Robert de Jouvenel was to put it famously in 1913, "There is less difference between two deputies one of whom is a revolutionary than between two revolutionaries one of whom is a deputy."[64] Most of the deputies saw nothing improper in delivering

64. Robert de Jouvenel, *La République des camarades* (Paris, 1913).

encomia for each other or in supporting causes in which they had a conflict of interest. Pelletan's praise of the Humberts in December, 1889, was not taken as unusual: only the high price he exacted for his performance was uncommon, and that was not revealed until 1903. Pelletan never satisfactorily explained the evidence. It was damaging not so much for its revelation of venality but for the implication that Pelletan knew, or strongly suspected, that Thérèse and Frédéric had undertaken an adventure that might end in catastrophe and therefore required an extraordinary fee for his endorsement. The disclosure and Pelletan's utter mismanagement of the Ministry of the Navy ended his career.

The charges of political intrigue were aimed not only at the Humbert allies but their antagonists. The most sensational target singled out by Thérèse and Frédéric was Waldeck-Rousseau. A figure of icy authority, the lover of reason and order and dimly lit offices, he was an attorney whose probity had never been challenged. As the premier who resolved the Dreyfus affair when some Frenchmen feared that it would lead to civil war, he was widely regarded as the savior of the Republic. In 1903, he was already dying of cancer. Thérèse claimed, and Labori repeated, that because Waldeck-Rousseau took no action against the Humberts when he was premier between June, 1899, and May, 1902, he must either have believed the Humberts innocent (in spite of his remarks in December, 1898 at Elbeuf) or have been planning the conspiracy that would destroy them in 1902 and biding his time until the proper moment. The insinuations are almost certainly unfair. As premier, Waldeck-Rousseau presided over three of the most difficult years of the Third Republic: the Dreyfus affair, the Associations law of 1901 that began an intense church-state conflict, and the pacification of Anglo-French relations after the Fashoda crisis of 1898. He could not spare time to follow up one case among the many in which he had participated before coming to power.

There is much more doubt about the role of Ernest Vallé, the minister of justice under Emile Combes. No documents have survived to validate Thérèse's claim that he accepted an enormous retainer, Fr 235,000, while still only a senator, to secure the downfall of the Humberts for Cattauï. Nevertheless, she had some basis to complain that Vallé acted as if he were still Cattauï's man even after he became minister of justice. There was abundant evidence that the charge of usury against the banker was accurate, and to it the parquet could have added the obstruction of justice in his sending account books out of France before they could be examined by the Sûreté. But on June 10, 1902, a month after the Humberts disappeared, Vallé ordered the charges dismissed.[65] After their arrest, the Humberts were accorded essentially the same considerations and treatment that most middle-class offenders received. Of course, they complained that Vallé singled them out for abuse, but in fact, they were placed in the Conciergerie, which, despite its age, was one of the most comfortable French prisons. Thérèse's resentment would have been far greater if she had been confined in Saint Lazare, where women were commonly held. The most intriguing question that can be raised, but not answered, about Vallé is his role in the search for the Humberts. He was in constant touch with the Sûreté, and it is not unreasonable to suspect that the Sûreté knew that the Humberts were in Madrid long before they were arrested. Certainly they made only token efforts at concealment. They left Paris openly from the Gare d'Orléans, taking the train south to Bordeaux and then to Madrid. Because Romain alone spoke Spanish, they would have been recognized there immediately as foreigners, and as foreigners who subscribed to numerous Paris newspapers, received other mail from France, and exchanged large amounts of French francs for Spanish pesetas. Barring extraordinary incompetence, this information, and a request for identities, would have been transmitted routinely by the Spanish authorities to the Sûreté and from the Sûreté to Vallé. If the minister of justice did learn that the Humberts were in Madrid early in the summer of 1902, the reasons for his not requesting their arrest by the Spanish police before December remain a mystery.

None of these questions of political intrigue came under serious scrutiny at the Humbert trial. When they were mentioned by the defense, it was for effect or to confuse the essence of the case, a long-running and successful fraud. If neither Thérèse nor Labori could convince the jury that the Crawfords existed, nothing else mattered. For the prosecution, it was the Humbert family on trial, not the French judicial system. And in the end, justice seemed to triumph: the Humberts were convicted. Why, then, came the finding of extenuating circumstances

65. *Le Figaro*, June 11, 1902.

that compelled the justices to impose extraordinarily light sentences? Five years' imprisonment at hard labor was a bargain for having enjoyed enormous proceeds from fraud for twenty years.

The jury might have been influenced by the depiction of the creditors as unscrupulous fools who deserved their fate. They might have succumbed to one of those familiar attacks of nationalism so common in France between 1870 and 1914 and suspended their certainty of Thérèse's guilt long enough to sympathize with the story of a poor little French girl deceived by a traitor. They might have done so, but it is unlikely. The jury saw the ghosts of political corruption and interference in justice staring at them in the courtroom. They understood that most of the guilty would never be charged and would escape without paying even Jacquin's price of resignation. With good cause, they suspected that the Humberts had come to disaster only because a banker capable of charging 63.14 percent interest had bought the services of the future minister of justice. Behind the defendants' rail, they saw la grande Thérèse, her husband, and her brothers; they had led a life of high drama and lived out the fantasy of a whole generation of lower-middle-class Frenchmen, to swindle not just the financiers but the whole social system: in short, to "arrive." The jury had pity. Their justice was not justice, but it was less hypocritical than the justice proposed by the state.

Chapter 3

THE CAILLAUX AFFAIR
Justice as a Political Statement

Justitia fiat, ruat coelum.
> William Murray, Earl of Mansfield, Judgment,
> *Rex v. Wilkes*

I

The woman sat alone in the waiting room of *Le Figaro* on the Rue Drouot. Slender, attractive, and well-dressed, she had arrived at 5 P.M. and asked to speak to Gaston Calmette, the editor in chief. After she was told that he was away from the office but expected back at least briefly within an hour, she sat down to wait, her face composed and resolute, her hands resting in a muff on her lap. No one on the staff recognized her, and with the next morning's edition to prepare, there was no time to speculate. At nearly 6 P.M., Calmette finally stepped into the office with his friend Paul Bourget, the novelist. They were in a hurry, and Calmette had stopped only to retrieve some papers. Just as he was preparing to leave again, one of his secretaries handed him a sealed envelope from the woman. Idly ripping it open as he moved toward the door, Calmette suddenly stopped as he read the name on the calling card: Madame Joseph Caillaux. The leader of the left-of-center Radical party, champion of an income tax for France, opponent of the defense spending that nationalists claimed was necessary to face up to the armed might of Germany, once premier, now minister of finance, Joseph Caillaux was the object of an extraordinary campaign of vilification by *Le Figaro*. Calmette showed the card to Bourget, who exclaimed, "You're not going to see her?" Calmette answered that he would take only a few minutes and that he could not refuse a woman.

With that, Calmette returned to his office and called for Mme Caillaux to be shown in. As soon as the door was closed, she said, "You must know why I am here." "But I do not," Calmette replied, rising from his seat behind his desk and indicating a chair. "Please sit down." He had hardly completed the sentence when she pulled a .32-caliber Browning automatic pistol from her muff and began firing at him. There were six shots in quick succession, four of the bullets striking Calmette, who fell in front of the desk. *Figaro* staffers raced into the office of their editor and found him lying in a pool of blood. While some of them attempted to loosen his garments or called for the police and medical assistance, a few turned to Mme Caillaux, who stood emotionless, the pistol smoking in her hand. When they approached, she warned, "Do not touch me! I am a lady. I have my car outside to ride in to the police station." As they looked dumbfounded, she added, "Since there is no justice in France . . . " and then left her sentence unfinished. Ten feet away from her on the floor, a dying Calmette tried to feel for important papers in his coat pocket, called in confusion for "My friends . . . my firm . . . " and then more coherently, "What I did, tell them, I did without hatred." While his friends and a physician worked on his wounds, he lost consciousness and died six hours later. Mme Caillaux, a murderess, rode to the police station in her own car. It was March 16, 1914, and the Caillaux affair had begun.[1]

Joseph Marie Auguste Caillaux, in whose name many in France saw his wife acting, was born on March 30, 1863, and bred for politics. The family was from the Sarthe and had money, some through inheritance and advantageous marriages, the rest through speculation in confiscated church lands during the 1789 Revolution. Eugène Caillaux, Joseph's father, was a state engineer who turned to politics in 1870, first

1. For the details of the assassination, see *Le Figaro*, March 17, 1914, and Peter Shankland, *Death of an Editor* (London, 1981). With the exception of Jean-Claude Allain's excellent new biography, *Joseph Caillaux: Le défi victorieux, 1863–1914* (Paris, 1978), nothing written by or about Joseph Caillaux is entirely reliable. His *Mes Mémoires* (3 vols.; Paris, 1942–47) are self-adulatory and fatuous but generally accurate as to event. Prior to Allain, biographical treatment of Caillaux had been either to deify him or to damn him. Alfred Fabre-Luce, *Caillaux* (Paris, 1933), Gaston Martin, *Joseph Caillaux* (Paris, 1931), and Rudolph Binion, *Defeated Leaders: The Political Fate of Caillaux, Jouvenel, and Tardieu* (New York, 1960) excuse Caillaux's every fault but usually make up for this lapse in interpretation by factual accuracy. Roger de Fleurieu, *Joseph Caillaux au cours d'un demi-siècle de notre histoire* (Paris, 1951), Paul Vergnet, *Joseph Caillaux* (Paris, 1918), Severance Johnson, *The Enemy Within* (New York, 1919), and above all, Berthe-Eva Gueydan (Caillaux's first wife), *Les Rois de la République* (2 vols.; Paris, 1925) are defamation only loosely supported by fact, and that often taken out of context.

Henriette Caillaux testifying at her trial, her "Mercury" hat plainly visible and her fist clenched

A cartoonist's rendering of the assassination of Gaston Calmette by Henriette Caillaux

Joseph Caillaux takes the witness bar at his wife's trial. Henriette Caillaux is at the extreme left of the picture, with Fernand Labori, her attorney, seated in front of her.

Gaston Calmette, editor in chief of *Le Figaro*

in the municipal council of Le Mans, then in the National Assembly of the nascent Third Republic, and finally in its Senate. The violence of the Paris Commune made him an Orleanist. In May, 1877, he served as minister of finance in the cabinet of Duke Albert de Broglie when President MacMahon attempted unsucessfully to frustrate the will of the republican majority in the Chamber of Deputies. He never lived down this stigma, and in 1887 it cost him his seat in the Senate. Twenty years of politics led him back to his beginnings. He ended his life president of the Paris-Lyon-Mediterranean Railway.

As the eldest son, Joseph was supposed to follow his father as an engineer. He prepped for the Ecole Polytechnique at the Lycée Fontanes, the Ecole Fénélon, and finally the Ecole de le rue des Postes, always among the scions of the aristocracy and the highest bourgeoisie, but he tired of science. He failed the examinations for the Ecole Polytechnique and rejected his father's exhortation to try next for the Ecole des Mines. Instead, he won admission to the Ecole de Droit and the Ecole des Sciences Politiques to study law and economics. After he received his degree in 1886, he decided to seek a position in the Inspection des Finances. In 1890, he passed the extremely competitive examinations to become an inspector. So he began a career as a public auditor, specializing in fiscal administration: probing local taxes and receipts, getting to know intimately the morass of indirect taxation that the nation had inherited from the seventeenth century. The system defied all logic, taxing even the number of windows and doors on houses while all but ignoring industry, which was often two hundred years younger than the taxes themselves. These contradictions came to fascinate Joseph Caillaux.

In 1898, two years after the death of his father, an astonished Caillaux was approached by a delegation of republicans from Mamers, an important town in the Sarthe, offering to nominate him for the Chamber of Deputies. From the beginning of the Republic, Mamers had been a monarchist stronghold and was at that point in the hands of the Duke Sosthène de La Rochefoucauld, a very old man. The republicans knew the traditions of the Caillauxs, but they also suspected the ambitions of Joseph Caillaux. At first he refused the offer and wrote to La Rochefoucauld pledging not to run against him. In return, the duke promised to smooth Caillaux's succession to the seat after he retired, thinking that the young man would remain a monarchist. Two weeks before the ballot, Caillaux broke his word, cast his lot with the republicans, and won on the first ballot. The famous name and La Rochefoucauld's age won Caillaux votes that had never forsaken monarchism before.[2]

In the legislature, Caillaux avoided controversy while building a quick reputation as a financial expert among the economically illiterate deputies. In June, 1899, Waldeck-Rousseau picked him to be minister of finance in his cabinet. Throughout the liquidation of the Dreyfus affair, Caillaux compiled a record of careful, orthodox administration, creating the most detailed budgets yet seen by the Republic. But his plans to balance the budget to the last sou were frustrated by the system of indirect taxes he knew so well. It was impossible to estimate them accurately, and they were highly inelastic. For these reasons, Caillaux came to favor their substitution by a single uniform tax on all income. The theory was simplicity itself, the practice something else. The parties of the Left planned to make any income tax progressive, whereas those of the Right and Center, horrified by this portent of socialism, riposted that the idea was the negation of republican *égalité*. In addition, almost no Frenchman—even to this day—relished having tax officials poring over his books. There were too many hatreds that went too deep and had lasted too long in France for there not to be fears that this manner of "inquisition" would be the prelude to a general expropriation.

In July, 1901, some deputies on the Left, the main support of the Waldeck-Rousseau ministry, attempted to force the issue by demanding that Caillaux write an income tax into the next budget. Within the ministry, there was no agreement on the kind of income tax to seek, and Caillaux temporized before the Chamber by praising the idea of the tax but calling its immediate introduction premature. It was brilliant obfuscation and won the support of both the defenders and detractors of an income tax. On the next day, he wrote a boastful letter on the letterhead of the Senate to his mistress, Mme Berthe-Eva Dupré,

2. For Caillaux's youth, family, and relations with La Rochefoucauld, see Allain, *Caillaux*, 19–60, 63–76, 145–72, 207–15; Fabre-Luce, *Caillaux*, 9–17; and Binion, *Defeated Leaders*, 17–21.

the wife of Jules Dupré, administrative assistant to Caillaux's colleague in the cabinet, Alexandre Millerand, the minister of commerce.

> In spite of the best will, I was unable to write you yesterday. I had to suffer through two crushing sessions of the Chamber, one at 9 A.M. that lasted until noon, the other at 2 P.M., from which I emerged exhausted at 8 P.M. I carried off a great success. I crushed the income tax while seeming to defend it; I was acclaimed by the Right and the Center without upsetting the Left. I barred the way of the Right, an indispensable task.
>
> Today, I had another session of the Chamber, which finished only at quarter to one. Now, I'm off to the Senate, where I am going to win the passage of the law on assessed taxes, and this evening, the legislature will recess. I will be exhausted, brutalized, perhaps ill, but I will have rendered a true service to my country.

He signed the letter "Ton Jo," a nickname he used only in the boudoir.

Boastful, he had much about which to boast: his life was a conscious and controlled creation. He had gained for himself the ministry of his father and at the age of forty-one had impressive possibilities in his political future. Although his native arrogance offended, his expertise impressed. Only the political extremes would have failed to welcome him to their ranks. His personal life was secure. The death of his parents and his brother left him possessing an inheritance of a million francs, an amount more than sufficient for a comfortable, if not extravagant, existence. Berthe Dupré, four years his senior and a handsome rather than beautiful woman, was an excuse for avoiding marriage.[3]

Between 1902 and 1909, this control would slip. Waldeck-Rousseau resigned after the 1902 elections, which brought the Chamber of Deputies under the domination of the Radicals and the Socialists. Caillaux left what he considered "his" ministry to become a mere deputy again, although one reelected by a strong majority in 1902. He published *Les Impôts en France* in 1903, an effort to link the French system of taxes to

3. For Caillaux's debut as a legislator and the "Ton Jo," see Allain, *Caillaux*, 215–49; Fabre-Luce, *Caillaux*, 18–32; Binion, *Defeated Leaders*, 21–24; and Floriot, *Deux femmes*, 99–101, with the "Ton Jo" cited in extenso, p. 100. Floriot's study conveniently quotes many of the major documents introduced at the trial of Henriette Caillaux.

the nation's history, and he continued to speak out in the Chamber on financial matters. In 1906, he was voted vice-president of the Chamber of Deputies and accepted the position of president of the Gauche Démocratique, a new small group of the Center. But the dignities were honorific and powerless, and he yearned to return to the Ministry of Finance in the north wing of the Louvre on the Rue de Rivoli. Caillaux got his chance in the cabinet of Georges Clemenceau in October, 1906, and thought he had a promise from the premier to press for passage of an income tax. Actually, Clemenceau's promise was made to ensure that the Socialists and Radicals, whose power in the Chamber had been diminished but not eliminated by elections in 1906, would support his ministry. When Caillaux presented his proposal for a comprehensive and progressive tax on all income in February, 1907, he found the cheering all on the Left, and to find support for his bill, he would be driven there himself. By refusing to place the prestige of the cabinet fully behind the proposal of his finance minister, Clemenceau abandoned Caillaux and the income tax to all the delays in procedure that the opposition could devise. And after the Chamber finally approved the tax on March 9, 1909, Clemenceau knew that similar delays and probably defeat awaited it in the Senate. With great cleverness, Clemenceau had isolated a potential rival, leaving Caillaux to assume the partisan title Man of the Income Tax and to appeal to a political constituency increasingly only of the Left.[4]

Caillaux's troubles were not all political. In 1905, Berthe Dupré divorced her husband and began to cajole Caillaux to marry her. This sacrifice and the appeal to his honor overcame misgivings at marriage to a mistress with whom he was beginning to be bored. In August, 1906, the wedding took place. Almost immediately, he deeply regretted giving in to his scruples. Berthe was a better mistress, he decided, than a wife. Her tastes were "plebeian" in comparison to his, and he was not entirely proud to have her by his side at formal receptions. He had also come to dislike her grown son, François Dupré, and her artist sister, Marie. Some of these tensions may easily be ascribed to a longtime bachelor's reaction to marriage. More seem the result of Caillaux's falling in love with a recent divorcée more than ten years younger than

4. Allain, *Caillaux*, 172–204, 240–54, 270–301; Fabre-Luce, *Caillaux*, 32–48; Binion, *Defeated Leaders*, 24–30.

Berthe. On June 14, 1908, his butler committed the indiscretion of bringing him, in Berthe's presence, a love letter signed "Riri." Caillaux pretended it was a hoax, but Berthe finally traced it to Henriette Rainouard, formerly the wife of writer Léo Claretie. In July, 1909, just as Clemenceau's cabinet lost its majority in the Chamber of Deputies and Caillaux left his ministry again, Berthe accused him of having betrayed her. He went on his knees to ask forgiveness, and she believed him for several weeks until September, when an anonymous letter warned her that the liaison was continuing. Searching in their house in Paris for new evidence, Berthe turned up a folder containing a complete correspondence between her husband and Henriette. Confronted a second time, Caillaux affected another reconciliation and even arranged for Henriette to write him in terms indicating that their passion had become only a friendship.

Berthe had known Caillaux long enough not to fall for this ruse, and he did not really expect her to do so. He was already planning a divorce and had provided for the expense by accepting the presidencies of the Banco del Rio de la Plata and two mortgage-loan societies, the Crédit Foncier Argentin and the Crédit Foncier Egyptien, which together paid him salaries of five hundred thousand francs to use his influence among politicians in their behalf. In mid-September, he traveled to Mamers on a campaign tour and wrote to Henriette in Paris twice, one time explaining in detail that his divorce from Berthe had to wait until after the 1910 elections in order not to provoke complications in his political career. As soon as he had written these letters, he regretted putting such thoughts on paper. He asked Henriette to send them back to him at Le Mans, poste restante. This was a second mistake; he should have had her burn them. Then, after picking the letters up at Le Mans, he failed to destroy them himself and carried them to his house in Mamers. He discovered Berthe waiting for him there and made a fourth mistake, locking the two letters in a desk in her presence. During the night, she found a skeleton key, opened the desk, and took the letters.

The scene between husband and wife the next morning was dramatic. Berthe demanded an immediate divorce, and Caillaux, thinking only of his reelection, threw himself at her feet, swearing his love and begging her not to act hastily. She had no intention of doing so: she had taken the letters not to obtain a divorce but to prevent one. By early November, she decided that she would give the letters back in return for a written admission by Caillaux of his transgressions. This was arranged for November 5. In the presence of Georges Privat-Deschanel, the director general of the Comptabilité publique (the highest civil servant in the Ministry of Finance), Berthe solemnly handed her husband the proof of his adultery with Henriette Rainouard in return for a statement signed by Caillaux naming a Mme X—— and expressing his profound apology for his acts. Caillaux then burned the letters that had caused him such difficulties, never thinking that Berthe would have arranged for them to be photographed before the ceremony of atonement. She must have realized that any reconciliation would be temporary. In fact, Caillaux resumed his liaison with Henriette in late December, 1909, and filed for divorce from Berthe as soon as he won reelection in April, 1910, just as he had planned.

Because the next legislative elections were four years away, long enough for any outrage at Caillaux's divorce to die down, the admission of guilt signed by him on November 5, 1909, and the photographs of the letters to Henriette had limited value for Berthe in her divorce case. She could name Henriette Rainouard as corespondent in a countersuit, but that would sully the names of all involved, herself not least, because she had been Caillaux's mistress for five years while still married to her first husband. Instead, Berthe brought out new ammunition, the "Ton Jo" letter of 1901, in which he had boasted of crushing the income tax while seeming to defend it. Never mind that the political circumstances, and the man, had been different in 1901 than in 1910: the publication of the letter might ruin the Man of the Income Tax. Caillaux capitulated and agreed to another ceremony in the presence of Privat-Deschanel. Berthe handed over the "Ton Jo" for burning while he signed a contract granting her a lump sum of Fr 240,000 and monthly alimony payments of Fr 18,000, a settlement that represented the greater part of his fortune. Needless to add, Berthe had secretly photographed the "Ton Jo." The divorce was pronounced on March 9, 1911, and seven months later in October, Caillaux married his mistress.[5]

5. Caillaux's adultery is given muted treatment in Allain, *Caillaux*, 77–85; Fabre-Luce, *Caillaux*, 48–57; and Binion, *Defeated Leaders*, 31–32. The letters from Caillaux to Henriette Rainouard and the November 5, 1909, confession are cited in extenso by Floriot, *Deux femmes*, 90–98.

Geneviève Josephine Henriette Rainouard was born on December 6, 1874, at Reuil (Seine-et-Oise) to a wealthy and strict bourgeois family. She never left home until her marriage in 1894 to Léo Claretie. They were an unfortunate couple, but for the sake of their two daughters, born in 1896 and 1900, they maintained the pretense of a marriage until 1908, when Henriette sued for divorce and won custody of the children. She established her affair with Caillaux in late 1907 and consciously set about to break up his marriage in order to free him to become her husband. The intervention by Berthe in September, 1909, almost brought Henriette to despair, because it coincided with the sudden death of her younger daughter. In the end Caillaux kept his promises to her, but she had to wait another two years. In 1911 at the time of her second marriage, Henriette was thirty-six years old and very pretty, her blond hair and vivacious face entirely charming. She shared Caillaux's arrogance and snobbery, but she hid them more effectively than he did. Proud of his distinction in society, she thought to please him, as she did, by playing the role of elegant hostess.

The new Mme Caillaux had no knowledge of politics when she married one of the best-known politicians in France. Even when Caillaux's mistress, she made no effort to understand the issues that preoccupied him or even to read the newspapers. An adoring wife, she assumed that whatever her husband did was unquestionably right for the country. She was genuinely shocked once she began to share a household with Caillaux to learn that he was an extremely controversial man. Some of the most vehement criticism of him came from her own milieu, the upper bourgeoisie, who were afraid of a progressive income tax. Within a few months, Henriette Caillaux came to detest politics and deeply to resent the condemnation of her husband that she read in the fashionable newspapers such as *Le Figaro* and *Le Gaulois* and heard at the salons and parties she attended. By the end of 1911, that condemnation was being voiced loudly because Caillaux was no longer merely the Man of the Income Tax but the "friend" of Germany.[6]

After the fall of the Clemenceau ministry in July, 1909, Aristide Briand became premier. Genial, shrewd, an eternal compromiser, he built a majority of moderate deputies for moderate policies. He was particu-

6. For biographical material about Henriette Rainouard Caillaux, see the sketch in *Le Figaro*, July 21, 1914.

larly conciliatory toward the conservatives of the Center-Right, abandoning the income tax proposal and calming the passions raised at the separation of church and state in 1905 by lowering the tone of government anticlericalism. For about a year, some segments of the Radical party—but not all, and certainly not the Socialists further left—followed Briand suspiciously because he promised vague social reforms. This support vanished when the premier crushed the strike of the railway workers by mobilizing the army reserve units of which they were a part and threatening to court-martial those who refused to work. Briand's tactics unified the entire Left against him and restored the idea of a purely leftist majority solidified by the issues of anticlericalism and an income tax. Jean Jaurès, the leader of the Socialist party, could not be considered to head up the coalition, because the collectivism and antimilitarism he espoused frightened too many Frenchmen. None of the older Radicals seemed vigorous enough, but there was the possibility that Caillaux, having edged into the Radical camp with his income tax, might have the ambition for the task.[7]

For more than a year after July, 1909, Caillaux found personal problems more pressing than political ones. He was one of the few men with whom Briand did not get along and so had no influence in the government. Late in the summer of 1910, from his position on the Chamber's Budget Committee, Caillaux began to snipe at Briand by involving himself gratuitously in the complicated and corrupt dealings of the N'Goko Sangha Company, and from there, in foreign policy. The N'Goko Sangha had been chartered to develop the northern region of the French Congo. Its possible field of operations was vastly enlarged by the Franco-German agreement of February 8, 1909, which provided that Germany would recognize France's "special political interests" and police powers in Morocco in return for the French government's undertaking to "associate [French and German] nationals" in commercial ventures. N'Goko Sangha immediately negotiated a trade consortium with the German Südkamerun Company of the Cameroons. In addition to the foreign policy considerations there were great sums of money at stake in several obscure and trumped-up claims by the company

7. For Briand, see Georges Suarez, *Briand: Sa vie, son oeuvre, avec son journal et de nombreux documents inédits* (6 vols.; Paris, 1938–52); for Jaurès, see Harvey Goldberg, *The Life of Jean Jaurès* (Madison, 1962).

against the French colonial administration. Briand considered it best to acquiesce quietly in these claims in order not to jeopardize the French presence in Morocco, which had been buttressed by the agreement of February, 1909. Caillaux saw the issue as an opportunity to embarrass Briand by claiming that bribery and corruption would be behind any settlement. Once Caillaux made the N'Goko Sangha maneuvers public, the question of its claims became politicized. Briand dropped his support of N'Goko Sangha, and the deal with the Germans collapsed. The premier's hatred of Caillaux deepened, and the German foreign office felt cheated.[8]

Compelled by his own policies and Caillaux's manipulations to rely upon an ever smaller and more conservative majority, Briand resigned as premier in February, 1911. As his successor, President Fallières chose Ernest Monis, an aging Radical leader, who in turn filled his cabinet with the most vigorous younger men of his political persuasion whom he could find: Maurice Berteaux at the War Ministry, Jean Cruppi at the Foreign Ministry, Louis Malvy at the Interior Ministry, and Joseph Caillaux back at the Finance Ministry. Caillaux had finally cast his political fate with the Radicals. Firmly allied with the Socialists for its majority, the cabinet promised to pursue militant anticlericalism and to secure the passage of a progressive income tax. Caillaux's restoration to power came almost simultaneously with his divorce from Berthe. While submitting the final bill for legal fees, his attorney, Maurice Bernard, mentioned that another client, a financier named Henri Rochette, needed a favor from the government, a postponement of his trial for fraud. Caillaux agreed to carry the request to Monis and soon involved himself and the cabinet in what came to be called the Rochette affair.

Henri Rochette began his business career as a busboy at the Melun train station and then moved up to running messages for a bank. He learned the jargon of the financial world quickly. Quitting his menial job, he dressed immaculately on borrowed money and set about to swindle credulous investors. His method was simple: to sell stock in fraudulent companies. By 1908, there were fourteen of them, the most important, the Crédit Minier, having attracted Fr 120,000,000 worth of

8. Allain, *Caillaux*, 354–57; Binion, *Defeated Leaders*, 32–34.

stock purchases. When one company experienced difficulties, he transfused capital from another. To keep his business quiet, he gave money liberally to newspapers and to important members of the Radical party. One of his particular allies was Edmond du Mesnil, editor in chief of *Le Rappel* and a close friend of Caillaux. But in 1908, the government was in the hands of the unpredictable Clemenceau, who ordered Rochette arrested. Caillaux, at the Ministry of Finance, made no objection. Unfortunately for the prosecution, Rochette had managed his swindles so carefully that none of the shareholders in his fraudulent companies believed the charges against him. In order to have a signed complaint, Clemenceau was forced to concoct a fictitious plaintiff, a certain Pichereau. This formality accomplished, the investigation by the Sûreté could proceed. As it did so, the shareholders grew nervous and were finally willing to testify. In 1910, Rochette was tried before the Tribunal Correctionnel de la Seine, convicted, and sentenced to twenty-four months in prison, all but five of which he had already served while awaiting trial.

Afraid that a conviction for swindling might adversely affect his ability to perpetrate such schemes in the future, he appealed the decision to the Cour d'Appel and retained Maurice Bernard, who had the greatest number of political contacts of any member of the Paris Bar. The hearing on the appeal was set for April 27, 1911, but Bernard plotted to have it set back to the fall. When the chief justice of the Cour d'Appel, Benoit Bidault de l'Isle, refused the postponement, Bernard took his request to Caillaux on March 9 at the conclusion of the divorce suit. A week later at the Ministry of Finance, he threatened that Rochette would make public his unsavory connections to the Radical party if the appeal date could not be put off. At that, Caillaux went to Monis, and together on March 22, they called in the public prosecutor, Victor Fabre, and pressured him to pressure Bidault de l'Isle. The appeal date was set back to October, and during the intervening six months, Rochette mounted successful new swindles that were not discovered until several years later. Before the Cour d'Appel, Bernard had the temerity to argue not only that the conviction of his client should be quashed because the original plaintiff had been fictitious but that because more than three months had elapsed between the decision of the Tribunal Correctionnel and the hearing of the appeal, Rochette had to be released on a technicality of French law. Bidault de l'Isle was scandalized and ruled against Bernard, but Rochette and his attorney took the appeal another step higher in 1912. Before it could be heard, the financier fled the country with millions of fraudulently gained francs in his baggage.

By then, Briand had become minister of justice. As he examined Rochette's dossier, he was shocked by the postponement of the first appeal and called in Fabre, the public prosecutor, to demand an explanation. Fabre replied by placing before Briand a memorandum he had drawn up nine days after the meeting with Monis and Caillaux.

> On Wednesday, 22 March 1911, I was called to the office of M. Monis, the premier. He wanted to talk to me about the case of Rochette. He said to me that the government did not want the appeal to come before the court on 27 April, a date fixed long ago; that the case could create difficulties for the ministry of finance at the moment when it had enough to deal with because of complications resulting from the liquidation of the religious congregations, from the Crédit Foncier, and from other sources. The premier ordered me to obtain from the chief justice of the Cour d'Appel the setting back of the hearing until after the judicial vacations of August and September.
>
> I protested with energy. I indicated how painful it would be for me to carry out such a mission; I begged him to allow the Rochette case to follow its normal course. The premier maintained his orders and required that I return to report on having fulfilled them.
>
> I was indignant. I was convinced that it had been the friends of Rochette who had provoked this unbelievable action.
>
> On Friday, 24 March, attorney Maurice Bernard came to the parquet: he declared to me that yielding to the entreaties of his friend the minister of finance, he was going to declare himself ill and ask the postponement of the Rochette case until after the vacation period.
>
> I replied to him that he looked in excellent health but that it was not my place to discuss the reasons of personal health invoked by an attorney, that I could only convey them to the chief justice for his consideration. He [Bernard] wrote a note to the chief justice. This magistrate, whom I did not see and whom I

did not want to see, replied with a refusal. Maurice Bernard showed himself very irritated. He began to make recriminations to me and made me understand, through hardly veiled allusions, that he was aware of everything.

What was I to do? After a violent interior conflict, after a true crisis to which the only witness was my friend and assistant Raoul Bloque-Laroque, I decided to obey, constrained by the violence exercised against me.

The same evening, that is, Thursday, 30 March, I went to the premier. I told him what I had done. He appeared very pleased.

In the antechamber of the premier's office, I saw M. du Mesnil, the editor in chief of *Le Rappel*, a newspaper very favorable to Rochette which slandered me often. He had come, no doubt, to ask whether or not I had submitted. I have never before suffered such humiliation. This 31 March 1911.

Victor Fabre

Briand rejoiced at this extraordinary ammunition against his enemy Caillaux, but he could think of no immediate use for it. Fearing that this Fabre memorandum might somehow disappear if he entrusted it to the files, he set it aside in his private papers to save for some future occasion when it might be used with maximum effectiveness.[9]

In April, 1911, the Rochette affair and Fabre were far from Caillaux's mind. A revolt against Sultan Moulay Hafid broke out in Morocco, and the European community in Fez was besieged. The cabinet dispatched a column of troops to relieve the city, but this unilateral action infringed the 1909 agreement with Germany. There were certain to be international complications, but on May 19, two days before the French troops entered Fez, Monis, the premier, was seriously injured and Berteaux, the minister of war, killed, in a freak accident at the Paris Air Show. Cruppi, the foreign minister, lost his nerve waiting for the German response. Caillaux and his friend Malvy were left in complete control of the cabinet. It became clear that Monis would be hospital-

9. For the Rochette affair, see the large dossier in AN, BB 18, 2377[2] (1908), which contains all of the relevant documents except, of course, the Fabre memorandum. See also the personnel dossiers of Fabre and Bidault de l'Isle, AN, BB 6 II, 850 and 670, respectively. See also Allain, *Caillaux*, 358–64; Fabre-Luce, *Caillaux*, 58–70; Binion, *Defeated Leaders*, 34; Floriot, *Deux femmes*, 114–17, with the Fabre memorandum cited in extenso, 116–17; David Robin Watson, *Georges Clemenceau: A Political Biography* (London, 1974), 213.

ized for many months, and on June 28, President Fallières called upon Caillaux to form a cabinet of his own. Three days later on July 1, the Germans delivered their reply to the French occupation of Fez: the gunboat *Panther* anchored off the Moroccan Atlantic port of Agadir "in order to protect German interests."

Caillaux had put his cabinet together hastily, and he did not know his foreign minister, Justin de Selves, well enough. He was stunned to find him so bellicose as to suggest that a French gunboat be sent to Agadir to join the *Panther.* Caillaux thought compromise might be better. After failing to conclude an agreement with the German foreign office through normal channels (de Selves and the French ambassador to Berlin, Jules Cambon), he began secret negotiations through Baron Oskar von der Lancken-Wakenitz, a counselor at the German embassy in Paris. De Selves and the permanent staff at the Quai d'Orsay knew of this duplicity, because the German diplomatic code had been broken, but they had no recourse but to file away the deciphered telegrams—called *documents verts* from the green diagonal bar in the margin. In the end, Caillaux's negotiations produced the relatively advantageous Treaty of Frankfurt, signed on November 4, 1911. By it, Germany would acquiesce in the establishment of a French protectorate in Morocco in return for the approximately 120,000 square miles of France's Congo territory connecting the German Cameroons to the Congo and Ubangi rivers. To some Frenchmen, this cession of territory seemed very like extortion, although almost everyone was willing to admit that unless France wanted war, Germany had to be given *something* in return for renouncing her economic rights in Morocco. Nevertheless, Caillaux's methods gave rise to suspicions that he had offered more than was necessary and that he had groveled for peace.

The Agadir crisis revived French antagonism toward Germany, and nationalism was again a potent force in the French legislature. Two-fifths of the Chamber's Foreign Affairs Committee abstained rather than vote for the Treaty of Frankfurt. On December 21, one-quarter of the Chamber as a whole did the same. Unless they were ready for war, the legislators could not risk the insult to Germany of repudiating the government's signature, but they could repudiate the signer. On January 9, 1912, before the Senate's Foreign Affairs Committee, Caillaux denied speculation that he had engaged in unofficial negotiations. Clemenceau, whose Jacobin nationalism had led him to hate Caillaux because of the treaty, at once demanded that de Selves confirm that declaration. The foreign minister, who had been humiliated by the conduct of the premier, declined to answer, the equivalent of a direct condemnation of Caillaux, and then resigned. Caught in a blatant lie and with the morale of his cabinet shattered, Caillaux had no alternative but to resign himself two days later. When the treaty came up for ratification by the Senate, Raymond Poincaré, the new premier, called it a disgrace but insisted that there could be no question of its rejection at this point. Clemenceau added that Caillaux had evidently misunderstood his patriotic duty during the negotiations. The Man of the Income Tax had "betrayed" the interests of France. For his opponents, Caillaux had become a species of traitor.[10]

The legislature was clearly not the friendliest spot now for Caillaux. Most of the Radicals did not forsake him, and his views were congenial to Jaurès and the Socialists. But Poincaré's ministry stood on a majority of the Center and the Right, for whom the slogans of no fiscal experiments, national unity, and a firm policy toward Germany meant barring the way to Caillaux's politics. Under the circumstances, Caillaux decided it opportune to spend the first half of 1912 on a long trip through the Middle East with his new wife. After their return, he passed most of the summer quietly at Mamers. In October, the Chamber of Deputies appointed a committee to look into rumors that Caillaux and Monis had interfered in the trial of Rochette, but nothing came of the investigation. Briand was not ready to use Fabre's memorandum; Fabre himself refused to reply to questions; and Monis acted affronted that his honor had been questioned: "I will be the victim if you like, of your injustice, but I will be the proud and silent victim." Caillaux was not even called as a witness, and the committee disbanded for lack of evidence.

What rallied Caillaux from his inactivity was Poincaré's decision to run for president of the Republic. Fallières' term expired in January, 1913, and Poincaré, who had attracted to his side such astute politi-

10. For the Agadir crisis, see Joseph Marie Auguste Caillaux, *Agadir, ma politique extérieure* (Paris, 1919); André Tardieu, *Le Mystère d'Agadir* (Paris, 1912); Binion, *Defeated Leaders*, 35–51; Fabre-Luce, *Caillaux*, 65–70; and Allain, *Caillaux*, 364–401. See also Benjamin F. Martin, *Count Albert de Mun: Paladin of the Third Republic* (Chapel Hill, 1978), 241–48.

cians as Briand and Louis Barthou, expected the new fervor of nationalism among the deputies and senators to carry him to victory. Fearing a strong man at the Elysée palace, one who was partial against them, Caillaux and Jaurès opposed him. They were joined by the quixotic Clemenceau, who admired Poincaré's patriotism and nostalgia for his lost natal province of Lorraine but who could not countenance a threat to the end of the legislative predominance that had characterized the Republic. He was pleased by the tradition of mediocrity in the office and declared, "I vote for the stupidest." It was not an effective campaign cry, and Poincaré was elected. This would be the last time Caillaux and Clemenceau would work together.

The allies of the new president, under the leadership of Briand and Barthou, celebrated the victory by postponing indefinitely any consideration of an income tax, dismantling the program of anticlericalism, and, most important, passing a bill raising from two years to three the period of required military training. The three-year-service law was France's only possible response to Germany's increase in the size of its active army: all of France's young men already were subject to the draft, and the population differential between the two rivals placed France at an ominous disadvantage. Clemenceau supported the law as the sole means of preventing subjection by Germany. Caillaux and Jaurès opposed it as militarism, and the political tie between them grew stronger and stronger. In October, the Radical party held its annual congress in Pau. The delegates elected Caillaux their president on a platform of alliance with the Socialists in the forthcoming 1914 legislative elections. The coalition would campaign for a progressive income tax and an unspecified "revision" of the three-year-service law. It took an open letter from the Gauche Démocratique to remind Caillaux that he had not bothered to step down as its president.[11]

In December, 1913, the nationalist majority split on the question of how best to pay for the new expenses imposed by the three-year-service law, thereby forcing the resignation of Barthou as premier. Conceding that some form of income tax might be necessary, Poincaré then named Gaston Doumergue, a very moderate Radical, as Barthou's

11. For this period, see Allain, *Caillaux*, 402–10; Fabre-Luce, *Caillaux*, 70–79; Binion, *Defeated Leaders*, 52–56; Brogan, *Modern France*, 452, for the quotation from Monis; Martin, *De Mun*, 253–64, the quotation from Clemenceau, p. 263.

successor, knowing that Caillaux would certainly return to the Ministry of Finance. But the Man of the Income Tax was not to touch foreign policy: that was the promise wrung from the new premier by Poincaré and enforced by threats from Clemenceau and Briand. Caillaux accepted this limitation, almost glorying in the hatred of those he scorned. He was already notorious for "making faces on the rostrum, spinning around on his axis, his hands in the armholes of his vest, disdainful, seemingly disgusted with so vulgar an audience as the Chamber." This "ploutocrate démagogue," Briand called him, sat with the Left but dressed as if headed for a soirée, his monocle, his spats, his cane, his top hat and suit of the costliest material an insolent reminder of his fortune; his polished bald pate, his carefully trimmed moustache, his mincing step and petulant, arrogant voice the evidence of his refinement and haughtiness. He was Caillaux and he was hated. He did not know how dangerous that could be.[12]

At the instigation of Briand, Poincaré, and especially Barthou, the editor in chief of *Le Figaro*, Gaston Calmette, personally undertook a virulent campaign against Caillaux. The goal was to discredit him before the elections in April, 1914, but driving him from office to be replaced by a less vigorous supporter of progressive income taxing was another motive. First, in late December, Calmette accused Caillaux of having failed to resign from the two mortgage-loan societies and of thus creating a conflict of interest in the Ministry of Finance. After curt denials from Caillaux, Calmette abandoned this tack for want of evidence. On January 8, there was a new charge in *Le Figaro*, that Caillaux had conspired to commit fraud with the heirs of a French merchant, Pierre Marcel Prieu, who had died a millionaire in Brazil. In return for France's support—in the person of the minister of finance—of their inflated claims against the Brazilian government for privileges allegedly won by Prieu but later confiscated, the heirs were to donate 80 percent of the proceeds to the Radical party. Again, Caillaux issued a denial, but this time Calmette persisted, quoting on January 12 from what he called "documents" in the case. He added for good measure the accusation that Caillaux had embezzled four hundred thousand francs from the treasury's Comptoir national d'escompte to use for personal political

12. Allain, *Caillaux*, 410; Binion, *Defeated Leaders*, 56–58; the description of Caillaux is quoted from Charles Benoist, *Souvenirs* (3 vols.; Paris, 1932–34), III, 165.

publicity. This charge prompted rebuttals not only from Caillaux but from the president, the vice-president, and the chief financial agent of the Comptoir national. On January 15 and 16, Calmette claimed that the Ministry of Finance had arranged illegal favors for the director of the Société Général bank, André Homberg, in return for kickbacks to Caillaux. There followed the monotonous round of denials.

Calmette found no particular resonance in any of these accusations, although their collective effect was to provoke increased suspicion of Caillaux. Fraud was difficult to prove and much more easily concealed. It was also boring to read about. Few of *Le Figaro*'s readers had the patience to struggle through the columns of figures Calmette used as proof of his charges. In late January and throughout February, *Le Figaro* attacked its target on more familiar grounds, Caillaux's sponsorship of a progressive income tax with "inquisition" and his "treason" during the Agadir negotiations. Almost every detail of these issues was raked over—almost, because there was one exception Calmette had to make. Poincaré had given him copies of the *documents verts* relating Caillaux's secret conversations with unofficial German intermediaries, but he had forbidden Calmette to publish them. Even so, the evidence in the *verts* could be cited. Eventually, Calmette was certain, the daily hectoring would take its toll on Caillaux; he would strike back, and in his anger and arrogance, he would make a mistake. Calmette was gambling that Caillaux's nerve would snap before the public revulsion at *Le Figaro*'s extraordinarily bitter campaign, already beginning to appear, forced him to stop.

On March 10, Calmette published a long editorial accusing Caillaux of intervening in 1911 to protect the convicted swindler Henri Rochette. All of the details were correct because Barthou had provided him with a copy of the Fabre memorandum, the original having been passed on to Barthou by Briand. The discovery that Rochette had continued his swindles during the postponement and the reality that he had escaped across the border with much of his proceeds made the accusation appear all the more serious. This was Caillaux, Calmette concluded, "the man of the Congo . . . the man who deals in favoritism, the man of kickbacks, the man of secret machinations and criminal interventions—there he is!" Inexplicably, Caillaux failed, for the first time, to issue a formal denial of the charge. On March 12, Calmette revealed that a memorandum composed by Public Prosecutor Victor Fabre provided absolute proof of Caillaux's concern for Rochette. But the Fabre memorandum did not appear in *Le Figaro*: Calmette's copy remained in his inside coat pocket because Barthou had insisted that it not be published until conditions were "appropriate." That moment, Barthou decided, had not yet come, and this refusal led Calmette to make a critical choice.[13]

The editor in chief of *Le Figaro* had in his possession three documents that he considered damning to Caillaux. He could not use the Foreign Ministry *verts* or the Fabre memorandum. The only possibility of maintaining the momentum of the campaign until he could persuade either Poincaré or Barthou to publish what they had entrusted to him was to try the third. On March 13, the front page of the newspaper was dominated by a photographic reproduction of the lines from Caillaux's "Ton Jo" in which he boasted of having "crushed the income tax while seeming to defend it"; the date had been deleted to make it appear current. Hard beside Caillaux's florid signature was an autographed campaign picture to allow readers to compare the handwriting. Calmette prefaced the document with an extraordinary statement: "This is the first time in my thirty years of journalism that I am publishing a private, intimate letter, against the wishes of its author, its owner, or its receiver. My dignity experiences true suffering at this act, and I excuse myself to those whom it distresses."[14]

The "Ton Jo" appeared on a Friday, and throughout the weekend the Caillaux household was in turmoil. On Saturday, *Le Figaro* published and ridiculed Caillaux's effort to place the words from 1901 in their context. Henriette Caillaux was near despair. Since January, she had suffered killing insults: At her dressmaker's, she had heard another lady describe her as "the wife of that thief Caillaux." At a luncheon, she had heard guests talking of the need for "bons français" to regain power in order to save France from bankruptcy. She had replied to them that "so long as my husband is in the ministry, there will

13. *Le Figaro*, January 4–31, February, 1–3, 5–7, 9, 12–21, 23–27, March 2–6, 8–12, 1914; Allain, *Caillaux*, 410–24; Binion, *Defeated Leaders*, 59–64; Martin, *De Mun*, 284; Floriot, *Deux femmes*, 103–20.
14. *Le Figaro*, March 13, 1914.

be a specialist in power, and it will not be he who will lead France to bankruptcy!" Now Henriette felt her entire reputation at stake. Despite the implication in Calmette's introduction to the "Ton Jo" that he had not procured it from its "receiver" and despite a telephone call from Berthe (who was now using her maiden name Gueydan) on March 14 assuring them that she had played no part in *Le Figaro*'s campaign, the Caillauxs assumed that Berthe was the source for the letter. If she had photographed the "Ton Jo" before its ceremonial burning, she had probably photographed the 1909 love letters before their destruction. The chain of presumptions led inexorably to the fear that Calmette would publish those love letters next. To Henriette, with a nineteen-year-old daughter in her charge and a presentation before George V on her social calendar, it seemed that Berthe had finally found the means of revenge: to destroy the career of her former husband and the reputation of her successor.

On Monday, March 16, *Le Figaro*'s front page featured an editorial by Calmette titled "Intermède Comique." It contained ridicule of Caillaux, always referring to him as "Jo." Caillaux's campaign manifesto of 1898, in which he promised to oppose any income tax, was reproduced beside it. Calmette promised a sensation for the following day, and Henriette became frantic after reading these words, certain that they referred to the 1909 letters. At breakfast, she asked her husband about filing charges of defamation against Calmette, but he counseled her to consult first with their friend Ferdinand Monier, chief justice of the Tribunal de la Seine. Because there was a cabinet meeting scheduled for the morning, Caillaux suggested that they see Monier in the afternoon. By telephone, they learned that the chief justice was free only at 10:30 in the morning but could actually stop by the Caillaux residence then. That would mean that Henriette would have to receive him by herself. Knowing his wife to be extremely overwrought, Caillaux was not entirely pleased with this arrangement because he feared that she might misconstrue the nuances in Monier's advice. To try to calm her, he promised to meet with Poincaré before the cabinet session to plead for the president's intercession with Calmette. Caillaux himself was not thinking as clearly as possible because he had another worry. *Le Figaro*'s charges about his dealings with Rochette had reawakened the interest of the Chamber of Deputies in the case, and Tuesday, March 17, had been set for formal questions to the cabinet about it.

Caillaux set off for the Elysée palace immediately after breakfast and asked for a private audience with Poincaré. He knew that Poincaré was at least partly behind Calmette's vendetta, but he feared to confront the president directly. Instead, he asked that Poincaré, as one of Calmette's friends, do what he could to prevent the publication of letters "reflecting on the conduct of Mme Caillaux." Poincaré replied blandly that he knew Calmette to be a gentleman who was too gallant to commit such a deed. Caillaux then exclaimed, "If he publishes a single one of them, I'll kill him!" With no discernible change of expression, Poincaré advised that if the minister of finance felt that strongly, he should consult an attorney and suggested Maurice Bernard. Caillaux left the office angrily.

While her husband sparred with Poincaré, Henriette Caillaux received Chief Justice Monier. He upset her by explaining that any prosecution for slander or defamation could take place only after the event. Because Caillaux was a legislator, the trial of the charges would have to take place before a jury in the Cour d'Assises, not a civil court. Press coverage would reopen all the wounds, and Caillaux's unpopularity would make a conviction of Calmette extremely difficult. These words left Henriette desperate, but she mastered her emotions and appeared calm as Monier left. She also seemed composed riding with her chauffeur from the house at 22 Rue Alphonse-de-Neuville to the offices of the Ministry of Finance at the Louvre. When she told Caillaux what Monier had said, he made a disastrous effort to reassure her by saying: "Since there is nothing else to do, I will take on the responsibility. I'll smash his face!" Timorously, Henriette asked when he expected to act. Caillaux replied, "In my own time, at my own hour, but that won't be long." Without further conversation, they rode home to have lunch together—a wretched meal prepared by a cook hired only the day before.

After lunch, Caillaux hastened off to make an appearance before the Senate while Henriette fired the cook and worried about finding a replacement. She would have to go to the employment agency, and as she prepared to leave, she thought of purchasing a pistol. She was accustomed to pistols, having carried one in her traveling bag all of her life at the suggestion of her father. Several months earlier, she had misplaced the one she had owned for many years, and she had been meaning to obtain another before she began a campaign trip with Caillaux through the Sarthe. The chauffeur, Arthur Carlier, brought the car around again, and Henriette directed him to the Agence Sainte-Solange, where the wealthy obtained servants. After concluding the arrangements for hiring another cook, she had herself driven to the door of Gastinne-Renette, the renowned gunsmith of Paris. She asked for a small but powerful pistol. One of the salesmen, Georges Fromentin, proposed the caliber .32 Smith and Wesson, but Henriette found the action too stiff. She much preferred his second suggestion, the popular caliber .32 Browning automatic, the gas operation of which allowed the trigger to be pulled and the pistol recocked with only the slightest effort. Fromentin led her down to the basement firing range, where she placed three shots out of five into the target silhouette. He was forbidden by law to load the pistol for her to take out of the shop, but he could show her how to do it. She watched carefully, purchased the Browning and a box of bullets, and once in her car, quickly inserted the rounds before she could forget the instructions. The chauffeur made one last stop, at her bank, where Henriette removed some papers from a safe-deposit box. At approximately 4 P.M, she arrived back at her house.

After changing her clothes, Henriette considered attending the reception at the Italian embassy to which she had been invited for later in the afternoon. Within a few moments, she rejected the idea and went to her writing desk to compose a note for Caillaux:

> My beloved husband,
>   This morning, when I told you about my meeting with chief justice Monier, who had explained to me that in France we have no law to protect us against the calumnies of the press, you replied only that one day you would smash the face of the ignoble Calmette. I understood that your decision was irrevocable. My decision was then taken: it would be I who would render justice. France and the Republic have need of you. I will commit the act. If this letter reaches you, I will have carried out, or tried to carry out, justice. Pardon me, but my patience is at an end. I love you, and I embrace you from the depths of my heart.
>
> Your Henriette

She sealed this note in an envelope, gave it to the English governess who tutored her daughter, and called for her automobile. Before she climbed in, she ordered the chauffeur to remove the cockade that identified the car as belonging to the minister of finance. Then she asked Carlier to drive her to the offices of *Le Figaro*. Henriette Caillaux arrived there at approximately 5 P.M.; less than an hour later, she had shot Calmette.[15]

II

Gaston Calmette was born in Montpellier on July 30, 1858, the son of a civil servant. His two brothers became physicians: Emile Calmette, a general practitioner who worked as an inspector in the health services of the military, and Albert Calmette, a specialist in internal medicine who spent many years with the navy, founding the bacteriological institute of Saigon and later becoming director of the Pasteur Institute of Lille. Gaston Calmette preferred law and later journalism. He published his first article in *Le Figaro* on October 20, 1885, and joined the staff the same year. By 1894, he was managing editor, and in 1902, he became editor in chief. Throughout fashionable Paris, he was known for his courtesy, his gentility, his excellent manners, and his perfect professional conscience. He was more timid than some editors, but he could be courageous when he felt great responsibility. His campaign against Caillaux had been out of character in its nastiness, but Calmette sincerely believed that anything was permissible in the effort to prevent Caillaux's regaining power.[16]

Because of the stature of *Le Figaro* and its editor in chief, the six shots fired by Henriette Caillaux stunned and shocked Paris. As soon as it became known through the black-bordered special edition of *Le Figaro* that Calmette had been pronounced dead at 12:15 A.M. on March 17, reaction in the capital split along political lines. François Thalamas,

15. For the reaction of the Caillaux household to the "Ton Jo," see Allain, *Caillaux*, 424; Floriot, *Deux femmes*, 103–31; Binion, *Defeated Leaders*, 62–64. For the session with Poincaré, see the deposition before Henriette Caillaux's trial, *Gazette des Tribunaux*, July 22, 1914. For Henriette's testimony, see *Gazette des Tribunaux*, July 21, 1914. For the testimony of friends and businesses Henriette visited, see *Gazette des Tribunaux*, July 23, 1914. See the reports of March–May, 1914, APP, B A/1625 and B A/1683, J. Caillaux. See also *Le Figaro*'s extensive coverage, March 13–14, 16, April 26, May 1, 9, 1914.

16. For biographical details about Calmette, see *Le Figaro*, March 17, 1914; Floriot, *Deux femmes*, 81–82; and APP, B A/988, G. Calmette.

hounded from his teaching career at the Sorbonne in 1908–1909 by conservatives and the neoroyalist Action Française for his criticism of belief in Jeanne d'Arc, then elected to the Chamber 1910, sent Henriette a remarkable letter: "I have not had the honor of meeting you, but I know by experience what is the infamy of the violent press against the most intimate and sacred sentiments and what a war it leads against those who combat the privileges of the rich and the plots of the clericals. You have killed one of them. Bravo! When a man places himself outside of the moral law and beyond civil penalties, he is no more than a bandit. When society will not give you justice, you must seek it yourself." When the letter leaked to the public, it did not win the Caillauxs, or Thalamas for that matter, any friends.[17]

The special treatment accorded Henriette by the police created almost as much scandal as the letter from Thalamas. She was allowed to have her chauffeur drive her to the nearest police precinct on the Rue Montmartre. Caillaux was called from the Senate and brought along his best friends, Louis Malvy and Pascal Ceccaldi, both deputies. Even with his wife accused of murder, Caillaux did not relax his arrogance: he snapped at the officer standing guard, "You might salute me! I am the minister of finance!" Examining Magistrate Henri Boucard began to interrogate Henriette only after her husband, an extremely powerful politician who had proved himself willing to meddle in the processes of justice, arrived. Even then, Boucard did not press her when she declared that despite firing six shots she had not meant to kill Calmette. Within a few hours, she was moved to Saint Lazare prison, where she was placed in the cell once occupied by Meg Steinheil. But Henriette did not have to share it, as Meg and all previous prisoners had had to do, and there was evidence of hasty but effective cleaning and scrubbing everywhere. She was given a new stove, a lamp, and a carafe. The warden offered her his own footrug—which she accepted. Later, another prisoner would be assigned to her as a maid. With all of this, Caillaux still complained that Henriette was confined "among common-law prisoners." Most serious, contrary to all regulations and practice, Henriette Caillaux was permitted to receive her visitors in her cell, and those visitors included her husband, her daughter Germaine,

17. The letter from Thalamas was read aloud in the Chamber of Deputies: JOC, Débats parlementaires, March 19, 1914.

and attorneys Fernand Labori, André Hesse, Henri Robert, and Maurice Bernard. This breach of procedure allowed her to coordinate her future testimony before she was interrogated seriously.[18]

Caillaux resigned from his ministry on the morning of March 17, but this act only began the political consequences of Calmette's death. Jules Delahaye, a conservative deputy, began that day's session of the Chamber with a demand for information about the Fabre memorandum, to which Calmette had alluded. First Ceccaldi, then Doumergue, and finally Monis denied in turn that there was such a document. Then, with great drama, Louis Barthou stood up to declare that the original Fabre memorandum did indeed exist because it was in his pocket. As he read it with deliberate solemnity, the conservatives rejoiced and the Radicals sat stunned. By an overwhelming vote, the deputies appointed a committee to "investigate abusive encroachments of the executive on the judiciary," naming Jaurès, an appropriate moralist for the occasion, as its chairman. There was a need for haste in the committee's deliberations if it planned to complete the investigation before the elections in late April, but Jaurès raced through eight days of hearings and approximately fifty witnesses—Rochette sent a letter from his hideout in Greece—so rapidly that he gave the impression of trying to protect his political ally. Certainly, the final report Jaurès wrote spread the blame widely. It censured Clemenceau for having created a fictitious plaintiff in 1908, Briand and Barthou for having concealed the Fabre memorandum, and, finally, Monis and Caillaux for "deplorable abuse of influence." No other sanctions were recommended against these five, but the report urged the Ministry of Justice to deal severely with Fabre and Bidault de l'Isle, whose only crime was to have succumbed to government pressure, or not to have been deputies. Both magistrates were ultimately demoted and their careers broken. The Chamber debated the report on April 3 and accepted it without modifications. It endorsed a resolution reproving abusive interventions of finance in politics and politics in finance and affirming the necessity for a law on conflicts of interest. The vote was 448 to 0, with a small number of abstentions, among them Caillaux.[19]

18. For the question of special treatment given Henriette, see *Le Figaro*, March 18–23, 1914; for Caillaux's reaction and quotation, see *Mémoires*, III, 148.
19. For the Rochette affair before the Chamber and in committee, see JOC, Débats

Since mid-March, there had been almost daily demonstrations against Caillaux in Paris led by Maurice Pujo of the Action Française, but these had no impact on the electors of Mamers. On the April 26 first ballot, Caillaux won reelection by 1,400 votes—the same margin as in 1910—over a candidate who had been so correct during the campaign that he never once mentioned the shooting of Calmette or the Rochette affair. The results overall of the voting on April 26 and May 10 were much less clear. France returned a Chamber of Deputies whose political allegiance was ambiguous. Ultimately, it would support a cabinet led by a former Socialist turned moderate Radical, René Viviani, who promised to impose some variety of income tax but not to touch the three-year-service law "until circumstances allowed." There were no conservatives manning the ministries in Viviani's cabinet, but Caillaux and Jaurès were also absent. The new premier was a temporary compromise, meant to last only until the Chamber could recess for the summer in July and then reconvene in October. In the end, Viviani lasted much longer because the first battles of World War I during August upset all plans.[20]

Henriette Caillaux's treatment at the hands of justice attracted almost as much attention as the political situation—and for the same reasons: curiosity at scandal and the sense of overt favoritism. Examining Magistrate Henri Boucard conducted an extraordinarily rapid *instruction* for a capital offense, concluding his investigation after six weeks. He interrogated Henriette only six times. The basic facts of the crime were relatively straightforward, and Henriette never denied shooting Calmette, although she continued to claim that she had not meant to kill him. Yet, unlike most examining magistrates, Boucard showed no inclination to delve into the dark corners of the case, to determine, for example, whether the many charges of *Le Figaro* against Caillaux had any validity. Caillaux's enemies complained that Boucard refused to listen to testimony that would carry the investigation beyond the narrow bounds he had set for it. In particular, they attacked him for accepting as genuine Henriette's statement that she had shot

---

parlementaires, March 17, April 3, 1914. See also AN, BB 18, 2377[2] (1908), for many memoranda from March and April, 1914. There are also good reports in *Le Figaro*, which had an important interest, March 18–28, April 2–4, 1914.

20. For the elections, see Martin, *De Mun*, 284–90.

Calmette to prevent his publishing the 1909 love letters. This interpretation of her motive made the crime an act of honor. But it was not difficult to suppose that she had fired to prevent the publication of documents such as the Fabre memorandum that could ruin her husband's career. That motive would seem considerably more cold-blooded to a jury.[21]

The magistrature and the Ministry of Justice did little to allay the suspicion that they were unenthusiastic about bringing Henriette Caillaux to trial. Victor Fabre, the public prosecutor and Caillaux's most powerful enemy in the Paris parquet, was unceremoniously demoted on April 7 and sent to faraway Aix-en-Provence to serve on the local appeals court. He was replaced by Jules Herbaux, a member of the Cour de Cassation, who owed his recent elevation to commander in the Légion d'Honneur to the Doumergue cabinet. One of Herbaux's first official acts as public prosecutor was to declare that he would personally conduct the case for the prosecution. On May 16, there was some reassurance about the impartiality of the parquet when Assistant Prosecutor Théodore Lescouvé supported Boucard's recommendation that the Chambre des Mises en accusation indict Henriette for the crime of premeditated murder, *assassinat*. But then came the incident of the jury selection.[22]

At the beginning of each year in Paris, the names of three thousand men taken from the voting list were placed in a wooden box, which was immediately sealed. In a public ceremony held each month, a six-judge panel withdrew the names of seventy-two men to serve as potential jurors in the Cour d'Assises during the forthcoming month, thirty-six for the first two weeks, thirty-six for the second two weeks. At the conclusion of the ceremony, the box was solemnly resealed. On May 21, as the bailiff carried the box into the courtroom, he stumbled and dropped it. When he retrieved the box and placed it before the judges, the seals were broken. No one could recall such a circumstance. Had the seals broken when the box hit the floor? Or had someone tampered with the names inside and then contrived the bailiff's

21. Reports of March–May, 1914, APP, B A/1625 and B A/1683, J. Caillaux. See Boucard's personnel file: AN, BB 6 II, 695. See also Floriot, *Deux femmes*, 131–33; and *Le Figaro*, March 17, 22, 24–29, 31, April 1–5, 7–13, 16–18, 22, 29–30, May 1–3, 5–10, 12, 1914.

22. See the personnel files: AN, BB 6 II, 850 (Fabre), 939 (Herbaux), and 1020 (Lescouvé); and *Le Figaro*, May 17–18, 1914.

accident? None of the judges knew how to proceed, and there was much emotion in the courtroom. Reluctantly, they agreed to carry out their duty as if nothing had happened. But because these jurors would provide the panel for the Caillaux trial, there was immediate suspicion that the names of Caillaux supporters had been inserted. A very questionable decision by the Ministry of Justice followed. Louis Albanel, a close friend of the Caillauxs, was designated as the presiding justice for the Cour d'Assises during the first two weeks of July, the time when the trial was scheduled to begin. When unforeseen delays forced the trial date back to July 20, Albanel's term as presiding justice was switched to the second two weeks of the month.[23]

The parquet was also remarkably uncooperative toward the *partie civile* in the case, a suit by Calmette's children against Henriette Caillaux for damages resulting from their father's death. The prosecution and the *partie civile* were traditionally partners, but they were not in the case of Henriette Caillaux. Although the Chambre des Mises en accusation bound her over to the Cour d'Assises by its decision of May 29, Herbaux refused to communicate the exact text of the indictment to the attorneys for the *partie civile*, Charles Chenu and Justin Seligman, until July 16, only four days before the trial opened. Suspicious of the jury, the presiding justice, and the prosecutor, Chenu, a brilliant member of the Paris bar, knew that his task would be very difficult.[24]

Like the two great sensational trials of the previous dozen years, those of Thérèse Humbert and Meg Steinheil, this one attracted an enormous crowd to the courtroom of the Cour d'Assises in the Palais de Justice. The first great moment for the crowd would be the appearance of the defendant, but the scene had to be set. The stout Albanel gathered his red robes around him and sat down beside his two assistant justices. The familiar Labori stood near the defendant's rail. Across from him, the slender, slack-shouldered Chenu, a political conservative, and the stocky, broad-shouldered Herbaux, a Radical, looked each other up and down warily. Finally, Henriette Caillaux was called. She

23. See the reports, all dated May 29, 1914, on the seventy-two potential jurors whose names were drawn on May 21, 1914: APP, B A/1683, J. Caillaux. Almost every one is identified as politically sympathetic to Caillaux. See also Albanel's personnel file, AN, BB 6 II, 616. The report in *Le Figaro*, May 22, 1914, is excellent.

24. *Gazette des Tribunaux*, May 30, 1914; *Le Figaro*, May 27–31, July 17, 1914.

entered dressed entirely in black, her hat's circular brim and tall plumes reminding some of Mercury. She was pale, her blond hair put up in a bun at the back of her head, her cheeks covered with too much powder. Her beauty was hard: a small thin nose, bloodless lips, and little gray eyes implacable in their gaze. She was elegant but without charm. From the first, her pride, her ambition, her arrogance would be apparent.

Albanel launched the *interrogatoire* immediately, but instead of asking questions, he allowed Henriette to speak for nearly three hours almost without interruption. She was not another Meg Steinheil. There was no panting, no tears, no evidence that her heart even beat faster. She introduced herself by stressing her origins: "Je suis une bourgeoise," and her situation: "In 1911, I married M. Caillaux, the premier," emphasizing the title. What she had feared since that marriage was the loss of her "situation," for she had learned that to be the wife of a minister was not to be mistress over public opinion. She spoke of her anguish at Calmette's campaign: sleepless nights, teary days, 138 malicious articles and editorials in 95 issues. It was upsetting to hear her husband's ideas and policies criticized in her social circles. It was her pride that was touched, and throughout her words, there was a preponderance of "me" and "my." The now-famous letters from 1909 represented for her the destruction of her honor, for a "lady" must have neither "adventures nor liaisons." Her father had told her that a woman who has a lover "is a woman without honor." She had no outlet for her emotions—her husband at least had the daily political battles. And yet, she had heard him say that he would smash Calmette's face. She feared that he would do so and ruin himself. From this fear, the idea of sacrifice pushed its way into her mind. She admitted all of this simply, and the jury seemed touched.

Henriette's most serious problem was to eliminate the idea of premeditation. She bought the Browning, she explained, to replace the pistol she had lost. She wanted to have one before campaigning with Caillaux through the Sarthe. She had not planned to use it against Calmette—how could she have, when she was not certain until the last moment that she would go to the offices of *Le Figaro* instead of to the reception at the Italian embassy. But why had she written the letter to Caillaux with the damning words "I will commit the act"? Henriette's reply was weak: "I did not know what I was writing. I attached no importance to it." She tried to repair any damage by soliciting sympathy. Calmette's death had publicized the 1909 letters and ruined not only her reputation but that of her daughter, whose chances for an advantageous marriage had been severely damaged. "And now," Henriette said in her disconcerting calm, "in order to satisfy the vengeance and hatred of journalists, I am obliged to blush in front of her." With great cleverness, she associated her cause with that of Berthe Gueydan: Calmette had marred Berthe's reputation by proving her the mistress of Caillaux while still married to her husband, and Calmette would have done the same to her. "For a women who has a sense of dignity, for a mother, that is too much!" To Albanel's question about the Fabre memorandum, she replied directly: "I did not fear the publication of that document because I was well acquainted with the role of my husband." Behind such threats, she asserted, was an attack not just on Caillaux and the Radical party but on the Republic itself!

Finally, she described her visit to the office of *Le Figaro*. She had to wait a long time for Calmette, and as she sat, she seemed to hear reporters and editors making mock of her husband. After she presented her card in the envelope, she thought a secretary cried, "Make way for Mme Caillaux!" In Calmette's office, she pulled the gun from her muff. She hoped to fire low, but "the gun went off all by itself." After a studied silence, she added, "I regret it infinitely." Even Albanel thought this expression of grief too limited and was moved to ask, "That's all you have to say?" With an absolute lack of sensitivity, she replied that what some of the newspapers had called her—Lady Macbeth—had deeply wounded *her* and that she had feared in March, and still feared, that her husband might be assassinated. At last, she managed feebly to say: "It was fate. I regret infinitely the unhappiness I have caused." Clearly, she had no more to say, and Albanel, removing his pince-nez and stroking his paternal beard, wondered for a moment at her frigid emotions before he recessed the court.[25]

This curiously passionless session was succeeded by six days of ex-

---

25. For overall descriptions of the trial, see Floriot, *Deux femmes*, 134–72; Binion, *Defeated Leaders*, 67–69; Allain, *Caillaux*, 441–43; John N. Raphael, *The Caillaux Drama* (London, 1914); and Charles-Maurice Chenu, *Le Procès de Madame Caillaux* (Paris, 1960). For the first day, see *Gazette des Tribunaux* and *Le Figaro*, July 21, 1914.

traordinarily heated testimony and controversy that surpassed anything the Steinheil trial had provided. The proceedings became less a trial of Henriette Caillaux than a continuation of the vituperative battle between Joseph Caillaux and *Le Figaro*. And beyond the political and human destinies at stake in the courtroom, there loomed the fears that the latest Balkan crisis would unleash the war between European states recurrently imminent since 1871. The Caillaux trial provided a focus for all of the tensions of a Paris stretched taut.

The court session of July 21 began with various secretaries and reporters from *Le Figaro* testifying to the conditions in their offices on March 16. No one remembered open criticism of Caillaux or hearing the name of Mme Caillaux. Paul Bourget, Calmette's close friend and the author of novels and plays calling France back to her conservative and religious traditions, added his version of the murder in sober eloquence. He finished with a eulogy of his friend, whose sense of delicacy, he said, would never have permitted him to publish the 1909 letters. Henriette listened in silence. The senior editors of *Le Figaro*, François Poncetton, Louis Quittard, and Louis Latzarus, confirmed that Calmette had made no attempt to obtain the 1909 letters and would not have published them if they had been given to him. With barely concealed distaste, they described Henriette's haughty attitude after the shooting and her amazing sangfroid.

Latzarus insisted that Calmette had in his pockets at the time of his death "documents of extraordinary importance from a political point of view and from which all good Frenchmen would conclude the infamy and treason of Caillaux." Latzarus was referring to the Fabre memorandum and the *documents verts*, which Calmette had shown him in late January, 1914, but which could not yet be published. In his desire to defame Caillaux as much as possible, Latzarus had taken a dubious step because the existence of the *documents verts* could not be officially acknowledged. Understanding this difficulty, Charles Chenu of the *partie civile* tried to focus attention on the Fabre memorandum. He feigned complete ignorance of it and asked that it be read aloud before the jury. This request was granted, but the impact was lessened by Henriette's insistence that preventing Calmette's publication of the Fabre memorandum could not have motivated her actions because Barthou retained the original of the document and had provided copies to Gustave Téry's *L'Oeuvre* and Léon Bailby's *L'Intransigeant* as well as to Calmette, with similar prohibitions against publication.

After a brief recess, the court heard a deposition from Poincaré describing in laconic fashion Caillaux's audience with him on the morning of March 16. This short statement provided an appropriate introduction to the first appearance of Caillaux himself in the courtroom. But before he entered, Presiding Justice Albanel pointedly read aloud the penalties for disturbances to ensure that there would be no hostile demonstrations. And then Caillaux appeared: head high, regard lofty, steps taut, almost prancing. As he took his place at the witness bar and arranged his notes, he looked haughtily about the court as if everyone there were to pass his inspection, as if he were Robespierre before the Jacobin club. When he spoke, Henriette shed her first tears.

Caillaux began what would be called technically a deposition—as a deputy, he was not required to take the oath and was allowed to consult notes—by recalling his first marriage. Brutally, he described his disillusionment with Berthe and, more tenderly, how he had found happiness with Henriette Rainouard. There followed the letters written in 1909, the theft of the letters by Berthe, the reconciliation with her, finally the divorce. At the time of the divorce, Berthe promised in writing that she had destroyed the originals and all copies of any letters in her possession that he had written. He trusted her until January, 1914, when rumors reached him that Berthe was attempting to sell copies of his correspondence. Quite naturally, he assumed that the "Ton Jo" came into Calmette's hands through Berthe and that the 1909 letters would be next. This thought was the motive for his meeting with Poincaré and his arrangements for Henriette to consult with Monier. He did not mention to his wife Poincaré's advice because he thought nothing would come of it.

Having spoken of his personal life, Caillaux felt compelled to defend his political record. The income tax was the "democratic tax of all great modern states," and if the legislature had passed it, "the finances of France would be in a better state." As for Rochette, his intervention as minister of finance was "an act of government" that he would do again: "the postponement avoided financial difficulties." The Agadir crisis was "the most arduous adventure that France had known," but the nation had triumphed through his masterful negotiations with Germany. Caillaux's conclusion was a startling mixture. He charged that *Le Figaro* was linked to German interests through the Dresdener bank and had accepted subsidies from political parties in Austria-Hungary in return for biased reporting. Having attacked Calmette's administration—through charges that were ultimately proved false—he added, "Whatever the evil he sought to do me, if I could bring Gaston Calmette back to life, I would do so." Finally, he offered the gratuitous comment that the jury should show themselves "good republicans."

After this two-hour performance, Labori insisted that Latzarus be recalled to the witness bar to explain what he had meant by documents that could make Caillaux seem a traitor. This challenge placed Latzarus in an awkward position. He now understood that if he persisted in claiming the existence of the *documents verts*, the French government would officially refute him and thereby cast doubt on his entire testimony. Taking his cue from Chenu, Latzarus refused to elaborate on his previous assertion. Labori, with Caillaux beside him, pressed the advantage, demanding that Latzarus either withdraw his "taint of M. Caillaux's patriotism" or produce the documents to prove his charges. Latzarus still refused to open his mouth. The public prosecutor, Herbaux, tried to end the incident by recalling that before the Chamber of Deputies on March 15, 1912, Poincaré, then premier and his own foreign minister, had declared that all the men who had held the office of foreign minister had acted "with a common ideal and had endeavored to carry out loyally their duties as good Frenchmen." This vague statement could not satisfy Caillaux and Labori. They realized that any unresolved question of Caillaux's patriotism might weigh unfortunately on the jury. They also understood that given the particular circumstances, they could force a denial of the existence of the *documents verts* and even obtain a certification of Caillaux's status as a patriot. Before Labori and Caillaux could exploit this discussion fully, Chenu tried to end it by referring directly to the papers found on Calmette's body and alleged to be copies of the *documents verts* from the Foreign Ministry at the Quai d'Orsay. The papers had been given to Albert Calmette, who in turn passed them to Poincaré. Chenu made much of promising not to use such uncertain evidence, but Labori saw through the scheme. At his urging, Caillaux exploded: "No more equivocations! . . . Furnish your proofs if you dare, for these are frauds!" And with that, Albanel had to declare a recess to allow for a consultation with the Quai d'Orsay and Poincaré.[26]

The morning newspapers for July 22 could not have pleased Caillaux. *Le Figaro* led the moderate and conservative press in condemning the presiding justice's favoritism toward the Caillauxs and in rejecting as patently false the allegations that Calmette had aligned his newspaper with the Central Powers of Germany and Austria-Hungary. In *L'Homme Libre*, Clemenceau published an angry editorial arguing that Caillaux should be tried for treason, with the Senate sitting as High Court.[27] Even so, Caillaux appeared content when Albanel opened the day's session by having Public Prosecutor Herbaux read aloud a formal declaration from the Ministry of Foreign Affairs: "The government declares that the *documents verts* are pretended copies of telegrams that do not exist and that have never existed. They can in no way be invoked to reflect upon the honor or the patriotism of M. Caillaux." As Herbaux sat down, Chenu congratulated Caillaux scornfully on a "superb diversion" in obtaining this "certificate of national loyalty."

The first witness for the day was Georges Prestat, president of the board of directors of *Le Figaro*, who assured the court that Calmette's campaign against Caillaux had had the complete confidence of the newspaper's ownership. While at the witness bar, he also expressed astonishment and genuine anger that Caillaux would invent lies to sully the reputation of the man his wife had shot. In defending the memory of Calmette one more time, he concluded by quoting an epigram: "The lion attacks the living, the jackal attacks the corpse." From the table of the *partie civile*, Chenu added, to general applause in the courtroom, "I know of no enterprise more shameful than coming before a public audience to profane the tomb one's wife has opened!" Caillaux did not even flinch. His conduct and tactics had shown, and would continue to show, that he had decided to defend his wife by attacking Calmette.

During the remainder of the day, the prosecution presented a series of witnesses to indicate Henriette Caillaux's state of mind and to explore the circumstances surrounding *Le Figaro's* publication of the "Ton Jo." Georges Fromentin and Anton Derviller of Gastinne-Renette re-

---

26. *Gazette des Tribunaux* and *Le Figaro*, July 22, 1914.
27. *Le Figaro*, *L'Homme Libre*, and *Le Temps*, July 22, 1914.

called Henriette as very calm and as having excellent aim for a woman. She had told them that she needed the pistol for traveling, and they had warned her that the Browning required so little trigger pressure that it could be dangerous if mishandled. Arthur Carlier, the family chauffeur who had driven Henriette about Paris during much of the day, did not think that she had acted in any unusual manner. They were contradicted by friends of the Caillauxs who had seen Henriette either on March 16 or during the preceding days: Emile Labeyrie, from the Cour des Comptes of the Ministry of Finance, Yvon Delbos, the editor in chief of *Le Radical*, Isidore de Lara, a composer of music, and Eugène Morand and Mme Jules Chartran, Henriette's confidants. Their more sophisticated view evoked a woman deeply affected by the bitterness of Calmette's campaign but trying to maintain a surface calm in order to avoid troubling her husband. Before the publication of the "Ton Jo" she had worried constantly that Caillaux's health would break under the strain of the constant criticism or that he would be provoked into a duel in which he would be killed. After March 13, concern about her reputation and the future of her daughter became paramount for her, and reassurances about Calmette's character had no effect.

The provenance of the "Ton Jo" and its relation to the 1909 letters remained entirely mysterious. Mme Chartran recalled that Léon Bailby, editor in chief of *L'Intransigeant*, had boasted of seeing photographs of *several* "intimate" letters by Caillaux, photographs circulated by Berthe Gueydan. During his turn at the witness bar, Bailby denied the allegation. Paul Painlevé, a Radical deputy from Paris, told the court of hearing Gaston Dreyfus, a conservative banker and enemy of any income tax, predicting to all who would listen to him on March 13 that there would be many more letters appearing in *Le Figaro*. Speaking for the senior editorial staff of *Le Figaro*, Auguste Avril repeated the denial of Calmette's intention either to acquire or to publish the 1909 letters. But what of the "Ton Jo" itself? Princess Juliette Mésagne-Estradère, who had for many years edited *Le Figaro*'s "Monde et Ville" section and who traversed so many social layers in Paris that she was on friendly terms with Calmette, Berthe Gueydan, and Henriette Caillaux, created a sensation by testifying that she had been Calmette's intermediary in an offer of thirty thousand francs to Berthe for the "Ton Jo." Berthe had refused. The Princess Estradère had told Henriette of the offer, using the ambiguous word *letter* for the "Ton Jo," but not of the refusal. Because she knew nothing of the "Ton Jo" before it was published, Henriette would have assumed that the "letter" was one of those from 1909. Abel Bonnard, a belle-lettrist and close friend of both Calmette and Berthe Gueydan, had also vainly attempted to obtain the "Ton Jo" for *Le Figaro*. He had supposed that Berthe's obdurateness had forced Calmette to abandon the effort. Suddenly, on March 12, Calmette sent Bonnard a note announcing that he had secured a copy of the "Ton Jo" and asking him to make apologies to Berthe for any pain the publication of it the following day might bring her. This revelation made previous claims of Calmette's high ethical conduct somewhat hollow, but it also removed Berthe Gueydan as a possible source for the "Ton Jo." If she had not dealt with Calmette on the "Ton Jo," she would not have supplied him with the love letters from 1909. Henriette's fears and bullets were needless and had ironically made certain that her secrets would become public property. But if the "Ton Jo" had not come to Calmette through Berthe and had actually appeared in *Le Figaro* contrary to her wishes, who had provided it? The court had to be adjourned for the day before there were any further attempts to answer that intriguing question.[28]

When the fourth session of testimony opened on July 23, there was as much anticipation in the courtroom as there had been before the first. Speculation about Calmette's sources had been rife overnight, and it was known that Berthe Gueydan would appear that day as a witness. The fascination with Berthe lay not entirely in the prospect of an emotional confrontation between the two women who had borne Caillaux's name or even in the likelihood of harsh words between Caillaux and his first wife. Berthe had become a very ambiguous figure in the case. She had been absolutely uncooperative during the *instruction*, and until Bonnard's testimony on July 22, Paris believed that she had provided Calmette with his documents and bore grave responsibility for the crime. Even now that Bonnard had spoken, it seemed certain that she alone knew the darkest secrets of the case and that she alone could communicate them to the court.

Before Berthe entered, the court heard several witnesses enlarging

---

28. *Gazette des Tribunaux* and *Le Figaro*, July 23, 1914.

on the confusing testimony presented the previous day about the provenance of the "Ton Jo." Gaston Dreyfus categorically denied making the remarks attributed to him by Paul Painlevé. Recalled, Painlevé maintained his declaration. Pierre Mortier, editor in chief of *Gil Blas*, took the witness bar to explain that in November, 1911, one of his best reporters, André Vervoort, came to him with an idea to discredit Caillaux, who was at that time facing bitter criticism from nationalists for his handling of the Agadir negotiations. Vervoort had been in contact with Berthe's sister, Marie, who told him that Berthe hated Caillaux so thoroughly that she was willing to deal in his private correspondence. Mortier had warned him not to consider the offer because no reputable journalist would publish a private letter. Vervoort, since 1912 the editor of his own newspaper, the Paris *Journal*, added detail: he had met with Berthe in a room on the sixth floor of the Hotel Astoria at the end of 1911, and she had shown him a typescript of the 1909 love letters. He recalled Caillaux's reference to Berthe as "la princesse" and use of "Riri" as a nickname for Henriette. Berthe had, he claimed, offered to sell him the typescripts, but he had refused. If she had been so willing in 1911 to traffic in intimate letters, why had she refused to do so in 1914?

At that point, the public prosecutor called Berthe Gueydan as a witness. She entered the courtroom dressed entirely in black except for white gloves. The outfit accentuated her pale face and hollow cheeks. She cut a ghastly figure, clearly in mourning, but for what was uncertain. Once she had taken the oath and her place behind the witness bar, she pulled from her purse a set of handwritten notes to aid her memory. The presiding justice sharply reprimanded her, insisting that a witness had to testify "spontaneously." When Berthe protested that Caillaux had been allowed notes, both Albanel and Herbaux reminded her that as a deputy he was a special case. Labori added the sarcastic comment that "Mme Gueydan has great sangfroid and can certainly manage on her own; I owe her that respect, at least provisionally." In the midst of this bullying, only Chenu tried to protect her.

Deprived of her notes, Berthe spoke first of her life with Caillaux. Throughout this part of her testimony, she would carefully avoid looking at Henriette, who, for her part, maintained an ironic grin. Berthe insisted that there had been much confusion about the correspondence between Caillaux, then her husband, and Henriette Rainouard. It began in 1908, not 1909, and consisted of eight letters, not two. Briefly, and with dignity, she described the first letter's arrival in June, 1908, her suspicions, Caillaux's avowals of love to her, the episode of the letters in September, 1909, and the reconciliation that led to the ceremony of November 5 six weeks later. She had agreed to burn the two letters from September, 1909—which worried Caillaux principally because they mentioned divorce—in return for Caillaux's written apology, but she had not trusted her husband. On the advice of her attorney, Raoul Rousset, she had secretly photographed the letters and kept the prints locked away in a deposit box at the Société Générale bank. The exposure of Henriette's adultery and calculated effort to destroy Caillaux's first marriage in order to win him for herself could not have been made more public if Calmette had published the 1909 letters on the front page of *Le Figaro*.

Labori then reminded Berthe that the divorce decree dissolving Caillaux's first marriage rendered in March, 1911, called on the former husband and wife to destroy any correspondence from the other. Labori insisted that the photographs and even the formal apology were included in this category and tried to argue that Caillaux had made the alimony payments contingent upon her carrying out this provision. Berthe protested that Labori was mistaken. At the time of the divorce, Caillaux had asked her word of honor that she would destroy all the correspondence in her hands. She had replied that she would not give *her* word and that she did not want *his* word of honor because she knew exactly what it was worth. The tenor of these words was damaging to Caillaux, and Labori petulantly demanded that there should be no reading of documents "that should have been destroyed." It was not Labori's best performance, and Chenu had no difficulty shaming him for attempting to suppress evidence and trying to badger a helpless woman. Albanel was compelled to side with Chenu, but he tried to introduce a complicating factor by arguing that a letter signed "Riri" might have to be regarded as unsigned, because the law did not recognize initials or diminutives as the equivalent of a full name.

No one knew yet how many letters Berthe had or when she might be able to produce them. Without prompting, she continued a catalog of griefs against Caillaux: his hiring a detective agency to follow her in an effort to find something discrediting in her activities, his sudden departure from their house in May, 1910, after the legislative elections and demand for a divorce—though she had left her husband in 1905 to marry him. After such conduct, she was justified, she asserted, in using the "Ton Jo" to obtain a favorable settlement. But she never attempted to use any of the correspondence against Caillaux later. It remained in her deposit box. Vervoort's testimony was a lie; in fact, he had approached her, and she had rebuffed him completely. She did not know how Calmette obtained a copy of the "Ton Jo": perhaps her sister, who had arranged for the photographs to be taken, had kept copies. Albanel asked her whether she was certain that the photographs were still in her deposit box. Berthe replied that they were now in her purse. And she pulled them out.

Henriette appeared faint; Caillaux nearly tipped over his chair. Berthe had refused to allow the examining magistrate to see the photographs, but here they were in her hand at the witness bar. When neither Albanel nor Herbaux seemed anxious to scrutinize them, Chenu asked for the letters. Turning coy, she replied, "They contain nothing terrible—except for me." She protested that the letters could contribute nothing to the trial and that she did not want to appear a vengeful woman. Labori quickly stood up to praise this discretion, but Chenu understood that the *partie civile* had an immense advantage on this issue. He joined Labori's encomium of delicacy but added that no one inside or outside the court would believe that the letters did not bear on the trial. After a moment of consideration, Berthe agreed with Chenu but said that she would follow the wishes of the jury. Stupified by the request, none of the jurymen uttered a word. There were several moments of silence. Berthe turned toward Labori and suggested that he decide whether any or all of the letters should be read before the court. Horrified by this poisoned gift, knowing that he would have to read at least some of the letters or have the jury believe that they contained something damaging to his case, Labori replied, "Never yet in my career, Madame, has anyone done me such an honor." Berthe Gueydan was then excused as a witness, and Labori agreed to present a report on the letters as soon as possible.

Caillaux required immediate revenge, and Albanel allowed him to return to the witness bar. There, in supreme arrogance, he recounted his meeting in 1900 with Berthe, then Mme Dupré. At that time, he was thirty-seven years old, a millionaire from birth, the minister of finance, the son of a minister of finance. In 1906, he married her, but it was a mistake because she was not of the same "nature" as he, not of the same "stock." Facing her across the courtroom, he hurled his hatred: they had never made a "perfect couple," but before their marriage, they had been "perfect friends." Berthe cried out: "Be quiet! You dishonor yourself!" But Caillaux continued: "When I left, my dignity no longer permitted me to live with you. I will say nothing more." And at her place, Berthe stood up, magnificent in courage and indignation: "No, I summon you to say everything. I demand it!" He was willing. His lips sneering, his finger pointing dramatically at her, he loosed his harshest condemnation. "Permit me to remind you that when you entered my house, you had not a single centime!" There were whistles and hoots from the audience, but he continued over them. "Rather than force a woman who has borne my name to live in penury, I made sacrifices equivalent to nearly half my fortune. I do not understand what protestations such a woman can raise!" Still standing, Berthe answered in a proud voice: "I will not reply to the insults of M. Caillaux. I pardon him." His own voice very low, Caillaux responded, "And I pardon Mme Gueydan." Behind the defendant's rail, Henriette sobbed.

It was difficult to continue the proceedings after this emotional confrontation, and Albanel allowed only one further major witness that day, Louis Barthou. A slight, wiry man with a thick moustache and an imperial beard, one year Caillaux's senior, Barthou had become a minister (in 1894) at an even younger age. Although both men served together in Clemenceau's cabinet, they had never been friendly and were now bitterly divided by the issues of nationalism and the income tax. Barthou's statement to the court was a series of denials. He had not talked to Berthe Gueydan about the publication of intimate letters, had not given Calmette a copy of the Fabre memorandum, had not played a role in *Le Figaro*'s campaign against Caillaux. He admitted that Calmette had intended to meet with him during the evening of March 16 to ask his advice about publishing the Fabre memorandum. But such a meeting, Barthou insisted, was planned only because he held the original of the document. After a pause, he added that he would have advised Calmette not to publish the memorandum. With an ironic smile, he concluded by saying that he would not have read the original before the Chamber of Deputies on March 17 if Calmette had not been killed the previous day. With much tact, Labori, and with considerably less tact Caillaux, disputed Barthou's declarations. Caillaux claimed to remember a meeting in January, 1914, during which Barthou practiced a form of extortion, urging Caillaux to consider resigning because otherwise Calmette might publish *three* intimate letters held by Mme Gueydan. Barthou replied courteously that he felt it necessary to question "the fidelity of M. Caillaux's memory."[29]

The trial was escaping the control of Presiding Justice Albanel. Through three more days of testimony, there would be a series of interruptions from the audience. Herbaux was uncomfortable conducting the prosecution and left it to Chenu of the *partie civile*. Caillaux almost took over the presentation of the defense from Labori, who was unwilling to attack his former friend Calmette. Throughout the proceedings, Caillaux stood beside Henriette, figuratively joining her behind the defendant's rail. During the first four days of the trial, there was more testimony about him than her. In shooting Calmette, she confounded his political destiny with her pride and reputation, and both Caillaux and his enemies knew that if she were convicted, his career would be irremediably broken. That was why passions were so high, why judicial procedures were flouted, why the trial was out of control.

The initial act of the next day's session, July 24, provided the proof. Labori proposed that he read before the court three of the eight letters communicated to him by Berthe Gueydan. He had chosen the three written by Caillaux and wanted to leave out of the record the four by Henriette and a single anonymous one that denounced Mme Rainouard as the "Riri" of the 1908 letter. Chenu protested what he argued was an arbitrary decision and asked why the choice should not cast suspicion on the motives of the defense. Public Prosecutor Herbaux suggested a compromise: Labori would read aloud three of the letters and allow Chenu to examine the other five. From the audience, Berthe exclaimed that since all eight letters concerned the same issue—Caillaux's adultery with Henriette—any division would be artificial. Ha-

29. *Ibid.*, July 24, 1914.

rassed and annoyed, Labori retorted that he would read either the three he had chosen or none at all. A belief began to spread that the defense feared something in the letters. Suddenly, Chenu, Labori, Herbaux, and Berthe Gueydan were all shouting at once. Albanel attempted to declare a recess, and one of the associate justices, Louis Dagoury, convinced that the chief justice would allow Labori and Caillaux a chance to escape an embarrassing moment, declared, "Sir, you dishonor us!" Eventually, when order had been restored, there was an agreement to argue the question of the letters after the close of the public session.

There was order but hardly calm. At Caillaux's request—Albanel honored all of Caillaux's requests—Pascal Ceccaldi, a deputy from Corsica and Caillaux's closest friend, was called to present a declaration. Dry, thin, eloquent, his body bending up and back as he underlined every word with several gestures, the Corsican made his statement as partial and as inflammatory as possible. Henriette's name hardly passed his lips; he was Caillaux's disciple, and in Ceccaldi's eyes, the Republic would not be the Republic without the Radical leader. For Caillaux's sake, he slurred Calmette, claiming without substantiation that *Le Figaro*'s editor had speculated in German stocks during the Agadir negotiations and manipulated the news in *Le Figaro* to influence the price of the stocks, thereby to make his fortune. There were also malignant words for Barthou. Ceccaldi dramatically pointed to the Fabre memorandum on the evidence table and argued that the words of a disgruntled "functionary" could not compromise Caillaux. Bloque-Laroque, Ceccaldi exclaimed, the man who Fabre insisted had shared the humiliation, had called the memorandum "the writing of a Southerner who was making fun." Yet Barthou and Calmette had attempted to defame Caillaux through this document, a despicable act by despicable men. This was the Barthou who wanted revenge for having been toppled from office by Caillaux in December, 1913, who had not even a word of sympathy for the plight of Henriette Caillaux, brought to the docket because of Calmette's ignoble campaign.

Barthou could tolerate this character assassination no longer. Rising to his feet in the audience and approaching the witness bar, he cried out: "I am here! You have spoken of the fall of my ministry, how I was broken into pieces. Look at me well, M. Ceccaldi! The pieces are still good!" When the justices made no effort to halt the exchange, he continued by denying one more time that he had given a copy of the Fabre memorandum to Calmette and repeating that he had prevented its publication until after Calmette's death. He would not be treated as a defendant by Ceccaldi or accept a condemnation for lacking pity. Henriette Caillaux had killed his friend. His pity would "go to the children who have lost their father and to this man who has been murdered." These words brought Caillaux to his feet, and all three men stood glaring at each other. Albanel still did not intervene. Caillaux repeated Ceccaldi's attacks; Barthou retorted that it was a badge of honor to be assailed by Caillaux. There were more angry exchanges until Barthou lost all discretion and gave voice to a resentment felt by many of Calmette's friends. He had, he insisted, followed the trial very closely and had noticed that with the exception of the reading of the act of accusation preceding the *interrogatoire*, the magistrature—Albanel and Herbaux—had raised not a single complaint against Henriette Caillaux's conduct, not even to condemn the murder! There was a hush. Albanel finally acted, but only to declare a recess before Barthou could continue.

After the recess, only two witnesses attracted any attention. Most of the testimony merely corroborated earlier accounts that Calmette had never intended to publish or even to acquire the 1909 love letters and that he was waiting for authorization to print the Fabre memorandum. There was much greater interest in the appearance of Henry Bernstein, the young playwright whose *Israël* (1908), inspired by the Dreyfus affair, had won him international renown. Despite the nearly twenty-year difference in their ages, Calmette and Bernstein had been close friends. Bernstein came to refute Princess Estradère's testimony: Calmette would never have tried to use her as an intermediary with Berthe Gueydan, because he trusted friends such as Abel Bonnard to act for him. Bernstein could not explain what motives she might have had to create such a fiction. He could state unequivocally that Calmette and Princess Estradère were not close and that she had been retained on *Le Figaro*'s staff partly because she was experiencing financial difficulties. Finally, in the simple, affecting words he used in his dramas, Bernstein eulogized his friend and concluded by asking how Caillaux could be so shameful as to attack the honor of the man his wife had brutally murdered.

Bernstein was a very effective witness for the prosecution, but the brother of the editor had even greater impact. Albert Calmette was one of France's most distinguished physicians and a pioneer in research on tuberculosis. With great dignity, he described how the senior editors of *Le Figaro* presented him with the papers found on his brother's body: a copy of the "Ton Jo," a copy of the Fabre memorandum, and copies of the *documents verts*. He recalled trembling as he read the *verts*, aware that he was privy to state secrets. Without delay, he turned them over to Poincaré, who thanked him gravely for "doing his duty." Calmette refused to believe the declaration by the Quai d'Orsay that the *documents verts* were frauds. Finally, he evoked his brother as a gentleman. Gaston Calmette would have told Henriette Caillaux that he had no intention of obtaining the 1909 letters—if she had given him the chance. Turning toward Labori, he asked the defense attorney, who had known the editor for more than a decade, whether this assertion was true. Labori's sense of honor compelled him to nod his head, although this was a damaging admission for the defense.[30]

The testimony by Albert Calmette would have been a brilliant finale to the prosecution's case, but Herbaux had clearly refrained from scheduling his witnesses in the order of greatest effect. The evidence from the attending physicians was left to be heard, and the following session, on July 25, would be their day. Before they spoke, the conflict over the letters presented to the court by Berthe Gueydan was resolved. Having forced the defense to appear evasive, Chenu graciously agreed that only two of the letters, those from Caillaux to Henriette in September, 1909, should be read aloud. It was a moment of acute embarrassment for husband and wife, and as Labori finished his task, Henriette fainted. In the audience, there was stupefaction. Why had Henriette murdered to prevent these letters from being published? Her reputation was besmirched, but there was nothing else. It was impossible to believe that Calmette would have considered publishing intimate letters that had no political content whatsoever.

After a brief recess to revive Henriette, Dr. Charles Paul, the medical examiner for the Paris police, described the autopsy he performed on

30. *Ibid.*, July 25, 1914. For the incident between Albanel and Dagoury, see their personnel files: AN, BB 6 II, 616 and 788, respectively, which contain considerable information about the resolution of the insult.

Gaston Calmette's body in the presence of his assistant, Dr. Jules So-
quet, and Examining Magistrate Boucard. There had been four bullet
wounds, three of them superficial. One bullet had penetrated the left
thigh, another the lower left side of the chest, and a third the heart area.
This last would have had serious consequences had not Calmette's
wallet, in the breast pocket of his coat, provided a baffle. The fatal
wound had come from a bullet entering the left side of the abdomen,
passing through the iliac bone, cutting the right iliac artery, and provoking a fatal hemorrhage. All of the shots appeared to have come from
close range. In his opinion, the hand firing the pistol had remained
steady, but Calmette had fallen to the floor as he was struck. The medical examiner thought that the first shot to strike Calmette caused the
wound in the thigh. Forced to the floor by this injury, Calmette inad-
vertently moved the more vulnerable parts of his body into the line of
fire. Dr. Paul emphasized that this reconstruction was only a theory,
but he noted that the parallelism of the wounds supported it. Dr. So-
quet joined in the findings and the hypothesis of his superior.

The physicians who had struggled vainly to save Calmette's life appeared next. Dr. Emile Reymond, a stately, bald man with a pointed
moustache, described his examination of Calmette at the offices of *Le
Figaro*. Even then, only minutes after the shooting, there was almost
no pulse. He called an ambulance and, during the wait for it, admin-
istered some stimulants. Just as the ambulance arrived, Dr. Antoine
Hartmann, professor of clinical surgery at the Faculté de médecine,
joined him, and the two rode with Calmette in the ambulance to a well-
equipped private clinic in Neuilly, several miles away across the city.
The surgeon on duty was Dr. Bernard Cunéo. All three physicians
thought Calmette's condition too unstable to attempt surgery and decided that the risk of waiting to determine the extent of the wound was
outweighed by the risk of immediate intervention. At 12:15 A.M., when
they could wait no longer, Calmette died as soon as the first incision
was made. Labori questioned these judgments, but Reymond defended them indignantly, noting that Calmette's brothers, both physicians, concurred in the decisions. But Labori pressed on, quoting from
a medical textbook that the transport of severely bleeding patients could
be dangerous. Choking back anger, Reymond replied that he had to

make such decisions every day, that an attorney was in no position to lecture on medical practice, and that he could think of no circumstances in which it would be preferable to operate in an editorial office rather than in a hospital. Then, he bitterly attacked the notion that the physicians should be held accountable in a murder trial: it would be, he argued, as if an arsonist set fire to a building but was released because the fire fighters could not control the blaze!

The tall, full-bearded Hartmann supported Reymond's position in every particular. He called himself a partisan of immediate surgery in most cases of massive hemorrhage but insisted that Calmette could not have survived such an operation. When Labori, as he had with Reymond, questioned this judgment, Hartmann answered with scorn that this was the first time he had ever seen a defense attorney attempt "to incriminate the surgeons." A similar reaction to this line of questioning came from Cunéo, a short man whose pince-nez rested unsteadily on an extremely large nose. As his colleagues on the case had done, Cunéo defended the decision to try to stabilize Calmette's pulse before operating. He added that he had despaired of saving Calmette from the beginning and that Labori, "in attempting to present the illusion to Calmette's children that their father could have been saved, in reality only assassinates him again."

The session concluded with testimony by two of Hartmann's colleagues on the Faculté de médecine, Dr. Pierre Delbet and Dr. Jean Pozzi. Delbet put on a masterful performance, almost a lesson in surgery for the courtroom. Above all, he insisted that it was impossible for any surgeon to issue an opinion of true merit on a patient he had not personally examined. He called the attending physicians eminent men whose judgment should not be questioned. There were statistics on their side: In 1899 during the Boer War, British physicians immediately operated on soldiers who suffered abdominal wounds, but the death rate was 95 percent. During the fighting in Manchuria in 1905, the Russian physicians preferred to wait until stimulating drugs stabilized the heartbeat, and they managed to save 37 percent of similar cases. Pozzi was less certain. He had been one of Calmette's close friends and had rushed to the clinic to offer his assistance. He would have preferred to risk an immediate operation, but he refused to criticize the attending physicians. Only they had examined Calmette, and Hartmann was his colleague and former student. Pozzi even declared that he would trust his own life to Hartmann's judgment.[31]

Henriette would trust her life to the brilliance of her husband and Labori. Pozzi was the last witness for the prosecution, and because the afternoon was already late, Albanel recessed the court before calling on the defense to present its case. Caillaux used the delay to good advantage. When the court convened on July 27, he insisted on making another declaration and was granted the witness bar. From his portfolio, he withdrew several sheets of paper which he identified as a copy of Gaston Calmette's will. By law, a will was a private document, and even the presiding justice was sufficiently shocked to demand how Caillaux had obtained it. With supreme arrogance, he replied, "In the same manner by which M. Calmette obtained his copy of the 'Ton Jo.' " Chenu asked what was the cause of this profanation, and just as haughtily, Caillaux answered that it was essential to the defense that Calmette's will be read to the jury. With these words, the long-simmering animosity between the two became more than the exchange of ironic remarks. Chenu abruptly began to refer to "M. Caillaux," refusing to grant him the courtesy of "Monsieur le ministre." Caillaux's prickly dignity immediately noticed, and when Chenu explained himself by implying that his adversary was "unworthy," Caillaux retaliated by calling him the attorney for the "other side," for antirepublicans such as Gabriel Syveton and the Ligue de la Patrie Française. By the time order was restored, both men were launching their words like cannonballs, and Caillaux was all the more eager to attack Calmette and the editor's friends.

Reading from Calmette's will, Caillaux explained how the editor of *Le Figaro* had died with an estate of thirteen million francs. Hippolyte Chauchard, the founder of the Société du Louvre stores, had left him two million francs, most of it in the company's common stock. Through careful investments, as in the Société du Casino of Vichy, Calmette had managed to accumulate five million francs himself. The remainder, six million, was a gift from Calmette's mistress, Mme Maria Boursin, who signed over to him this enormous fortune with only the stipulation that

31. *Gazette des Tribunaux* and *Le Figaro*, July 26, 1914.

she receive the interest on the various stocks and bonds for the rest of her life. This was the honorable, the gentleman, Calmette, Caillaux said mockingly, a man who would make his fortune from his mistresses. He stopped just short of calling Calmette a gigolo. "In our bourgeois families," he continued, "it would take a hundred and fifty years to acquire this large an estate." Who would defend such a man? It required a Henry Bernstein, Caillaux replied in answer to his own question, a man "in whose past there are certain facts." Chenu—but not Albanel or Herbaux—challenged him to make this insinuation precise, and Caillaux seemed delighted to add, "When one has not fulfilled one's duty to the nation, one is ill-equipped to give certificates of morality to others."

The witness bar was Caillaux's at this moment. He could attack with all of the virulence that his wrath and thwarted ambition had stored inside him. Lashing out, creating an almost gunpowder smell to the air with his explosions of fury, this was the Caillaux of the Chamber of Deputies, for good reason the best-hated man in France. When Chenu was finally able to demand how any of these denunciations of Calmette, Bernstein, Barthou, and others attenuated or even related to the case under trial, Caillaux could permit himself to say, "There is something worse than to lose one's life, and that is to save it when one, by turns, attacks women and enriches oneself at their expense!"

After this sensational performance by Caillaux, there was a recess while Labori's assistants set up a number of charts for the first defense witness, Dr. Eugène Doyen, a celebrated surgeon who had won great notoriety during the last decade by differing with his academic colleagues on surgical procedures. Doyen, an energetic, corpulent man of mammoth ego, proclaimed himself an expert not only in surgery but also in ballistics. He savagely attacked the decision of the attending physicians to delay an operation until nearly six hours had passed after the shooting. His reasoning was simple: if Calmette had lived that long with massive bleeding, he would have survived an operation. Then, turning to his charts, he argued that the medical examiner was incorrect in his reconstruction of the scene in Calmette's office. Instead of remaining steady, Henriette's arm had been forced upward by the recoil of the Browning. It was this effect and Calmette's efforts at self-defense that produced the fatal shot. According to Doyen, Henriette aimed her first two shots at the floor and would have fired the final four there also, for she meant only to frighten Calmette. But the recoil forced those last four shots higher at the same moment that Calmette dropped downward at the noise of the first two. The combination of the rising arm and falling body had fatal consequences.

Chenu and the partisans of Calmette listened to this explanation in amazement and consternation. It was not sufficient for the defense to argue that Calmette's physicians had killed him. Now, Doyen seemed to say that Calmette died because he threw himself in front of the bullets. Chenu insisted on an immediate confrontation between Doyen and the physicians who had appeared earlier. Pozzi merely dissociated himself from everything Doyen had argued. Hartmann and Reymond were less circumspect, saying that Doyen's testimony and explanations would be unsatisfactory in a first-year medical student. Delbet served the prosecution best by asking Doyen to name a single instance in which a patient with a severed iliac artery had been saved through an immediate operation. Doyen had to reply that he could not name one.

Just as the medical controversy was finishing, there was a commotion in the rear of the courtroom. Henry Bernstein, who was not present at the beginning of the session but who had learned of Caillaux's attack on his past through a friend's telephone call, was shouting toward the table of the defense. "Caillaux! Are you there? Because I do not insult adversaries in their absence!" Walking quickly to the front of the audience—once again, no one attempted to control the interruption of the proceedings—he addressed the court: "We are present at an inconceivable affair, a man climbing atop the coffin of his wife's victim in order to speak to you more loudly!" Holding everyone's attention through the intensity of his emotion and voice, he reminded all that Caillaux had committed a crime in obtaining and reading Calmette's will. He warned with a sneer, "Don't let yourself be assassinated by a minister, or the next day your testament will be read before the court." More and more in a frenzy, he claimed that the *documents verts* proved Caillaux a traitor. But of himself: he deserted his unit after five months of service in 1894 and fled to Belgium. It was a mistake of youth. He returned to France under an amnesty and in 1911 enlisted in the army, choosing a combat branch. "I am an artilleryman," he continued. "I leave on the fourth day of mobilization, and"—here he voiced the fears of nearly everyone in the courtroom—"the mobilization may be tomorrow. I do not know what day Caillaux leaves for the front, but I must warn him that during a war, he cannot have himself replaced by his wife: he will have to fire himself!" Bernstein spoke these words directly at Caillaux, who sat not four feet away. The courtroom audience erupted in such acclamation and cheers that Albanel had to suspend the session.

With considerable bravery, Caillaux returned to the witness bar as soon as there was order. Very calmly, he admitted that Bernstein had paid his debt to the nation but insisted that anyone who made such a mistake forfeited forever his right to act as a character witness. Caillaux wisely did not provoke the audience further and quickly sat down, having made his twelfth intervention during the trial.

Labori concluded the case for the defense by calling Colonel Charles Aubry, commander of the Twenty-first Artillery regiment. At the witness bar, Aubry, like Doyen before him, declared himself an expert in ballistics. According to his analysis, Henriette Caillaux fired the first shot at the floor in front of Calmette. The other five shots, all involuntary and the result of the extraordinarily light touch of the Browning trigger, formed a rising pattern. Like Doyen, he attributed this pattern to the shock to her arm from the recoil action of the pistol. Calmette's attempt to avoid her aim by falling to the floor was the final ingredient in a fatal coincidence. The conclusion, Colonel Aubry asserted, was obvious: Henriette did not mean to kill. And with that controversial opinion, expressed with force and conviction, Labori rested his case.[32]

The final summations came on July 28, just as the Paris newspapers reported that France and its ally Great Britain were undertaking preparatory military measures in case of war. For the first time in ten days, the reports of the Caillaux trial were crowded onto the second page. Justin Seligman, who had quietly assisted Chenu throughout the trial for the *partie civile*, made the first summation. In the division of labor with Chenu, he was to refute the allegations of corruption and venality leveled by Caillaux against *Le Figaro* and to elicit sympathy for Calmette's family. Conscientious but dull, Seligman carried out this

32. *Ibid.*, July 28, 1914.

strategy in a carefully crafted speech to the jury. Calmette, he began, was part of a family that had made signal contributions to France. His father established the hold of the French government in the department of Alpes-Maritimes after it was ceded by Italy in 1860. Calmette's brothers served the nation's military as physicians, and Calmette himself made *Le Figaro* a newspaper of commanding reputation, the "daily bread of intelligence."

In a despicable act, Caillaux attempted to destroy the reputation of the man his wife had murdered. But was there any truth to the rumors Caillaux cited? Through a complicated series of documents, Seligman proved that there was not. The Dresdener bank had no control over *Le Figaro*; the money from Austria-Hungary was payment for advertisements of that country's spas, not a subsidy; the information about German stocks that appeared in *Le Figaro* during the Agadir negotiations had been published earlier in other Paris newspapers. Where was the corruption or venality? As for Calmette's will, what right had Caillaux to violate its secrecy? The court had poorly served justice, Seligman argued, in allowing the will to be read, and the parquet should immediately undertake an investigation to determine how Caillaux had obtained his copy from the Administration de l'Enregistrement. In his desperation to defend his wife, Caillaux had slandered Calmette, saying that he attacked women. But which ones? Calmette did not attack Henriette Caillaux; instead, she murdered him. Far from being the unprincipled rascal Caillaux called him, Calmette had been a sensitive gentleman, whose friends—among them such distinguished men of letters and politics as Jules Claretie, Louis Barthou, Pierre Loti, Albert de Mun, and Edmond Rostand—had already contributed eighty thousand francs for a monument to his memory.

Seligman's summation defended Calmette; Charles Chenu's would be a brilliant attack on Joseph and Henriette Caillaux. Chenu began by insisting that the portrait the defense painted of Henriette Caillaux, that of a woman unnerved by the unremitting criticism of her husband and driven to fire warning shots at Calmette, shots that her agitation made high and fatal, lacked any verisimilitude. The court saw the true Henriette, a woman of extraordinary sangfroid, so rational and cold that she yielded ground in her argument only inch by inch, a woman who boasted of her past and flaunted the humiliation she suffered at her own hands. She spoke of her rearing as a bourgeoise, but she initiated a liaison with Caillaux aiming to break up his marriage to Berthe Gueydan. Together since 1911, Joseph and Henriette Caillaux shared their lives, their sentiments, their ambitions, and their hatreds, all of which they professed before the court. The flaw in their lives was this ambition, especially Caillaux's, an ambition "without brake, without limit, curiously impatient at obstacles, authoritarian, sworn to crush by any means those who resisted him, who embarrassed him, who stood in his way." It was this Caillaux who thought of censorship "by the bullet" when the free press began to attack him.

What upset Caillaux, Chenu asked rhetorically? The "Ton Jo" was published on March 13, but the hints about the Fabre memorandum appeared on March 10–12. Calmette's editorial on March 16, "Intermède comique," which so frightened Henriette was clearly the prelude to the verbatim publication of Fabre's complaint. If Caillaux had really worried about the 1909 love letters, he would have told his wife about Poincaré's promised intervention, and that would have reassured her. Instead, he refrained from doing so and pushed her into murder. During that fateful afternoon, she picked up papers from a lockbox for him—almost certainly documents he could use to try to counter the Fabre memorandum—and bought her Browning. After she returned home, she wrote Caillaux a note in a firm and confident hand and then headed for the offices of *Le Figaro,* having taken the precaution of making the chauffeur remove the ministerial cockade from the automobile. While waiting for Calmette during an entire hour, she was calm and composed. She did not even hesitate when she finally entered his office. After the shots were fired, she declared that justice had been done. Was this a nervous woman who meant only to terrify Calmette? The defense argued first that Henriette Caillaux did not mean to kill and second that she did not kill: it was the failure of the physicians that allowed Calmette to die. Chenu's tone made it clear that he considered this reasoning beneath his contempt.

For Chenu, the idea that the 1909 letters precipitated the murder was untenable. No one outside the Caillaux household seriously believed that Calmette would publish such letters, and it was very doubtful that Caillaux himself could have believed this, although he allowed Henriette to think so. Calmette made not a single effort to obtain the 1909 letters. And what was in them? Nothing of any note! The Caillauxs consistently overemphasized the importance of the letters; this lie was revealed only when they were read aloud in open court. Calmette had in his possession the *documents verts* and the Fabre memorandum, but he had promised not to publish either without authorization. Why, then, had Henriette killed Gaston Calmette? It was, Chenu declaimed, to pay the editor and *Le Figaro* for the harm they had already done to Caillaux.

Another ingredient was the Fabre memorandum. The defense asserted that Caillaux had no reason to fear it, that Calmette could not publish it without the permission of Barthou and Briand, and that because other newspapers had copies, killing Calmette could not prevent its appearance. With an ironic laugh, Chenu admitted that these arguments appeared to answer all speculation. The flaw, he continued, lay in the contention that the Rochette affair was unimportant: "That a premier and a minister of finance should accord to a man who had drained so much of French savings and won the title 'Prince of Swindlers' a postponement solicited by him and obtained this result by violating the consciences of two magistrates—that is of no importance?" Caillaux dismissed the deed as "an act of government" that he would do again. But the Chamber of Deputies did not agree. In approving the report of its committee of inquiry, the Chamber endorsed the finding that Caillaux and Monis committed "a deplorable abuse of influence" and that this act was "a symptom of the evil of the disdaining of procedures and the independence of the magistrature, the unmeasured influence of finance and the confusion of finance, the press, and power." On April 3, the deputies passed a resolution censuring these abuses by a vote of 448 to 0; Caillaux abstained. After a prolonged dramatic pause to ensure that the jury properly appreciated the attitudes Caillaux had displayed, Chenu concluded by demanding justice in the name of Calmette's children.

After these incisive, accusatory words, Herbaux's summation as public prosecutor was remarkably mild, especially for a murder trial. There could be no doubt, Herbaux began, that Henriette Caillaux killed Gaston Calmette; the argument that the physicians shared blame was specious. There could also be no doubt that she meant to fire. There was conclusive evidence of premeditation in the note and the purchase of a pistol. Yet this crime was unusual because it arose from a combination of wrath and fear, both the result of believing that Calmette would publish "letters of grand passion." It was here that Herbaux's reconstruction clashed absolutely with the one Chenu had just presented before the jury. Herbaux insisted that since 1911, the Caillaux household had dreaded the possible appearance of the 1909 letters and that in Henriette, this dread became a mania. He willingly accepted the defense's contention that Caillaux was not seriously alarmed by the threatened publication of the Fabre memorandum and certainly could not prevent that through Calmette's death. Thus, the letters were behind the crime. Henriette made a "horrible mistake" because Calmette did not have the letters and would not have published them if he had them. She killed. Here was murder, and murder premeditated. There had to be a judgment, for no one had the right to do justice outside the law. But justice in this case, he concluded, would have to be justice tempered by mercy. The jury should return a verdict of guilty and at the same time a recommendation of the minimum sentence.[33]

As soon as Herbaux took his seat, Labori replaced him before the jury. He wanted to explain that the minimum sentence to which Herbaux referred was five years in prison at hard labor, a sentence that could not be suspended. Was this moderation, he asked, was this justice? Adopting an indignant tone and waving his arms dramatically, he denied that Henriette was accorded special treatment at Saint Lazare "despite what some would say, and what Barthou would say if he were here!" Having dispensed that gratuitous insult, he reminded the jury of two cases similar to Henriette's. In both 1885 and 1898, the wives of deputies shot and killed men who slandered their husbands. Both were acquitted, and *Le Figaro* applauded the verdict in 1898. How could the editors of *Le Figaro* act differently now, Labori questioned. These precedents alone seemed to him sufficient grounds for a verdict of innocent.

Labori also did not allow Chenu's characterization of the Caillauxs to go unchallenged. Continuing the indignant tone, he assailed his "dear colleague" for attempting to complete Calmette's work in black-

33. *Ibid.*, July 29, 1914.

ening their reputations. For Labori, Caillaux was a man who "commands the respect even of his adversaries through his intelligence, his energy, his courage, and—I have the right to add—his personal probity." It was the letters, not the Fabre memorandum, that motivated the crime. Henriette was mistaken, but it was a mistake that Calmette encouraged. And in an audacious conclusion, Labori even evoked Calmette, who, he said, "would ask for an acquittal if he were here. I believe that he would declare himself wrong to have waged so atrocious a campaign against the Caillauxs. I can imagine him now, smiling and gentle, at the witness bar, the Gaston Calmette whom I once saw shriveled with hate." After a pause even longer than the one held by Chenu, Labori made an eloquent plea to the jury. "Yes, I wish he were here. Put an end to this nightmare by an acquittal. May we save our wrath for our enemies beyond the borders. Let us stand always united and determined against the perils that advance upon us!"

After the audience broke into prolonged applause and cheers for all of the summations, Albanel read his instructions to the jury. They were to consider only two questions: First, was Henriette Caillaux guilty of premeditated murder (*assassinat*)? Second, was Henriette Caillaux guilty of murder without premeditation (*meutre*)? If they replied with an affirmative answer to either question, the minimum term that the court could impose would be five years in prison at hard labor, as Labori had explained. The law did not allow this penalty to be suspended. The jury departed at 7:55 P.M. Less than an hour later at 8:50, they returned. By a vote of 11 to 1, the twelve declared Henriette Caillaux innocent of both charges. She flung her arms to the ceiling and then embraced Labori and her husband. In the melee, her hat with the Mercury brim fell to the floor and was trampled.[34]

III

Earlier on July 28, 1914, Austria-Hungary declared war on Serbia. On July 30, Austrian artillery bombarded the Serbian capital of Belgrade. In retaliation, Tsar Nicholas II ordered a total mobilization of Russian

---

34. *Ibid.*, July 29–30, 1914. From 1901 through 1913 (no records were published for 1914), there were 1,603 cases of *assassinat* charged in French courts, with 2,019 defendants. Of the defendants, 433 were acquitted, enabling the French parquet to claim a conviction rate of 79 percent. See the *Compte général.*

troops. This action provoked Germany on July 31 to proclaim a "state of threatening danger of war." France could not afford to desert its ally Russia. It was clear that war was now certain—only the naïve and foolish believed that mobilization could be halted once begun.

Among the naïve was Jean Jaurès and the leadership of the French Socialist party. Desperate to prevent war between the working classes of France and Germany for what he dismissed as "national" causes, he was capable of telling Louis Malvy, the minister of the interior, on July 31, that "the France of the Revolution has been drawn by Russian Cossacks against the Germany of the Reformation." Jaurès thought that he could tread a narrow path between pacifism and patriotism, but when the nation is in danger, tepid patriotism is treason. On July 31, Urbain Gohier's newspaper, *Sociale*, carried the warning: "If there is a leader in France, Jaurès will be nailed to the wall at the same time as the mobilization bulletins!" Before the day was over, Raoul Villain would do the deed with bullets instead of nails and precede the announcement of mobilization by several hours.

Villain's father was the clerk of court at the Reims tribunal. In 1914, he was sending his son Fr 125 a month to study Egyptology at the Museum of the Louvre because he could think of nothing else for Raoul to do. The young man finished his military service in 1910 after having taken a degree from the agricultural school at Reims. In the next three years, he failed first as a farmer in the Ardennes—the peasants refused to follow his orders, because his theories about agriculture were divorced from reality—and next as a preceptor at the Collège Stanislaus—where he was unable to command the respect of the students. He reacted to these failures by cultivating the life of an aesthete and by wearing them as a badge of honor: only the crude could succeed with dirt, peasants, and adolescent boys. He began to oil his hair and to grow a moustache, to think himself sensitive and a dreamer. He swore to do great things. For a time, he was attracted to the Christian socialism and idealism of Marc Sangnier's Sillon organization. The Sillon was already in decline after its condemnation by Pope Pius X in 1910, but in any case, Villain soon lost interest. Next, he joined the Jeunes Amis d'Alsace-Lorraine (Young Friends of Alsace-Lorraine) and made a tour of Alsace. He stared across the border at the German guards, felt that he had conceived a mighty hatred for them, and swore to kill the kaiser for the insult to France rendered by the German occupation of Alsace and Lorraine. Vacuous, turning with the wind, Villain then saw a production of *Le Cid* in December, 1913. Under the inspiration of its antique conception of honor, he came to believe that the kaiser was only fulfilling his duty to Germans. The true criminal, Villain decided, was the enemy within, and that enemy was Jaurès.

And so Villain followed Jaurès on the night of July 31 to the Café du Croissant. There, Jaurès sat with the general staff of the Socialist party and its newspaper, *L'Humanité*—Pierre Renaudel, Georges Weill, Jean Languet, and Philippe Landrieu. Their table was on the sidewalk, but partitioned by a curtain from the busiest part of the café. At 9:30 P.M., Villain reached his hand through a gap in the curtain and fired the pistol he was carrying. Within moments, Jaurès was dead.[35]

With some reason, there were fears—and hopes by a few—that Caillaux would be next. The prefect of police notified him by telephone and advised him to leave Paris at once. He and Henriette spent the night packing their belongings and left the following morning for Mamers. There, he was so isolated and forgotten that in August when there was a reorganization of the cabinet he was not even informed. With Jaurès dead, Caillaux was the most prominent politician identified with a policy of friendship toward Germany. War made this position obsolete and relegated its author to political oblivion. But because Poincaré, Viviani, and the rest of the French cabinet wanted to maintain democratic freedoms while waging war, another politician, now Caillaux's deadly antagonist, was also condemned to a political wasteland. This was Georges Clemenceau.[36]

In 1914, Clemenceau was seventy-three years old. He was born in the Vendée to a family of petty nobility that had long been at war with its class. Following the tradition of his father, grandfather, and great-grandfather, he was trained in medicine, but he never practiced. From 1866 to 1869, he traveled in the United States and taught French at a finishing school for girls. Elected mayor of Montmartre in the midst of the Franco-Prussian War for his Jacobin chauvinism, he ran into trou-

---

35. For Villain and the shooting of Jaurès, see Goldberg, *Jaurès*, 467–74.
36. For Caillaux's reaction, see Binion, *Defeated Leaders*, 70. For Clemenceau, see Watson, *Clemenceau*; Theodore Zeldin, *France, 1848–1945* (2 vols.; Oxford, 1973–77), I, 698–714; Georges Suarez, *La Vie orgueilleuse de Clemenceau* (2 vols.; Rev. ed.; Paris, 1932); and Edgar Holt, *The Tiger: The Life of Georges Clemenceau, 1841–1929* (London, 1976).

ble during the Commune for his relative moderation. After returning to the Vendée, he won election to the National Assembly, and later the Chamber of Deputies, consistently on a platform of Radicalism. Within the Chamber, he established an unmatched reputation for invective that stung and brought down cabinets. For his savage and wild destructiveness, he was called the Tiger; for his bitter anticlericalism, the Priest-eater. A loner who attracted allies more through fear than love, he was vulnerable to any hint of scandal. A marginal participation in the Panama Canal affair provided the focus for his enemies and caused his defeat for reelection in 1893. During the next nine years, he remade his reputation through journalism, striking wildly until he found his issue in the Dreyfus affair. He rode the rehabilitation of Dreyfus to a seat in the Senate in 1902. During a crisis over the separation of church and state in 1906, he was brought into the cabinet of Jean Sarrien to add strength at the Ministry of the Interior. Within six months, he maneuvered Sarrien's resignation and his own elevation to premier. Still calling himself a Radical, he promised seventeen major social reforms in his ministerial address, but he was unhappy with the new tilt of the party toward the pacifism and collectivism of the Socialists. During three years as premier, he would specialize in breaking strikes and divorce himself from his party and only base of support. After his fall in 1909, he was as isolated as in 1893 until the revival of nationalism made him and *L'Homme Libre*, the newspaper he founded in 1913, sometime allies of Poincaré's brand of conservatism.

Clemenceau's program was summarized in the two-word Jacobin tradition of 1792, justice and nationalism. It provided him with an ideal for which to struggle in a life that was otherwise unrelievedly negative: negative because he gloried in his misanthropy, a struggle because he saw the world as a theatre of carnage, a gladiatorial battle of each against all. In his study of Demosthenes, Clemenceau wrote, "Call that man happy—for it is the lot of all to suffer—who has suffered for a noble cause, and grieve for him who, having sought nothing outside himself, has known only the cinders of life, of egoism vainly consumed." And in a letter from the 1920s to his grandson Pierre: "One might fight for one's self and make up to one's self for the failings of others. The strong make their way alone. The weak get together and try to prevent them from doing so." The less likely of success, the more unpopular, the better he liked his causes. "We shall be alone. We shall have all the world against us," he would say in recruiting supporters for Dreyfus, "but we shall win." Fiery, implacable, an eternal duelist, he lived to fight.[37]

There were no causes in his private life. Almost friendless, Clemenceau was the eternal outsider, looking down at the world with a bitter haughtiness. Short, never handsome, he nonetheless had a certain attraction in his youth because of the almost Oriental cast to his face. To ensure publicity for his conquests, he had affairs with a series of actresses. The naïve American girl, Mary Plummer, who fell in love with him in French class, married him against her family's wishes, and bore him three children, was left to herself. When she finally took a lover in 1892 out of desperation for companionship, Clemenceau found them out and had them arrested. He threatened her with imprisonment for adultery if she did not agree to be divorced at once and to leave the country. As he became older, he grew fat, bald, and asthmatic. The thick, drooping moustache he cultivated all of his life turned white, and he presented an impression that was almost simian. He lived alone in a fashionable apartment in Passy with a rose garden in the courtyard, needing no one but his two cowed servants and sometimes not wanting to see even them. His children all led wretched lives and embarrassed him so much that he ignored them for years at a time. Selfish, impatient, unpleasant, he lived only for politics and his comfort. It was easy to understand why Jaurès called him "an evil man."[38]

After the fall of his cabinet in 1909, Clemenceau seemed to slow, even to mellow. Increasingly, he placed comfort before politics. In the summer of 1910 when leaving for a speaking tour of South America, he chose the Italian liner *Regina Elena* in preference to a slower French vessel with fewer amenities. Two years later when he had to undergo an operation for prostate difficulties, he elected to recuperate not at a state hospital but at a nursing home in Paris on the Rue Georges Bizet staffed by the Little Sisters of Charity. His failure to block Poincaré's bid for the presidency in 1913 led some politicians to joke that when

---

37. For the words about Demosthenes and the letter to Pierre, see Holt, *Tiger*, 238–39, 274. For Clemenceau's attitude during the Dreyfus affair, see Caillaux, *Mémoires*, I, 301.

38. Zeldin, *France*, I, 702.

tigers grow old, they are made into bedside rugs. As if to belie these thoughts, Clemenceau founded *L'Homme Libre*, where he raked his still formidable claws across the political world. After the war broke out, his criticism of the government's leadership, especially in the inadequacy of medical services, provoked the censor to demand deletions. When Clemenceau's vigorous protests were useless and the newspaper was temporarily banned, he renamed *L'Homme Libre* (*The Free Man*), calling it *L'Homme Enchaîné* (*The Chained Man*).[39]

As always, his issues were justice and nationalism, but despite his long political career, Clemenceau had never reconciled his two great causes. He championed a veneration for an almost anarchic individualism limited only by the obligation not to infringe another's absolute freedom. At the same time, he held as an unshakable belief that only the nation-state, the *patrie*, could guarantee this individualism and the justice that made it possible and thus that the *patrie* had claim to the ultimate loyalty of its citizens. Clemenceau begged the questions that this creed posed: at what point must justice intervene in the relations of individuals, and at what point does the nation have the right to demand the ultimate loyalty that can override questions of individualism and justice? His own career provided no answers. He had taken up the cause of Dreyfus and "justice" against the government and the army, the cause of a convicted traitor. During the first months of the war in 1914, he defied the censor and called the nation's leaders a band of incompetents who were leading France to defeat. In one of his most famous witticisms, he derided the military leadership: "War is too serious a business to be left to the generals." But Clemenceau called it treason for others to question the conduct of the war or doubt that its outcome would be complete victory for France.

Joseph Caillaux and Georges Clemenceau learned to mistrust each other during the nearly three years of Clemenceau's cabinet from 1906 to 1909. In the next five years, the mistrust became antagonism. By turning to the Socialists for support of the income tax, Caillaux made the Radical party increasingly inhospitable to Clemenceau. Caillaux's conduct of the Agadir negotiations and opposition to the three-year-service law provoked Clemenceau's patriotic rage. Caillaux also had

39. Holt, *Tiger*, 157; Suarez, *Clemenceau*, II, 146–47; Benoist, *Souvenirs*, III, 185.

awkward friends and acquaintances. After serving briefly and disastrously as a paymaster in the army, he accepted a mission to South America in November, 1914. There, he and Henriette foolishly struck up a friendship with the rather mysterious Count James Frank Minotto, a German agent with an implausible cover as investigator for the Guaranty Trust Company. An introduction to Count Hellmuth von Luxburg, the German ambassador to Argentina, followed. Minotto and Luxburg were delighted to hear Caillaux rashly denounce the entire French government for having blundered into an "unnecessary" war. After their return to Europe in March, 1915, the Caillauxs spent several weeks at Biarritz as the guests of Paul Bolo-Pasha, a French financier formerly in the service of the Egyptian government whose immense wealth seemed to have suspicious sources. In Paris, Caillaux maintained contact with Eugène Bonaventure Vigo. He called himself Miguel Almereyda, edited the extreme left-wing newspaper *Le Bonnet Rouge*, and had won Caillaux's esteem by providing some of the damaging information against Calmette. Another of his informants against Calmette, the Austrian Leopold Lipscher, continued to correspond with Caillaux. Baron Lancken, Caillaux's intermediary in 1911 and now director of German espionage in France, tried to use Lipscher to sound out Caillaux about peace talks, once sending an agent, Thérèse Duverger, to Mamers. Caillaux refused to pursue any of these direct contacts with the enemy, but he was not categorical in breaking off all relations.[40]

Booed in the streets of Paris, his wife hissed when she volunteered as a nurse at the military hospital in Vichy, Caillaux came to resent ever more his isolation from power and the war that had caused it. There would come a time, he was certain, when France would have no more hope on the battlefield and would turn to him. That would be a time of reckoning. To prepare for the day, Caillaux prepared working papers entitled "Rubicon." He envisioned a fantastic plan of proroguing the legislature, rewriting the constitution, ruling by decree, and open-

---

40. For Caillaux's wartime activities, see the reports of January 13, February 13, May 28, September 3, October 23, November 22, December 3–29, 1917, APP, B A/1683, J. Caillaux; and *Affaire Caillaux, Loustalot, et Comby, inculpés d'attentat contre la sûreté de l'état; procédure générale; interrogatoires* (Paris, 1919). See also Binion, *Defeated Leaders*, 71–83; Fabre-Luce, *Caillaux*, 127–41; and Brogan, *Modern France*, 534–39.

ing peace talks with Germany. With the faithful Ceccaldi heading the Sûreté Générale (state security police), there would be a limited reign of terror. The "direct and indirect authors of the war" and "certain newspaper publishers" would be brought to trial. Those who slandered legislators would be guilty of treason. Perhaps realizing that it was unwise to have put these ideas on paper, Caillaux rented a deposit box under his wife's maiden name when he was on a brief trip to Florence in August, 1916. In it, he left "Rubicon" and several other sensitive documents, among them Briand's tax records.

In October, 1916, at Mamers, Caillaux entertained Bolo-Pasha, who the previous March had purchased the Parisian newspaper *Le Journal* and was using it to spread as many rumors of French war-weariness as could be slipped past the censor. Earlier that fall, Henriette, who was recovering from French slights through an extended stay in Rome, met another of Bolo-Pasha's friends, the charming Signor Filippo Cavallini. When Caillaux joined his wife in Rome in December, 1916, he began social relations with Cavallini, who soon introduced him to Italian politicians who opposed participation in the war and favored a negotiated peace with Germany. Among them was former premier Giovanni Giolitti. As in South America, Caillaux was much less than circumspect in his language. The French ambassador to Italy, Camille Barrère, sent reports of his words and his company to the Quai d'Orsay. Briand leaked them to the Paris press. Immediately, Caillaux was denounced publicly for "defeatism," a word coined for the occasion.

In January, 1917, Caillaux learned that Cavallini was a former felon and under investigation in France for espionage. He returned to Paris to find that there was also an investigation into the affairs of Bolo-Pasha, who was suspected of having received the funds to purchase *Le Journal* from German secret agents acting in Switzerland. Caillaux refused to give up Bolo, calling him a patriot and a gentleman. It was easy to misinterpret these remarks as more than support for a friend. In July, Baron Lancken sent to Mamers H. A. Marx, a banker from Mannheim who carried a forged Swiss passport, to approach Caillaux about a separate peace between France and Germany. Caillaux turned him out, but the contact appeared extremely suspicious when it was proved that Marx had carried with him funds for Almereyda's *Le Bonnet Rouge*. Arrested in August, Almereyda was allowed to strangle himself with his bootlaces. In November, it was the turn of Bolo-Pasha and his confederate Margaret Gertrud Zelle, the famous Mata Hari, who were shot in 1918 after conviction for espionage.

The year 1917 was a devastating one for France. First came a series of military disasters during the spring in the Aisne and the Champagne. The losses were so severe and the evidence of incompetent leadership so pervasive that soldiers in several divisions mutinied rather than take up positions on the front line. By midsummer, it was clear that the Russian Revolution had removed that nation as a functioning ally and provided a focus for pacifist propaganda. The only cheering news was that the United States was joining the side of France and Great Britain, but many months would have to pass before American reinforcements arrived in great numbers. Until that time, France had to hold to the last man, had to spend her last strength, to prevent defeat. Under these circumstances, the French government had to act with the utmost firmness against defeatism, and Poincaré, as president of the Republic, had no choice but to place that government under the leadership of the most uncompromising of French patriots, Georges Clemenceau.

The arrest of the group around *Le Bonnet Rouge* placed in jeopardy Joseph Caillaux, who had associated with them, and Louis Malvy, who as minister of the interior since June, 1914, had permitted them to operate with impunity for three years. At the outbreak of the war, Malvy made no use of Carnet B, the list of those who might, according to the Sûreté Générale, undermine the war effort. Malvy took this decision largely on the advice of Almereyda, who had won his trust and who convinced him that if he did not detain the socialists and pacifists on Carnet B, *Le Bonnet Rouge* could mediate between the government and the militant Left. Malvy had been reluctant to consider cracking the facade of national unity by embarking on mass arrests and was so grateful for Almereyda's proposal that he subsidized the newspaper with government funds. Thus it was that Malvy was duped by a German agent and that antimilitarists could spread pamphlets among the troops, undermine morale, call for peace, and even act as spies without being seriously hindered by the Ministry of the Interior. Malvy had not tracked down the authors of seditious publications, not kept the army informed about the circulation of pacifist propaganda, not even prevented the travel within France of enemy aliens. Yet he was not a traitor. His gravest failures came from laziness. There was also his tie to Caillaux, who would certainly become premier if France opted for a negotiated peace and who seemed to be pursuing such a settlement through illicit contacts. Malvy considered it politic to be gentle toward conciliators, pacifists, and pro-Germans who might make up the ruling class if Caillaux returned to power.

Before the Senate on July 22, 1917, Clemenceau spoke of Malvy's toleration of defeatism, using the words, "You have betrayed the interests of France!" Malvy managed to hang onto his office for another month before resigning on August 31, but on October 4 he was compelled to defend himself before the Chamber of Deputies against a charge of treason published in the reactionary *L'Action Française*. Rashly demanding a trial to clear his name, he was taken at his word, although the Senate, sitting as the High Court, did not try him until August, 1918. It was clear that no treason could be proved, but the senators convicted him of having "failed in, violated, and betrayed the duties of his office," euphemisms for the slackness he had displayed. Sentenced to five years' banishment, Malvy left immediately for Spain.[41]

The attack on Malvy marked the beginning of Clemenceau's offensive to return to power. But even now, when he seemed the only man with sufficient energy and will to lead France to victory, he was resisted. He was feared and detested by the great majority of senators and deputies. Poincaré accused him of grave defects: pride, jealousy, hatred, and rancor. For his part, Clemenceau merely despised Poincaré. There had been several opportunities for Clemenceau to join cabinets since the beginning of the war, but he had always refused to be a subordinate. Everything he said, everything he wrote in *L'Homme Enchaîné* suggested that if he were called to be premier, it would be to run the government and the war his way: he would be a one-man Committee of Public Safety. The legislators recoiled before the specter of a dictator in spite of the excellent Jacobin tradition. Throughout the late summer and early fall, they tried to make do with substitutes. When the crisis of confidence on the battlefield and at home became critical in mid-November, there were no more substitutes. The Germans had

41. For Clemenceau's denunciation of Malvy, see JOC, Débats parlementaires, July 22, 1917.

long predicted that Clemenceau was France's last card. Poincaré played it, hoping that it would be trump.

Clemenceau formed his cabinet on November 16, 1917, at the age of seventy-six. Four days later, he outlined his policy before the Chamber of Deputies.

> Gentlemen, I wage war! . . . In domestic affairs, I wage war! In foreign affairs, I wage war! Always, everywhere, I wage war! Russia has betrayed us, and I continue to wage war! Unhappy Romania has been forced to capitulate, but I still wage war! Before Paris, I wage war! Behind Paris, I wage war! If we retreat to the Pyrenees, I shall continue to wage war, and I wage war until the last quarter hour, because the last quarter hour will be ours! . . . Mistakes have been made. Do not think of them except to rectify them. Alas, there have also been crimes, crimes against France which call for prompt punishment. We promise you, we promise the nation, that justice will be done according to the law. . . . Weakness would be complicity. We will avoid weakness, as we will avoid violence. All the guilty before courts-martial. The soldier in the courtroom united with the soldier in battle. No more pacifist campaigns, no more German intrigues. Neither treason nor semitreason. The war! Nothing but the war! Our armies will not be caught between fire from two sides. Justice will be done. The nation will know that it has been defended.

Winston Churchill, present that day in the balcony of the Chamber, would describe the scene in his *Great Contemporaries:* "He ranged from one side of the tribune to another, without a note or book or reference or scrap of paper, barking out sharp, staccato sentences as the thought broke upon his mind. He looked like a wild animal pacing to and fro behind bars, growling and glaring; and all around him was an assembly that would have done anything to avoid having him there, but having put him there, felt they must obey." [42]

Before this brilliant and galvanizing performance, Clemenceau told Wythe Williams, correspondent for the New York *Times* in Paris since 1913: "Now that I am boss around here, I intend to accomplish two

42. For Clemenceau's ministerial declaration, see *ibid.*, November 20, 1917. Winston Churchill, *Great Contemporaries* (New York, 1937), 310–11, describes it brilliantly.

things. One, I will destroy the German Empire. Two, I will destroy Caillaux." That same day, Poincaré wrote him a note suggesting that Caillaux be brought to trial: "Fate has placed him at the crossroads of all the paths of treason." Clemenceau replied: "Caillaux is a bandit. I do not know whether the High Court or the Council of War will try him, but justice will be done." On December 11, Clemenceau asked the Chamber of Deputies to strip Caillaux of his parliamentary immunity from prosecution. The question was sent to a committee, and by December 22, it was so evident that Clemenceau would have his way that Caillaux emulated Malvy in demanding a trial to clear himself. He was willing to admit some imprudence in company and language but claimed to be under attack for his ideas, not his deeds. His proper judges, he insisted, were not military officers but the senators, sitting as the High Court.[43]

Caillaux underestimated the enmity toward him and Clemenceau's determination to exploit it. In late December, he wrote to Henriette in Rome asking her to retrieve the contents of the deposit box in Florence. Ambassador Barrère learned of this mission and arranged with the Italian police to arrest her as she carried it out. With much delight, he was able to forward to Paris the "Rubicon" plans, the sensitive documents like Briand's tax records that Caillaux had no right to possess, and some bonds, coupons, and jewelry—all taken from the deposit box. "Rubicon" appeared to be a projected coup d'état, the tax records material for blackmail of a cabinet minister, and the securities and jewelry perhaps a bribe from the Germans. At nearly the same time, the United States government communicated to the Quai d'Orsay newly obtained information about Caillaux's travels in South America. Minotto, whose improbable career included marriage in 1915 to Chicago meat-packing heiress Ida May Swift, had been arrested as a German agent and had described his contacts with Caillaux to American authorities. There were also two intercepted telegrams from Ambassador Luxburg to Count Albrecht von Bernstorff, the German ambassador to Washington, discussing Caillaux's possible value to Germany. None of this evidence was conclusive proof of treason, but it was extremely

43. Wythe Williams, *The Tiger of France: Conversations with Clemenceau* (New York, 1940), 153; Raymond Poincaré, *Au Service de la France* (10 vols.; Paris, 1926–33), IX, 382; JOC, Débats parlementaires, December 11, 22, 1917.

suspicious and suggestive. Poincaré and Briand declared themselves "disgusted" by it; Clemenceau crowed: "We've got him!" On January 14, 1918, they ordered Caillaux's arrest, confining him in La Santé prison among the common-law criminals he had so despised in 1914 when they surrounded Henriette.[44]

Despite Clemenceau's best efforts, and more than fifty interrogations of Caillaux by military authorities, there was insufficient evidence to convene a summary court-martial. After six months, Assistant Prosecutor Théodore Lescouvé, who had recommended the murder indictment of Henriette, assumed the role of examining magistrate for the case. He quickly completed an *instruction* for civilian justice and on October 29, 1918, secured an indictment against Caillaux for treason. Thirteen days later on November 11, Germany signed an armistice ending the fighting and admitting defeat: Clemenceau had won the war in less than a year after taking office. He did not intend to ruin the celebration by bringing Caillaux to trial immediately, and he saw no reason why his old enemy should not fester in prison for a time. The months of incarceration and anxiety had their effect, and by September, 1919, Caillaux had to be transferred from La Santé to a nursing home in Neuilly. Clemenceau finally set February 23, 1920, as the date for Caillaux's trial before the Senate. He carefully arranged it to follow senatorial elections that would take place in an atmosphere of white-hot nationalism.

During the trial, Caillaux faced almost every accusation that had ever been flung at him during his political career. The doubts about his Agadir negotiations were revived, and much was made of his opposition to the three-year-service law in 1913. But it was his wartime activities that led to the charge of treason. Caillaux associated too closely, far too closely, with Minotto, Almereyda, Bolo-Pasha, and Cavallini, all of them spies. He received letters from Lipscher and visits from Thérèse Duverger and Marx, all three agents directed by Baron Lancken. In South America, in Italy, and in France, he made himself the focus of conversations about a negotiated, compromise peace. The working papers of "Rubicon" betrayed his affinities for a personal, au-

44. For the remarks of Poincaré, Briand, and Clemenceau, see Suarez, *Briand*, III, 329; and Poincaré, *Au service*, X, 7–8.

tocratic rule. Put together, did these actions equal treason? For a France that had suffered through four and a half years of war and won victory at the cost of a million and a half men dead and millions more mutilated, Caillaux had stepped too far out of bounds. *Legally*, he might be innocent; *morally*, he was surely guilty. Charles Demange, who defended Dreyfus only after assuring himself that the charges were baseless, took Caillaux's case on the same condition. He impressed the senators with his plea of justice for Caillaux, but they were convinced that justice for France demanded some penalty. On April 22, by a vote of 213 to 28, the High Court found Caillaux innocent of treason or "intelligence with the enemy," the crimes covered in Articles 77 and 79 of the Criminal Code. By a vote of 150 to 91, it declared him guilty of Article 78, "damage to the external security of the state . . . such correspondence with the subjects of an enemy power as, without being directed toward treason, nonetheless results in furnishing the enemy with information deleterious to the political or military situation." He was sentenced to serve three years in prison, to lose his political rights for ten years, to banishment from all cities of over fifty thousand inhabitants except Toulouse, and to pay the expenses of the trial, fifty-three thousand francs. Because he had spent more than two years in La Santé awaiting trial, the prison term was set aside, and he was allowed to go immediately to Mamers.[45]

Eleven months earlier, Raoul Villain had finally been brought to trial for the assassination of Jaurès. He had spent the entire war in prison. Before the court, he claimed that he had killed Jaurès to prevent disorder during mobilization and that the thought of his nation had been uppermost in his mind as he pulled the trigger. His attorney, Alphonse Zévaès, urged leniency "in the name of victory which is now filling our hearts with joy." On March 29, 1919, the verdict was handed down: innocent. Mme Jaurès and her children, who brought suit as the *partie civile*, were ordered to pay the expenses of the trial. Reminiscing about the case and the war a few years later, Clemenceau would say, "I can never think without a shiver of the first, the very first, cause of

45. For Caillaux's trial, see *Gazette des Tribunaux*, November 11–12, 1918, September 21, October 24–25, 1919, February 18–19, 22, 26–28, March 5–7, 11–13, 17–18, 21, 24–27, April 2–3, 21–22, 28–29, 1920; and *Procès Caillaux; compte-rendu sommaire fait pour le syndicat de la presse parisienne; réquisitoire, plaidoiries, arrêt de condemnation* (Paris, 1920).

victory: the murder of Jaurès."[46] The ambiguity and relativism of "justice" is nowhere better illustrated than in the contrast between the Clemenceau of 1898 and the Clemenceau of 1919–20. To free Dreyfus, he pleaded the basic rights of the individual against the interests of the state. Two decades later, he vindicated the conviction of Caillaux and the acquittal of Villain on the grounds of national necessity.

IV

There is an interlocking pattern formed by the trials of Henriette Caillaux, Joseph Caillaux, and Raoul Villain. In their essence, all three were about political power and influence in France. This contest had been carried on throughout the Third Republic, but the stakes had never been so high. Politics ceased to be a game within the "Republic of pals"—as Robert de Jouvenel put it—and became literally a deadly struggle. The trials bracket World War I, providing a prelude and postlude to the event that would so markedly change life in France. The Belle Epoque died with the first charges on the western front. The justice rendered to Caillaux and Villain in 1919 and 1920 cleared up a residue left behind after that death, providing a last settling of scores. It was a reminder of a past so close but now so unrecoverable. It was also Calmette's revenge for Henriette's acquittal in 1914.

The trial of Henriette Caillaux resembled less a judicial hearing than a circus. The irregularities of procedure were impossible to overlook. It was absurdly easy to raise disturbing questions about the selection of the jury, about the zeal of Public Prosecutor Herbaux, and about the impartiality of Presiding Justice Albanel. There should have been cause for alarm because of suspicion about any single one of these elements in the process of justice. Suspicion about all three meant that Labori and the Caillauxs entered the courtroom with a verdict of innocence nearly foreordained.

No evidence exists that the seals on the box containing the names of potential jurors for the trial were tampered with, but there was no precedent for the judges charged to draw the names to find the seals broken when the box was presented to them. Certainly, the jury that emerged was highly favorable to the Caillauxs, and its composition was

46. For Villain's trial, see *Gazette des Tribunaux*, March 24–31, April 1, 1919. For Clemenceau's remark, see René Benjamin, *Clemenceau dans la retraite* (Paris, 1930), 139.

heavily weighted toward those groups that normally voted for the Radical party, small shopkeepers, artisans, and government workers: Paul Ferré (furrier), Louis Berthier (distiller), Antoine Mullet (piano tuner), Paul-Emile Barcat (secretary to the mayor of a Paris *arrondissement*), Félix Galopin (tax collector), Louis Besombes (demolitions worker), Emile Colbach (printer), Louis Rameau (architect), Victor Audouy ("worker"), Athanase Bardet (landowner), Jean Muraour (rentier), and Victor Obermayer (mechanic). They voted 11 to 1 for acquittal on all charges in spite of the fact that Henriette never denied firing the shots that killed Calmette.

Even if scrupulously impartial, the jurors could well have voted for acquittal because the case for the prosecution was so poorly presented. Herbaux was extremely reluctant to pose any questions that would cause the discomfiture of Henriette and her husband. And yet he made the first act of his elevation to public prosecutor the announcement that he would personally conduct the case for the state. If Herbaux had remained aloof, the task would have fallen to Assistant Prosecutor Théodore Lescouvé, who, unlike his superior, had no links to the Caillauxs. Charles Chenu for the *partie civile* managed to present a closely reasoned and very effective case against Henriette, but the jury was bound to regard his efforts with skepticism when Herbaux, as the representative of the Ministry of Justice and the state, refused to make as much of the same evidence and came to strikingly different conclusions about the motive in the crime. During the preparations for the trial and throughout the proceedings, there was a noticeable lack of cooperation between the parquet and Chenu, another testimony to Herbaux's disinclination to press the case against Henriette.

If Herbaux lacked ardor, Albanel was partisan. A friend of the Caillauxs, he solicited the case, although his announced term as presiding justice of the Cour d'Assises had to be shifted to accommodate it. During the trial, his bias was so obvious that one of the associate justices publicly rebuked him. Albanel maladroitly and unsuccessfully sought to prevent a reading of the letters turned over to the court by Berthe Gueydan. More serious, he permitted the defense to transform the trial into an attack on Gaston Calmette and *Le Figaro*. Caillaux was allowed to direct the proceedings of the court, although he had no standing except as the husband of the accused. Albanel sat quietly as Caillaux defamed *Le Figaro* and its editor, cast aspersions on the president of the Republic, Raymond Poincaré, and on two former premiers, Louis Barthou and Aristide Briand, and lashed out wildly at any friends of Calmette, like Henry Bernstein, loyal enough to defend his honor. Albanel also did not budge when Ceccaldi denounced Victor Fabre, a fellow magistrate, and claimed that Fabre's assistant, Bloque-Laroque, shared this opinion. Bloque-Laroque would publicly deny the insinuation and demand satisfaction from Ceccaldi for this lie. Finally and most important, Albanel worded his instructions to the jury in a manner that made acquittal more likely. He was authorized to require replies from the jury to four questions: (1) Did Henriette Caillaux fire the shots that hit Calmette? (2) Did she mean to cause his death? (3) Did she mean to fire the shots? (4) Did she do so with premeditation? The jury could not have avoided returning a guilty verdict on the first question because Henriette could not deny that, willfully or not, it was her finger that pulled the trigger. Instead, Albanel had the jury consider only the latter two questions, to which they replied that she was innocent.

Caillaux won his wife's freedom, but through the invocation of principles that would eventually be turned on him. The first, never explicitly elaborated in the courtroom but never absent from thought, was a version of *raison d'état*, of expediency. To convict Henriette Caillaux was to end the career of Joseph Caillaux. He often stood beside her at the defendant's rail to emphasize this point, the figurative beside the literal defendant. But the nation, he assured the court, had need of him: he was the glory of the Republic, the only man who could enact the income tax and maintain peace with Germany. To destroy him would be to do the work of Calmette and his antirepublican friends at *Le Figaro*. Despite the evidence, Henriette would have to be acquitted in order for Caillaux to continue the great work he had begun. The other principle, more dangerous still to justice, was the notion of a "higher law." Calmette, so this argument went, made himself an outlaw by publishing a private letter. Never mind that the letter did not touch Henriette or that her fears about letters naming her were groundless, Calmette deserved to be shot. The law might declare otherwise, but there were times when the law was insufficient, when what was legal was not what was moral, when "justice" demanded a sanction, when honor was a "higher law." To argue in this fashion, to invoke *raison d'état* for no purpose grander than his own career, to identify himself with the destiny of the nation, to justify murder and censorship by the bullet through the pathetic excuse of preventing the appearance of adulterous love letters, Caillaux revealed himself as an arrogant, opportunistic egomaniac. Calmette's campaign to remove such a man from a position of power found its ultimate justification.

Qui culpae ignoscit uni, suadet pluribus: pardon one offense and you encourage the commission of many. If Henriette Caillaux could kill Gaston Calmette with impunity, Raoul Villain could kill Jean Jaurès and expect to be freed. He was brought to trial in Paris at a time when the euphoria of victory was still fresh and at a time when extravagant gains could still be expected from the peace negotiations. Villain's defense wrapped him in this cloak of victory. He had acted, his attorney claimed, from misplaced patriotism, from a surfeit of zeal, from the mistaken belief that Jaurès would oppose the mobilization. The shot was fired only to assure that France would win the war. In contrast to Henriette's trial, there was no sustained attack on the victim by the defense. Jaurès was termed a patriot, although a pacifist, and France's loss through his death was said to be great. But his intemperate language was also recalled: how he had urged the proletariat of all European nations to rise in general strike rather than answer the call of mobilization, how he had opposed French imperialism in Morocco and when criticizing the government's policy had referred to *your*, not *our*, soldiers. Jaurès would have supported the French war effort in 1914, the defense readily agreed, but he had given hostages to fortune by his words. And so Villain had fired his gun.

Villain spent nearly five years in prison before his trial. He missed all of the fighting in which more than a third of the male members of his generation died. The court found this combination of penalty and blessing sufficient expiation for his crime and ordered his release. He was freed in spite of the evidence, for he never denied shooting at Jaurès with premeditation. His act was excused because left unspoken at the trial was the belief—the certainty in the minds of many—that had Jaurès lived, he would have been a constant critic of the conduct of the war and a rallying point for all those who hoped for a compromise peace. His greatest influence had been among the intellectuals and the working class, both of whom shared in the zeal of nationalism early in the war but lost their taste for it by mid-1916. During the crisis of 1917, Jaurès would surely have opposed Clemenceau's policy of total war at a time when France could not have afforded division. For the sake of national unity, Clemenceau might have had to order his arrest. Villain's bullet saved France that agony. Expediency demanded that he be acquitted and released. The notion that he had acted in the best tradition of patriotism, risking his life to serve his nation, provided the justification. For daring to challenge this "higher law," Mme Jaurès and her children were condemned to pay the expenses of the trial.

Because Jaurès had not lived, Caillaux became, in Poincaré's phrase, the "crossroads of all the paths of treason." His arrest in 1917 was as necessary to the French war effort as the removal of Malvy from the Ministry of the Interior a few months earlier. It was a symbol of France's determination to fight the war to the finish and to reject any conditional peace. It was Clemenceau's means of placing his domestic opponents on notice that disunity would not be tolerated. With Caillaux in prison on a charge of treason, there was no alternative to Clemenceau and no alternative to a Clemenceau policy. France's victory less than a year later supplied as much vindication as history has ever provided.

Caillaux's conviction when he was brought before the High Court in 1920 was all but predetermined. No senator had forgotten his arrogance and his disdain: those who have no mercy are rarely granted it. Some senators recalled their anger at how Henriette escaped punishment in 1914, and more understood that her acquittal had allowed Caillaux to play his role during the war. But clearly, Caillaux's semi-treasonous wartime activities were paramount. To acquit him was to find Clemenceau a tyrant and the total victory by France too costly; to acquit was to desecrate victory. Caillaux had to be punished for failing to believe in French destiny. There are times when justice must fit the crime despite the evidence and despite the law. Gaston Calmette would have smiled.

POSTSCRIPT AND CONCLUSION

Plus ça change, plus c'est la même chose: the more things change, the more they remain the same.

Serge Alexandre "Sacha" Stavisky was born in 1886 to Russian Jewish parents of modest circumstances in Kiev. At the turn of the century, the family moved to Paris, where his father set himself up as a dentist in one of the poorer quarters. In 1908 at the age of twenty-two, the young Stavisky had his first brush with the law over fraud and worthless checks. A second arrest brought him his first prison sentence in 1912—over which his father committed suicide in despair. It was clear that Stavisky had drifted into the petty underworld of Paris with its pimps, prostitutes, drugs, confidence games, and fencing of stolen property. The prison experience merely placed him among experts at these trades, and he graduated with new talents and the advice to win friends in high places.

Throughout his life, Stavisky never really altered his activities. He was always the confidence man, but he grew more sophisticated in his tactics, more ambitious in his targets, and more careful to acquire the trappings of respectability. After accumulating money through various shady practices, he bought the Empire Theater in Paris and a string of racehorses, financed some newspapers, and began to frequent gambling houses where he attracted fancy mistresses. He now had a secure place in the demimonde and mixed with socialites, adventurers, dissolutes, and politicians. Any of them could be useful friends, and to secure his future even further, Stavisky ingratiated himself with the

Sûreté by occasionally acting as an informer. Nevertheless, he mishandled a major deception in 1926 and finally landed in serious difficulty. Two stockbrokers charged him with defrauding them of seven million francs, and while the magistrature endeavored to discover where his deceits began and ended, Stavisky was held in the Santé prison. In 1927, after serving eighteen months, he was released on provisional liberty with the intention that he finally face trial.

During the next seven years, the trial was postponed nineteen times. In the end, it never took place at all. Stavisky had friends among the police, among politicians, and therefore in certain ministries and the legislature. These in turn had friends and could exercise their influence in Stavisky's favor. Bureaucracies work slowly at best, and in France during the 1920s and 1930s they worked somewhat more slowly than usual. Postponements were easy to obtain; files were misplaced, found only later, and then misplaced again. Doing a favor for a friend of a friend was not corrupt in the venal sense of the word, and Stavisky was not unique in avoiding trial and punishment. He actually spent very little money guaranteeing the postponements, although some small amounts went to professional go-betweens and to a few others who were paid to remain quiet.

While free, Stavisky returned to his old practices, growing richer and enlarging his circle of friendships among useful politicians, ministers, police officials, magistrates, and newspaper editors. The attention of the police was called to his affairs no less than forty-five times during these seven years, but nothing was done about them. Among these rackets was Stavisky's well-honed tactic of using his influence with politicians to be named the agent in the floating of a city's municipal bonds. He would cover the bonds with deposits of stolen property—largely jewels—or by skillfully dishonest bookkeeping. He would then discount the bonds through a legitimate bank and use the funds for yet another devious scheme. The maturity date on the bonds imposed a time limit for the enterprise, but Stavisky always managed to cover each set of bonds legitimately through the proceeds of another operation. In this manner, he absconded with ten million francs of bonds from the city of Orléans in 1928 but managed to repay them through the profits he made on the use of the money. At Bayonne, Fr 239 million of bonds were issued from 1932 to 1933 through the municipal pawnshop, as Stavisky carried out his operation with the support of the mayor, who was also a Radical-Socialist deputy. This time, however, there was no way to cover the bonds legitimately, and on Christmas Eve, 1933, one of his confederates, a certain Tissier, lost his nerve and confessed. Almost everyone connected with Stavisky was quickly arrested: Tissier, Joseph Garat, the deputy and mayor, Albert Dubarry, from the left-wing *La Volonté* and the reigning blackmailer of Paris, and Camille Aymard, from the right-wing *La Liberté*. Clearly, Stavisky had maintained a wide variety of contacts, but now he disappeared.

On January 3, 1934, the Stavisky case came to national attention when *L'Action Française* published two letters from Albert Dalimier, then the minister of colonies, in which as minister of labor and social welfare during 1932 he recommended the purchase of Bayonne Municipal Pawnshop bonds. Evidently, a minister had gone out of his way to endorse a fraud. The Paris press also quickly established that Stavisky had been under indictment for fraud since 1927 and that his trial had been postponed those nineteen times. This revelation involved Antoine Pressard, the public prosecutor, in the controversy. Because Pressard was the brother-in-law of the premier, Camille Chautemps, long a power in the Radical party, the trial of corruption had the possibility of leading to the highest ranks of the government. There were immediate demands from many sectors for Dalimier's resignation and for the appointment of a committee to investigate and clarify the responsibilities involved in the affair.

Initially, the police claimed that Stavisky could not be found. There was much reason to suspect that they did not want to find him, and a rumor circulated that the Sûreté had recently furnished him with a false passport in the hope that he would flee abroad. But by the end of the first week in January, with headlines in the Paris newspapers demanding that Stavisky be produced and compelled to testify about his protectors, the Sûreté finally grew serious about locating him. By what seemed a remarkably fortuitous coincidence, it was announced on January 8 that Stavisky had been tracked to a villa above Chamonix but had committed suicide as the agents were breaking down the door.

Few Frenchmen accepted this account from a police they had long believed to be brutal and corrupt. Awkward men had a way of dying in their custody. Much of the aroused press echoed these sentiments openly: some wrote *suicide* in quotation marks, some flatly termed Stavisky's death a murder. The truth, finally revealed by a special legislative investigating committee in 1935, was more complicated. "Beyond the shadow of doubt," Stavisky shot himself in the head as the Sûreté broke into the villa, but to call his death a suicide was "somewhat forced." Stavisky failed to inflict a lethal wound, but the agents left him unattended on the floor for more than an hour while he died very slowly. A shocked committee concluded that "this extraordinary negligence finished the task which Stavisky had begun. . . . Would it have been possible to take Stavisky alive? We believe the answer is yes. Beyond doubt, there was no attempt by the police to make a normal arrest and conserve for justice an accused of his importance."

Six weeks later, at the end of February, there was another mysterious death. The drugged body of Albert Prince, an assistant prosecutor and the man said to have carried out Pressard's orders to postpone the Stavisky trial so many times, was discovered tied to the railroad tracks not far from Dijon. It had been dismembered by the passage of the Paris express. Prince was rumored to have been holding documents that would prove the guilt of his superior, but these were never found. Only the memory of his allegations remained. But even allegations were enough to rekindle the charges of police murder. The respectable *Journal des Débats* asserted that "public opinion believes in the existence of a gangster organization, driven insane with fear, capable of anything and ready to do anything to hide the truth and thwart justice." When Prince's death was labeled a suicide, the newspapers mounted their own inquiry by hiring detectives, including Georges Simenon and the former chief of Scotland Yard, Sir Basil Thompson. The truth was never established, the mystery of this horrible and complicated death never solved. After many weeks, the investigation was quietly dropped.[1]

World War I changed much about French society, but as the Stavisky affair demonstrated so clearly, justice remained as far from the ideal as it had during the Belle Epoque. Between 1890 and 1920, five elements combined to produce the hypocrisy of justice: political interfer-

1. For the Stavisky affair, see APP, E A/85, Affaire Stavisky; and the Rapport général in JOC, Documents, 1935, No. 4886. There is a good summation in Eugen Weber, *The Action Française: Royalism and Reaction in Twentieth-Century France* (Stanford, 1962), 319–22, 348–49. For the atmosphere of the period, see Alexander Werth, *The Twilight of France, 1933–1940*, ed. Denis W. Brogan (New York, 1942).

ence in the judicial process, government corruption and inefficiency, the structure of the magistrature, nationalism as a hidden agenda, and the Republic as a stalemate society. Only nationalism was absent from the sordid saga of Stavisky, and that was because victory in 1918 ended its sway over French emotions. What must be explained is the prevalence of these five elements in the justice of the Belle Epoque and their cheerful acceptance by the Third Republic.

The men of government, politicians and high civil servants, traversed the multiple layers of a Parisian society the outward stratification of which was illusory. They inhabited a glittering world of power and incredible hauteur but also maintained contacts with the Bohemian enclave of the arts and felt the enticement of the demimonde. Propriety and respectability had ambiguous meanings when "to pay a call on the president of the Senate" was the euphemism among not just politicians but all men of the world for soliciting the favors of a great courtesan. Meg Steinheil walked in the half-light of this region, as did Thérèse Humbert, each looking for the wealthy who would provide the sustenance of her dreams. This was also the world of Rochette, of Bolo-Pasha, Almereyda, and Cavallini, of Daniel Wilson, and of the Panama Canal scandal's Cornelius Herz and Baron Jacques de Reinach. Few politicians were immune to the lure held out by this world of easy virtue where the rules were forgotten, where money and friendships were easy—too easy, for the money and friends of this world were haunting. The money too lightly invested or accepted, the favors too lightly granted, the women too lightly confided in, all were the sort of the demimonde. And like pitch, the demimonde stuck.[2]

There were embarrassments that had to be suppressed when brought up in the future and friends who remembered too much after a man became important. And so there was political interference in the process of justice, occasionally in a savage fashion. This factor was decisive in the cases of Alfred Dreyfus, Joseph Caillaux, and Henri Rochette. Dreyfus and Caillaux were convicted because "France," in the person of Minister of War Mercier and Premier Clemenceau, respectively, re-

2. See, for example, Anne Manson, "Quand les Trois Grandes régnaient sur Paris," in Gilbert Guilleminault (ed.), *Le Romain vrai de la Troisième République: La Belle Epoque* (Paris, 1957), 163–96. See also Karen M. Offen, "Aspects of the Woman Question During the French Third Republic," *Third Republic/Troisième République*, III–IV (1977), 1–19.

quired a traitor. Rochette received his postponement and additional time in which to continue his frauds and to make his escape, because he threatened to embarrass the party of the cabinet in power. In the cases of Serge Stavisky, Raoul Villain, Henriette Caillaux, Thérèse Humbert, and Marguerite Steinheil, the impact of political interference is less clear but also apparent. Stavisky's case was postponed and postponed but not dropped. Instead, in order to avoid his revelations about this favoritism, he was allowed to die in what was very close to a police murder. Raoul Villain's trial was delayed until the furor over the assassination of Jaurès had been replaced by euphoria over victory, thus guaranteeing his acquittal. To save the position of Henriette Caillaux's politically powerful husband, there may have been tampering with the entire trial process—prosecution, presiding justice, and jury—in her case. During twenty years of civil suits, Thérèse Humbert benefited from her father-in-law's influence—active or passive. The magistrates laid aside their skepticism when the daughter-in-law of a former minister of justice appeared before them and told remarkable tales about missing American millionaires. The best explanation of Meg Steinheil's baffling case assumes the intervention of an examining magistrate to cover up the participation of an important figure from an allied nation.

Justice also fumbled because like many figures in the government—Camille Pelletan comes immediately to mind—the police were venal and incompetent. Anatole France's Crainquebille had much basis in fact: an old hawker arrested for blocking a policeman while waiting for several sous owed him for vegetables and at the precinct station falsely charged with having shouted, "Down with the *flics!*" Burlingham, Couillard, and Wolff in the Steinheil affair were as defenseless and as innocent as Crainquebille and nearly suffered trial for murder. Evidence was trumped up against them as it was against Dreyfus and Caillaux. Just as the police could persecute the guiltless, so they could understand how the demands of *raison d'état* could dictate ignoring complaints filed against Stavisky or Thérèse Humbert, acquitting the clearly guilty Henriette Caillaux and Raoul Villain, and overlooking the complicity of Meg Steinheil. But not all of the failures of the police were by design. The investigation of the Steinheil murders demonstrated an alarming laxity in procedure. The inability to track down the Humberts in no fewer than seven months when there was such a clear trail was incapacity so extraordinary that the chief of the Sûreté was replaced and charges were made that this hunt, like the one later for Stavisky, was pursued with less than alacrity.[3]

The magistrature accepted, tolerated, or ignored this interference and incompetence, because its justices, prosecutors, and examining magistrates were civil servants whose struggle for promotion made them susceptible to political influence. Attorneys and magistrates pursued their careers separately, each law student electing one of the two routes upon completion of his degree. The greatest members of the Paris bar commanded enormous fees, but the chances of failing in this intensely competitive atmosphere were great. Magistrates had security of tenure, but they were poorly paid at every level and had only promotion as a means of increasing their income. To be stricken from the promotion list even at the relatively important level of examining magistrate in Paris, as Leydet was in 1908, meant the end of any hope for a successful career. Too often, advancement was dependent upon catering to the whims of the current minister of justice or permanent officials at the ministry like Jacquin. When men of influence had the power to advance a magistrate from the provinces to a position in Paris—or the reverse, as in Fabre's case—and to elevate a magistrate suddenly in the hierarchy, as was Herbaux's good fortune in 1914, justices and prosecutors became more nearly government officials than impartial arbiters.[4]

Procedure compounded the possibilities for injustice. During the investigation of a crime, there was often more competition than cooperation between the ordinary police and the better-paid, more celebrated Sûreté or between the parquet and the Sûreté, as occurred during the search for the Humberts. The examining magistrate assigned to the case had extraordinary powers. He could order a suspect confined to prison while he gathered evidence against him, even if the

3. Jacques Anatole Thibault [Anatole France], *Crainquebille, Putois, Riquet* (Paris, 1904).
4. See Maurice Garçon, *Histoire de la justice sous la Troisième République* (3 vols.; Paris, 1959); Robert Charles Kirkwood Ensor, *Courts and Judges in France, Germany, and England* (Oxford, 1933); René David and Henry de Vries, *The French Legal System* (New York, 1958); George O. Junosza-Zdrojewski, *Le Crime et la presse* (Paris, 1943); and Benjamin F. Martin, "The Courts, the Magistrature, and Promotions in Third Republic France, 1871–1914," *American Historical Review*, LXXXVII (October, 1982), 977–1009.

process required many months, as it did in the cases of Meg Steinheil and Thérèse Humbert. Without any formal conviction, he could also condemn suspects to ten days of solitary confinement in a cell without windows or light. During the trial, the defendant was required to submit to the *interrogatoire* with the knowledge that a refusal to respond to questions would be regarded by the jury as tantamount to a confession. At the same time, defendants and attorneys were permitted enormous latitude in making dramatic speeches, gestures, and summations to appeal to the emotions of the jury. This tactic was successful for Meg Steinheil, who revealed herself a Sarah Bernhardt of the Assises; it made Thérèse Humbert appear a mummer and a charlatan. Attorneys were always aware that juries were charged not just with determining whether the defendant had committed the crime but whether that guilt was culpable. The trick in defending a guilty client lay in convincing the jury that the act was not blameworthy, as the juries did decide in the cases of Henriette Caillaux and Raoul Villain. Some few attorneys like Charles Demange and Henri Robert preferred to make a simple, rational summation. More often, the jury was confronted with a melodramatic appeal by an accomplished orator such as Antony Aubin or Fernand Labori.

Few of these appeals had more power than nationalism. In proclaiming France's need for revanche to expunge the shame of the defeat of 1870–1871 and the loss of Alsace and Lorraine, Léon Gambetta set the pattern by cautioning Frenchmen never to speak of it but always to remember it. The theme acted as a hidden agenda throughout the entire first half of the Third Republic. Corruption in government was denounced as enfeebling the state at a time when it should be preparing for tests to come; General Georges Boulanger's brief fling as a man on horseback in the late 1880s was made possible by his reputation as the only Frenchman to stand up to Bismarck; the huge new empire of "France d'outre-mer" was a substitute for victory in Europe. For between 1870 and 1914, the Third Republic grew to maturity in the shadow of defeat by Germany and consequently suffered from intense ambivalence toward its eastern neighbor. There was an admiration for things German—because they seemed modern and successful—but at the same time, and within the same Frenchmen, a revulsion toward them as the traditions of the enemy. French economic, intellectual, and political institutions and thought were often purposely the antithesis of German equivalents. And behind this subtle influence of Germany on the whole of French society was the thought that on some future day the black crepe of mourning veiling the statue representing the city of Strasbourg in the Place de la Concorde would be removed as the French marched victoriously into Alsace and Lorraine.[5]

In the interim, and for good reason, nationalism was an intensely emotional issue that played a curious role in the sensational trials of the first half of the Third Republic. Were Alsatians and Lorrainers potential traitors or the most passionate of the *revanchistes*? The Alsatian origins of Alfred Dreyfus counted against him because most of his family had chosen to remain behind under German jurisdiction after 1871. Yet Meg Steinheil used her own Alsation birth to good purpose, evoking sympathy for a girl who had lost the land of her childhood. Thérèse Humbert also tried to exploit the issue of the lost provinces by claiming that the Crawford millions had their source in the Franco-Prussian War and that she had been the dupe of the traitor Régnier. In his summation for Henriette Caillaux at the end of July, 1914, Labori concluded with a stirring call to set aside intestine quarrels to face the hereditary foe: the French should rise as one man to seize the moment of revanche. Joseph Caillaux was convicted of a form of treason precisely because he refused to believe that revanche was worth the cost. Raoul Villain was acquitted of Jaurès' assassination because he considered revanche so vital that even murder could be excused in its name.

The trials of Meg Steinheil, Thérèse Humbert, and Henriette Caillaux were the most sensational criminal cases between 1900 and 1914. The lives of these women, and the investigations into the shocking crimes with which they were charged, illuminate the specific tangle of politics, money, and sex that was an important ingredient in the stalemate society of the Belle Epoque. All three were women of strong character, and two of them, Meg Steinheil and Thérèse Humbert, were exceptionally able. They dedicated their lives to the creation, and committed their crimes for the maintenance, of an artificial existence. Meg

5. See Claude Digeon, *La Crise allemande de la pensée française, 1870–1914* (Paris, 1959); Herbert L. Tint, *The Decline of French Patriotism, 1870–1940* (London, 1964); Eugen Weber, *The French Nationalist Revival, 1905–1914* (Berkeley, 1959); and Alan Mitchell, *The German Influence in France After 1870: The Formation of the French Republic* (Chapel Hill, 1979).

Steinheil became a species of prostitute whose meretricious salon attracted the glittering elite of the Third Republic. The gigantic fraud mounted by Thérèse Humbert seemed such an alluring and lucrative scheme that bourgeois investors abandoned their proverbial financial caution to make reckless loans. Henriette Caillaux gambled her reputation and future on a successful liaison with a prominent politician only to discover that the price of victory—marriage—was having to defend the gamble forever from revelation. In a world that was less male-dominated and less the product of simulation, these women might have discovered outlets for their talents and energies that were more conventional and honorable. All three women married men who were essentially dilettantes, part of a culture that may be termed anti-necessitarian. Each husband lived on the reputation and wealth of his father. Adolphe Steinheil dabbled at his art with no compulsion toward creativity and little toward sales; Frédéric Humbert played at politics and law and saw life as a confidence game; Joseph Caillaux ultimately made politics his passion, but he entered public life as a pastime. These men and their wives were part of a social order that the great mass of Frenchmen could rarely aspire to—that is what made Thérèse Humbert so unusual in her extraordinary ascension from peasant origins. Except for their crimes, the lives of Meg Steinheil, Thérèse Humbert, and Henriette Caillaux would never have become dependent on the decisions of their social inferiors who sat in judgment of them on the jury.

Political liberties were largely illusory in Third Republic France in spite of the slogan LIBERTÉ, EGALITE, FRATERNITÉ. In the absence of truly organized political parties to finance legislative elections, most candidates had to be so wealthy that they were entirely unrepresentative of their constituents. Even the deputies of the Socialist party were middle-class almost to a man. Jury decisions were one of the few realms of complete freedom in which the manners and mores of the society were revealed without a veil. And yet, because the answers to the presiding justice's questions were presented without commentary, it is not always easy to interpret what a decision disclosed. In Henriette Caillaux's case, there was a declaration that the traditional rights of honor and revenge could not be trammeled by artificial laws against them. Mere legislation could not understand the dark and tragic side of human life: public opinion approved, or at least condoned, the crime of passion and granted it a sympathetic awe. "I shall kill him and I shall be acquitted" was an expletive that provoked no rebuke. The extenuating circumstances granted Thérèse Humbert seem to have derived from a genuine admiration for her success in beating the system, in bilking the haughty and hated financiers, and from her having to pay the penalty of prison when the magistrature and political system that made her frauds possible escaped without punishment. Meg Steinheil's acquittal is less easy to explain. An oddly ineffective prosecution and the baffling evidence were factors in her favor, and she won support through a brilliant performance at the defendant's rail. Most important, she appeared to have been a victim not just of strange intruders, as she claimed, but of the machinery of state justice.

Is there a justification for these decisions? They were clearly at variance with the ideal of justice as the discovery of truth and the due apportionment of guilt and innocence to each individual. Could more have been expected? It is reasonable to presume that the Third Republic and the Belle Epoque, hypocritical as they were in other respects, should have experienced hypocrisy in justice.[6]

6. See Howard Zehr, *Crime and the Development of Modern Society: Patterns of Criminality in Nineteenth-Century Germany and France* (Totowa, N.J., 1977); Mary S. Hartman, *Victorian Murderesses: A True History of Thirteen Respectable French and English Women Accused of Unspeakable Crimes* (New York, 1977); Jean-Louis Costa, *Liberté, ordre publique et justice en France* (3 vols.; Paris, 1967); Marcel Rousselet, *Les Cas de conscience du magistrat* (Paris, 1967); Louis Casamayor, *La Justice, l'homme, et la liberté* (Grenoble, 1964); Maurice Aydalot, *Magistrat* (Paris, 1975); Raoul de La Grasserie, *De la justice en France et à l'étranger au XXe siècle* (3 vols.; Paris, 1914); Antonin Besson, *Le Mythe de la justice* (Paris, 1973); Denis Langlois, *Les Dossiers noirs de la justice française* (Paris, 1977); Jean Imbert and Georges Levasseur, *Le Pouvoir, les juges, et les bourreaux* (Paris, 1972); André Cambréal, *Le Jury criminel* (Paris, 1937); René Bondoux, *Les Incohérences de la justice* (Paris, 1946); and Georges Guilhermet, *Souvenirs d'un avocat de la Belle Epoque* (Paris, 1952).

BIBLIOGRAPHY

I. Unpublished Government Documents

Archives Nationales, Series BB 6 I, Dossiers de mouvement des magistrats, Premiers Cours et Tribunaux, An VIII–1925
   524^4 Registres du personnel de la magistrature, 1864–99
   524^5 Registres du personnel de la magistrature, 1899–1925
Archives Nationales, Series BB 6 II, Dossiers personnels de magistrats, 1842–1942
   445 Baudouin, Louis
   616 Albanel, Jean Marie Louis
   620 André, Jean Louis
   650 Baudouin, Manuel Achille
   670 Bidault de l'Isle, Benoit Marie Albert
   679 Blondel, Louis Marie Joseph
   690 Bonnet, François Gaston
   695 Boucard, Louis Emile Henri
   788 Dagoury, Louis René
   850 Fabre, Victor Albin
   939 Herbaux, Jules Emile
   951 Jacquin, Etienne Edmond
   1009 Lemercier, Charles Louis Athanase Abel Joseph
   1020 Lescouvé, Théodore Paul
   1025 Leydet, Félix Pierre Joseph
   1083 Monier, Ferdinand
   1256 Trouard-Riolle, Paul Adolphe
   1267 de Valles, Charles Bernard Théodore Médéric

Archives Nationales, Series BB 18, Correspondance de procureurs généraux avec la garde des sceaux (division criminelle)

  2314 (1905)

  2339^2 (1906)

  2358^2 (1907)

  2369 (1908)

  2377^2 (1908)

  2388 (1908)

  2417 (1909)

  2435 (1910)

  2441 (1910)

  2444 (1911)

  2457 (1911)

  2460 (1911)

  2462 (1911)

  2462^1 (1911)

  2466 (1911)

  2467 (1911)

  2471^2 (1911)

  2474 (1911)

  2475 (1911)

  2491 (1912)

Archives Nationales, Series BB 20, Comptes-rendus d'assises au ministère de la justice, 1800–95

  284–285 Comptes-rendus des assises-prisons, 1820–71

  286–293 Comptes-rendus des affaires jugées par les cours d'assises, 1877–95

Archives de la Préfecture de Police, Paris, Series B A

  81–85 Crimes

  497 Faits divers

  878 Seliverstoff—Xau

  988 G. Calmette

  1017 Mort de M. Félix Faure

  1072 Mort de M. Félix Faure

  1584 Affaire Steinheil

  1612 Crimes

  1625 J. Caillaux

  1683 J. Caillaux

  6022–6027 Mort de M. Félix Faure

Archives de la Préfecture de Police, Paris, Series E A
    85 Affaire Stavisky
    118 Affaire Humbert

II. Parliamentary Papers

Journal Officiel. Chambre des Députés, Débats parlementaires
Journal Officiel. Chambre des Députés, Documents

III. Newspapers

L'Aurore, 1899
L'Echo de Paris, 1900–20
Le Figaro, 1898–1920
La Gazette des Tribunaux, Journal de jurisprudence et des débats judiciaires, 1898–1920
L'Homme Libre, 1913–14
Le Journal du Peuple, 1899
La Libre Parole, 1895–99
Le Matin, 1902–14
Le Temps, 1914

IV. Books, Articles, and Dissertations

Affaire Caillaux, Loustalot, et Comby, inculpés d'attentat contre la sûreté de l'état; procédure générale; interrogatoires. Paris, 1919.
Allain, Jean-Claude. *Joseph Caillaux: Le défi victorieux, 1863–1914*. Paris, 1978.
Amiel, Henri Frédéric. *Journal Intime*. Translated by Van Wyck Brooks and Charles Van Wyck Brooks as *The Private Journal of Henri Frédéric Amiel*. Rev. ed. New York, 1935.
Ammar, Catherine. *La Tête qui roule*. Paris, 1951.
Aujol, Jean-Louis. *Les Mains de Pilate: Adresse à la justice politique*. Paris, 1976.
Aydalot, Maurice. *Magistrat*. Paris, 1975.
Barrès, Maurice. *Dans le cloaque*. Paris, 1914.
———. *En regardant au fond des crevasses*. Paris, 1917.
Bellanger, Claude, *et al.*, eds. *Histoire générale de la presse française*. 5 vols. Paris, 1969–76.

Benjamin, René. *Clemenceau dans la retraite*. Paris, 1930.

Benoist, Charles. *Souvenirs*. 3 vols. Paris, 1932–34.

Besson, Antonin. *Le Mythe de justice*. Paris, 1973.

Binet-Valmar, Gustave. *Une femme a tué*. Paris, 1924.

Binion, Rudolph. *Defeated Leaders: The Political Fate of Caillaux, Jouvenel, and Tardieu*. New York, 1960.

Bondoux, René. *Les Incohérences de la justice*. Paris, 1946.

Boniface de Castellane, Count Marie Paul Ernest. *Confessions of the Marquis de Castellane*. London, 1924.

Braibant, Charles. *Félix Faure à L'Elysée: Souvenirs de Louis Le Gall*. Paris, 1963.

Brogan, Denis W. *The Development of Modern France, 1870–1939*. London, 1940.

Caillaux, Joseph Marie Auguste. *Agadir, ma politique extérieure*. Paris, 1919.

———. *Mes Mémoires*. 3 vols. Paris, 1942–47.

Cambréal, André. *Le Jury criminel*. Paris, 1937.

Casamayor, Louis. *Le Bras séculier: Justice et police*. Paris, 1960.

———. *La Justice, l'homme, et la liberté*. Grenoble, 1964.

Chapman, Guy. *The Dreyfus Case: A Reassessment*. London, 1955.

Charles, Ernest. "Camille Pelletan." *Revue politique et parlementaire*, June, 1900, pp. 625–54.

Charles, Raymond. *La Justice en France*. 3rd ed. Paris, 1964.

Charvin, Robert. *Justice et politique: Evolution de leurs rapports*. Paris, 1968.

Chastenet, Jacques. *La France de M. Fallières, une époque pathétique*. Paris, 1950.

Chenu, Charles-Maurice. *Le Procès de Madame Caillaux*. Paris, 1960.

Chrestien, Michel. *L'Affaire Steinheil*. Paris, 1958.

Churchill, Winston. *Great Contemporaries*. New York, 1937.

Cobb, Richard. "The Memoirs of Marie Besnard." In *A Second Identity: Essays on France and French History*. London, 1969.

Costa, Jean-Louis. *Liberté, ordre publique et justice en France*. 3 vols. Paris, 1967.

David, René, and Henry de Vries. *The French Legal Sysem*. New York, 1958.

Digeon, Claude. *La Crise allemande de la pensée française, 1870–1914*. Paris, 1959.

Dominique, Pierre. "Les Cinq coups de revolver de Madame Caillaux (16 Mars 1914)." In *Le Roman vrai de la Troisième République:*

Avant 14, Fin de la Belle Epoque, edited by Gilbert Guilleminault. Paris, 1957.

Dudley, Ernest. *The Scarlett Widow.* London, 1960.

Durand, Claude. *Les Rapports entre les jurisdictions administrative et judiciaire.* Paris, 1956.

Durand-Barthez, Pascal. *Histoire des structures du Ministère de la justice, 1789–1945.* Paris, 1973.

Elwitt, Sanford. *The Making of the Third Republic: Class and Politics in France, 1868–1884.* Baton Rouge, 1975.

Ensor, Robert Charles Kirkwood. *Courts and Judges in France, Germany, and England.* Oxford, 1933.

Eschaich, René. *Les Monstres sacrés de la IIIe République.* Paris, 1974.

Fabre-Luce, Alfred. *Caillaux.* Paris, 1933.

Fleurieu, Roger de. *Joseph Caillaux au cours d'un demi-siècle de notre histoire.* Paris, 1951.

Floriot, René. *Au banc de la défense.* Paris, 1959.

––––––. *Deux femmes en cour d'assises: Madame Steinheil et Madame Caillaux.* Paris, 1966.

––––––. *Les Erreurs judiciaires.* Paris, 1968.

France, Ministère de la Justice. *Compte général de l'administration de la justice criminelle.* Paris, 1825–.

Garçon, Maurice. *Histoire de la justice sous la Troisième République.* 3 vols. Paris, 1959.

Goldberg, Harvey. *The Life of Jean Jaurès.* Madison, 1962.

Gorsse, Pierre de. *La Justice égarée par les femmes.* Paris, 1946.

Gueydan, Berthe-Eva. *Les Rois de la République.* 2 vols. Paris, 1925.

Guilhermet, Georges. *Souvenirs d'un avocat de la Belle Epoque.* Paris, 1952.

Guimard, Paul. "Thérèse Humbert." In *Le Roman vrai de la Troisième République: Prélude à la Belle Epoque,* edited by Gilbert Guilleminault. Paris, 1956.

Hamlin, Jean. "Interview with Marguerite Japy, veuve Steinheil, Scarlett-Abinger." *Ici Paris,* April 15, 1947.

Hartman, Mary S. *Victorian Murderesses: A True History of Thirteen Respectable French and English Women Accused of Unspeakable Crimes.* New York, 1977.

Heppenstall, Rayner. *A Little Pattern of French Crime.* London, 1969.

Hoffman, Stanley, et al. *In Search of France.* Cambridge, Mass., 1963.

Holt, Edgar. *The Tiger: The Life of Georges Clemenceau, 1841–1929.* London, 1976.

Howard, Michael. *The Franco-Prussian War: The German Invasion of France, 1870–1871*. London, 1961.

Imbert, Jean, and Georges Levasseur. *Le Pouvoir, les juges, et les bourreaux*. Paris, 1972.

Johnson, Douglas W. *France and the Dreyfus Affair*. London, 1966.

Johnson, Severance. *The Enemy Within*. New York, 1919.

Jouvenel, Robert de. *La République des camarades*. Paris, 1913.

Junosza-Zdrojewski, Georges O. *Le Crime et la presse*. Paris, 1943.

Kelsen, Hans. *What Is Justice? Justice, Law, and Politics in the Mirror of Science*. Berkeley, 1957.

La Grasserie, Raoul de. *De la justice en France et à l'étranger au XXe siècle*. 3 vols. Paris, 1914.

Langlois, Denis. *Les Dossiers noirs de la justice française*. Paris, 1977.

Lanoux, Armand. "L'Affaire de Mme. Steinheil." *Paris-Presse-L'Intransigeant*, December 20–28, 1955.

————. "La Mystérieuse affaire Steinheil." In *Le Roman vrai de la Troisième République: La Belle Epoque*, edited by Gilbert Guilleminault. Paris, 1957.

Larnaude, Ferdinand. *La Séparation des pouvoirs et la justice en France et aux Etats-Unis*. Paris, 1905.

Laurent, Jean Charles. *Principes de droit judiciaire français*. Paris, 1962.

Léautaud, Paul. *Journal littéraire*. 4 vols. to date. Paris, 1954–.

Leuthy, Hubert. *Frankreichs Uhren gehen anders*. Translated by Eric Mosbacher as *France Against Herself*. New York, 1955.

Lewis, David L. *Prisoners of Honor: The Dreyfus Affair*. New York, 1973.

Locard, Edmond. *Le Crime et les criminelles*. Paris, 1925.

————. *Traité de criminalistique*. 7 vols. Paris, 1931–40.

Manson, Anne. "Quand les Trois Grandes régnaient sur Paris." In *Le Roman vrai de la Troisième République: La Belle Epoque*, edited by Gilbert Guilleminault. Paris, 1957.

Marrus, Michael R. "Social Drinking in the Belle Epoque." *Journal of Social History*, VII (Winter, 1974), 115–41.

Martin, Benjamin F. "The Caillaux Affair: Justice as a Political Statement." *Laurels* (American Society of the Legion of Honor Magazine), LII (Winter, 1981), 143–62.

————. *Count Albert de Mun: Paladin of the Third Republic*. Chapel Hill, 1978.

————. "The Courts, the Magistrature, and Promotions in Third Republic France, 1871–1914." *American Historical Review*, LXXXVII (October, 1982), 977–1009.

————. "Law and Order in France, 1980 and 1912." *Contemporary French Civilization*, VI (Winter, 1981), 205–12.

————. "The Steinheil Affair, 1908–1909." *Laurels* (American Society of the Legion of Honor Magazine), L (Winter, 1979), 137–52.

Martin, Gaston. *Joseph Caillaux*. Paris, 1931.

Mayeur, Jean-Marie. *Les Débuts de la IIIe République, 1871–1898*. Paris, 1973.

Mitchell, Alan. *The German Influence in France after 1870: The Formation of the French Republic*. Chapel Hill, 1979.

Montal, Pierre, *L'Affaire Steinheil*. Paris, 1909.

Morand, Paul. *1900*. Translated by Mrs. Romilly Fedden as *1900 A.D.* New York, 1931.

Morcos, Saad. *Juliette Adam*. Cairo, 1961.

Nadaud, Marcel, and André Fage. *Les Drames passionels: De Casque d'or à Mata Hari*. Paris, 1926.

Nye, Robert A. "Crime in Modern Societies: Some Research Strategies for Historians." *Journal of Social History*, XI (Summer, 1978), 491–507.

Offen, Karen M. "Aspects of the Woman Question During the French Third Republic." *Third Republic/Troisième République*, III–IV (1977), 1–19.

Partin, Malcolm Overstreet. *Waldeck-Rousseau, Combes and the Church: The Politics of Anti-Clericalism, 1899–1905*. Durham, 1969.

Perelman, Chaïm. *The Idea of Justice and the Problem of Argument*. New York, 1963.

Poincaré, Raymond. *Au service de la France*. 10 vols. Paris, 1926–33.

Procès Caillaux; compte-rendu sommaire fait pour le syndicat de la presse parisienne; réquisitoire, plaidoiries, arrêt de condemnation. Paris, 1920.

Raphael, John N. *The Caillaux Drama*. London, 1914.

Rawls, John. *A Theory of Justice*. Cambridge, Mass., 1971.

Régnier, Edmond. *Quel est votre nom? N.   ou M.   ? Une étrange histoire dévoilée*. 5th ed. Brussels, 1870.

Reveillon, Tony. *Camille Pelletan*. Paris, 1930.

Rousselet, Marcel. *Les Cas de conscience du magistrat*. Paris, 1967.

Rouvier, Louis. *La Chancellerie et les sceaux de France*. Marseille, 1950.

Schacht, Roland E. *Madame Steinheil: Drama in Elf Bildern*. Berlin, 1933.

Shankland, Peter. *Death of an Editor*. London, 1981.

Shattuck Roger. *The Banquet Years: The Origins of the Avant-Garde in France, 1885 to World War I*. Rev. ed. New York, 1968.

Sorlin, Pierre. *Waldeck-Rousseau*. Paris, 1966.

Steinheil, Marguerite. *My Memoirs*. London, 1912.

Stephens, Winifred, *Madame Adam (Juliette Lamber), la grande française: From Louis Philippe Until 1917*. New York, 1918.

Suarez, Georges. *Briand: Sa vie, son oeuvre, avec son journal et de nombreux documents inédits*. 6 vols. Paris, 1938–52.

————. *La Vie orgueilleuse de Clemenceau*. 2 vols. Rev. ed. Paris, 1932.

Tardieu, André. *Le Mystère d'Agadir*. Paris, 1912.

Tavernier, René. *Madame Steinheil, ange ou démon: Favorite de la République*. Paris, 1976.

Thibault, Jacques Anatole [Anatole France]. *Crainquebille, Putois, Riquet*. Paris, 1904.

Tint, Herbert L. *The Decline of French Patriotism, 1870–1940*. London, 1964.

Varenne, Henri [Henri Vonoven]. *La Belle Affaire*. Paris, 1925.

Vergnet, Paul. *L'Affaire Caillaux*. Paris, 1918.

————. *Joseph Caillaux*. Paris, 1918.

Walser, John Raymond. "France's Search for a Battlefleet: French Naval Policy, 1898–1914." Ph.D. dissertation, University of North Carolina, 1976.

Watson, David Robin. *Georges Clemenceau: A Political Biography*. London, 1974.

Webb, James. *The Occult Establishment*. La Salle, Ill., 1976.

Weber, Eugen. *The Action Française: Royalism and Reaction in Twentieth-Century France*. Stanford, 1962.

————. *The French Nationalist Revival, 1905–1914*. Berkeley, 1959.

————. "Inheritance and Dilettantism: The Politics of Maurice Barrès." *Historical Reflections*, II (Summer, 1975), 109–31.

————. *Peasants into Frenchmen: The Modernization of Rural France, 1870–1914*. Stanford, 1976.

Werth, Alexander. *The Twilight of France, 1933–1940*. Edited by Denis W. Brogan. New York, 1942.

Williams, Wythe. *The Tiger of France: Conversations with Clemenceau*. New York, 1940.

Wische [pseud.]. *Le Vert-Logis et Mme. Steinheil*. Lille, 1909.

Zehr, Howard. *Crime and the Development of Modern Society: Patterns of Criminality in Nineteenth-Century Germany and France*. Totawa, N.J., 1977.

————. "The Modernization of Crime in Germany and France, 1830–1913." *Journal of Social History*, VIII (Summer, 1975), 117–41.

Zeldin, Theodore. *France, 1848–1945*. 2 vols. Oxford, 1973–77.

INDEX